Fourth Workshop on Computational Linguistics for Literature 2015

Held at NAACL HLT 2015

Denver, Colorado, USA
4 June 2015

ISBN: 978-1-5108-0441-8

Printed from e-media with permission by:

Curran Associates, Inc.
57 Morehouse Lane
Red Hook, NY 12571

Some format issues inherent in the e-media version may also appear in this print version.

Printed by Curran Associates, Inc. (2015)

For permission requests, please contact the Association for Computational Linguistics at the address below.

Association for Computational Linguistics
209 N. Eighth Street
Stroudsburg, Pennsylvania 18360

Phone: 1-570-476-8006
Fax: 1-570-476-0860

acl@aclweb.org

Additional copies of this publication are available from:

Curran Associates, Inc.
57 Morehouse Lane
Red Hook, NY 12571 USA
Phone: 845-758-0400
Fax: 845-758-2634
Email: curran@proceedings.com
Web: www.proceedings.com

Preface

Welcome to the 4th edition of the Workshop on Computational Linguistics for Literature. After the rounds in Montréal, Atlanta and Göteborg, we are pleased to see both the familiar and the new faces in Denver.

We are eager to hear what our invited speakers will tell us. Nick Montfort, a poet and a pioneer of digital arts and poetry, will open the day with a talk on the use of programming to foster exploration and fresh insights in the humanities. He suggests a new paradigm useful for people with little or no programming experience.

Matthew Jockers's work on macro-analysis of literature is well known and widely cited. He has published extensively on using digital analysis to view literature diachronically. Matthew will talk about his recent work on modelling the shape of stories via sentiment analysis.

This year's workshop will feature six regular talks and eight posters. If our past experience is any indication, we can expect a lively poster session. The topics of the 14 accepted papers are diverse and exciting.

Once again, there is a lot of interest in the computational analysis of poetry. Rodolfo Delmonte will present and demo SPARSAR, a system which analyzes and visualizes poems. Borja Navarro-Colorado will talk about his work on analyzing shape and meaning in the 16th and 17th century Spanish sonnets. Nina McCurdy, Vivek Srikumar & Miriah Meyer propose a formalism for analyzing sonic devices in poetry and describe an open-source implementation.

This year's workshop will witness a lot of work on parallel texts and on machine translation of literary data. Laurent Besacier & Lane Schwartz describe preliminary experiments with MT for the translation of literature. In a similar vein, Antonio Toral & Andy Way explore MT on literary data but between related languages. Fabienne Cap, Ina Rösiger & Jonas Kuhn explore how parallel editions of the same work can be used for literary analysis. Olga Scrivner & Sandra Kübler also look at parallel editions – in dealing with historical texts.

Several other papers cover various aspects of literary analysis through computation. Prashant Jayannavar, Apoorv Agarwal, Melody Ju & Owen Rambow consider social network analysis for the validation of literary theories. Andreas van Cranenburgh & Corina Koolen investigate what distinguishes literary novels from less literary ones. Dimitrios Kokkinakis, Ann Ighe & Mats Malm use computational analysis and leverage literature as a historical corpus in order to study typical vocations of women in the 19th century Sweden. Markus Krug, Frank Puppe, Fotis Jannidis, Luisa Macharowsky, Isabella Reger & Lukas Weimar describe a coreference resolution system designed specifically with fiction in mind. Stefan Evert, Thomas Proisl, Thorsten Vitt, Christof Schöch, Fotis Jannidis & Steffen Pielström explain the success of Burrows's Delta in literary authorship attribution.

Last but not least, there are papers which do not fit into any other bucket. Marie Dubremetz & Joakim Nivre will tell us about automatic detection of a rare but elegant rhetorical device called *chiasmus*. Julian Brooke, Adam Hammond & Graeme Hirst describe a tool much needed in the community: GutenTag, a system for accessing Project Gutenberg as a corpus.

To be sure, there will be much to listen to, learn from and discuss for everybody with the slightest interest in either NLP or literature. We cannot wait for June 4 (-:).

This workshop would not have been possible without the hard work of our program committee. Many people on the PC have been with us from the beginning. Everyone offers in-depth, knowledgeable advice to both the authors and the organizers. Many thanks to you all! We would also like to acknowledge the generous support of the National Science Foundation (grant No. 1523285), which has allowed us to invite such interesting speakers.

We look forward to seeing you in Denver!

Anna F., Anna K., Stan and Corina

Nick Montfort (http://nickm.com/)

Short bio

Nick Montfort develops computational art and poetry, often collaboratively. He is on the faculty at MIT in CMS/Writing and is the principal of the naming firm Nomnym. Montfort wrote the books of poems *#!* and *Riddle & Bind*, co-wrote *2002: A Palindrome Story*, and developed more than forty digital projects including the collaborations *The Deletionist* and *Sea and Spar Between*. The MIT Press has published four of his collaborative and individual books: *The New Media Reader*, *Twisty Little Passages*, *Racing the Beam*, and *10 PRINT CHR$(205.5+RND(1)); : GOTO 10*, with *Exploratory Programming for the Arts and Humanities* coming soon.

Invited talk: *Exploratory Programming for Literary Work*

Abstract

We are fortunate to be at a stage when formal research projects, including substantial ones on a large scale, are bringing computation to bear on literary questions. While I participate in this style of research, in this talk I plan to discuss some different but valuable approaches to literature that use computation, approaches that are complementary. Specifically, I will discuss how smaller-scale and even ad hoc explorations can lead to new insights and suggest possibilities for more structured and larger-scale research. In doing so, I will explain my concept of exploratory programming, a style of programming that I find particularly valuable in my own practice and research and that I have worked to teach to students in the humanities, most of whom have no programming background. I am completing a book, *Exploratory Programming for the Arts and Humanities*, to be published by the MIT Press next year, which I hope will foster this type of programming. In my talk, I will provide some examples of how both generative approaches (developing system that produce literary language) and analytical approaches can be undertaken using exploratory programming, and will explain how these can inform one another. While some of this work has been presented in literary studies and computer science contexts, my examples will also include work presented in art and poetry contexts.

Matthew Jockers (http://www.matthewjockers.net/)

Short bio

Matthew L. Jockers is Associate Professor of English at the University of Nebraska, Faculty Fellow in the Center for Digital Research in the Humanities, Faculty Fellow in the Center for Great Plains Studies, and Director of the Nebraska Literary Lab. His books include *Macroanalysis: Digital Methods and Literary History* (University of Illinois, 2013) and *Text Analysis Using R for Students of Literature* (Springer, 2014). He has written articles on computational text analysis, authorship attribution, Irish and Irish-American literature, and he has co-authored several amicus briefs defending the fair and transformative use of digital text.

Invited talk: *The (not so) Simple Shape of Stories*

Abstract

In a now famous lecture, Kurt Vonnegut described what he called the "simple shapes of stories." His thesis was that we could understand the plot of novels and stories by tracking fluctuations in sentiment. He illustrated his thesis by drawing a grid in which the y-axis represented "good fortune" at the top and "ill fortune" at the bottom. The x-axis represented narrative time and moved from "beginning" at the left to "end" at the right. Using this grid, Vonnegut traced the shapes of several stories including what he called the "man in hole" and the "boy meets girl". At one point in the lecture, Vonnegut wonders why computers cannot be trained to reveal the simple shapes of stories. In this lecture, Matthew Jockers will describe his attempt to model the simple shapes of stories using methods from sentiment analysis and signal processing.

Program Committee

Apoorv Agarwal (Columbia University)
Cecilia Ovesdotter Alm (Rochester Institute of Technology)
David Bamman (Carnegie Melon University)
Peter Boot (Huygens Institute for Netherlands History)
Julian Brooke (University of Toronto)
Hal Daumé III (University of Maryland)
David Elson (Google)
Micha Elsner (Ohio State University)
Mark Finlayson (MIT)
Pablo Gervás (Universidad Complutense de Madrid)
Roxana Girju (University of Illinois at Urbana-Champaign)
Amit Goyal (University of Maryland)
Catherine Havasi (MIT Media Lab)
Justine Kao (Stanford University)
David Mimno (Cornell University)
Saif Mohammad (National Research Council Canada)
Rebecca Passonneau (Columbia University)
Livia Polanyi (LDM Associates)
Owen Rambow (Columbia University)
Michaela Regneri (Saarland University)
Reid Swanson (University of California, Santa Cruz)
Rob Voigt (Stanford University)
Marilyn Walker (University of California, Santa Cruz)
Janice Wiebe (University of Pittsburgh)
Bei Yu (Syracuse University)

Invited Speakers

Matthew Jockers (University of Nebraska)
Nick Montfort (MIT)

Organizers

Anna Feldman (Montclair State University)
Anna Kazantseva (University of Ottawa)
Stan Szpakowicz (University of Ottawa)
Corina Koolen (Universiteit van Amsterdam)

Table of Contents

Conference Program

Thursday, June 4, 2015

Session 1

8:57–9:00 Welcome

9:00–10:00 *Exploratory Programming for Literary Work* (invited talk)
Nick Montfort

10:00–10:30 *Tools for Digital Humanities: Enabling Access to the Old Occitan Romance of Flamenca*
Olga Scrivner and Sandra Kübler

Coffee break

Session 2

11:00–11:30 *RhymeDesign: A Tool for Analyzing Sonic Devices in Poetry*
Nina McCurdy, Vivek Srikumar and Miriah Meyer

11:30–12:00 *Rhetorical Figure Detection: the Case of Chiasmus*
Marie Dubremetz and Joakim Nivre

12:00–12:30 *Validating Literary Theories Using Automatic Social Network Extraction*
Prashant Jayannavar, Apoorv Agarwal, Melody Ju and Owen Rambow

Thursday, June 4, 2015 (continued)

Rule-based Coreference Resolution in German Historic Novels
Markus Krug, Frank Puppe, Fotis Jannidis, Luisa Macharowsky, Isabella Reger and Lukas Weimar

A computational linguistic approach to Spanish Golden Age Sonnets: metrical and semantic aspects
Borja Navarro

Session 5

16:30–17:00 *Automated Translation of a Literary Work: A Pilot Study*
Laurent Besacier and Lane Schwartz

17:00–17:30 *Translating Literary Text between Related Languages using SMT*
Antonio Toral and Andy Way

17:30–17:33 Farewell

Tools for Digital Humanities: Enabling Access to the Old Occitan Romance of Flamenca

Olga Scrivner
Indiana University
Bloomington, IN, USA
obscrivn@indiana.edu

Sandra Kübler
Indiana University
Bloomington, IN, USA
skuebler@indiana.edu

Abstract

Accessing historical texts is often a challenge because readers either do not know the historical language, or they are challenged by the technological hurdle when such texts are available digitally. Merging corpus linguistic methods and digital technology can provide novel ways of representing historical texts digitally and providing a simpler access. In this paper, we describe a multi-dimensional parallel Old Occitan-English corpus, in which word alignment serves as the basis for search capabilities as well as for the transfer of annotations. We show how parallel alignment can help overcome some challenges of historical manuscripts. Furthermore, we apply a resource-light method of building an emotion annotation via parallel alignment, thus showing that such annotations are possible without speaking the historical language. Finally, using visualization tools, such as ANNIS and GoogleViz, we demonstrate how the emotion analysis can be queried and visualized dynamically in our parallel corpus, thus showing that such information can be made accessible with low technological barriers.

1 Introduction

In the past, historical documents and manuscripts were studied exclusively by a manual, paper-based approach. This limited the access to such documents to scholars who, on the one hand, know the historical variety of the language and, on the other hand, had access to the manuscripts. However, recent achievements in corpus linguistics have introduced new methods and tools for digitization and text-processing. Similarly, the progress in digital technology has created novel ways of data visualization and data interpretation. Finally, "by accessing linguistic annotation, we can extend the range of phenomena that can be found" (Kübler and Zinsmeister, 2014). That is, a digital corpus enriched with linguistic annotation, such as syntactic, pragmatic, and semantic annotation, can amplify our understanding of the literary or historical work. With such a corpus, a researcher can overcome many of the challenges provided by the historical nature of the manuscripts as well as by the technological barrier provided by many available query tools. For example, one of the challenges in working with historical texts consists in the variation in spelling or in lexical variation. In such cases, instead of performing a direct lexical search, researchers can access this information via linguistic annotation if lemma information is available.

However, there are challenges for which standard linguistic annotations are not useful. First, searching in text is usually restricted to known phenomena or explicit occurrences of data. For example, some phenomena may involve a variation between explicit and implicit tokens, e.g., null subjects or zero relative clauses. While some corpora allow for a query of null occurrences, such as in the MCVF (Martineau et al., 2010), most of the monolingual corpora do not provide such an annotation. Furthermore, it is essential for the researcher to be aware of all possible forms and contexts for queries, which is a difficult task in monolingual corpora. That is, there is always a possibility that "some relevant form will be overlooked because it has never been studied"

Proceedings of NAACL-HLT Fourth Workshop on Computational Linguistics for Literature, pages 1–11,

(Enrique-Arias, 2013, 107). For example, consider the study of Medieval Spanish discourse markers, e.g., *he*, *evás* 'behold'. Enrique-Arias (2013) shows that only by using a parallel corpus is he able to observe unexpected linguistic structures conveying the same discourse function, e.g., *sepas que* 'know that' and *cata que* 'see that'. Finally, monolingual corpora are usually accessible only to an audience with prior knowledge of a given historical language, leaving a large public aside.

We propose to address these challenges by using a parallel corpus. In our case, the two documents consist of the original, historical text and its translation into modern English. Until recently, parallel corpora have been almost exclusively used in the fields of machine translation, bilingual lexicography, translator training, and the study of language specific translational phenomena (McEnery and Xiao, 2007). With the increased availability of historical parallel corpora, we have seen the emergence of their use in historical linguistics (Koolen et al., 2006; Zeldes, 2007; Petrova and Solf, 2009; Enrique-Arias, 2012; Enrique-Arias, 2013).

In this paper, we introduce a parallel annotated Old Occitan-English corpus. We show how the alignment with modern English makes this historical corpus more accessible and how the word alignment can facilitate the cross-language transfer of emotion annotations from a resource-rich modern language into a resource-poor language, such as Old Occitan. Finally, we demonstrate how emotion visualization techniques can contribute to a richer understanding of the literary text for technically less inclined readers.

The remainder of this paper is organized as follows: Section 2 reviews the use of corpora in historical studies, and section 3 describes work on transferring annotations via alignment. Section 4 describes the textual basis of our corpus, the 13th-century Old Occitan *Romance of Flamenca*. In section 5, we explain the compilation of the parallel corpus. Section 6 describes the emotion annotation, which was carried out for English and then transferred to Old Occitan. Section 7 introduces emotion queries via ANNIS, a freely available on-line search platform, and visualization methods with motion charts in GoogleViz. Section 8 draws general conclusions and provides an outlook on future steps for the project.

2 Using Corpora in Historical Linguistics

Parallel corpora are collections of two or more texts consisting of an original text (source) and its translation(s). Generally, such parallel corpora are annotated for word *alignment* between the source text and its translation. Word alignment can be carried out automatically via tools such as GIZA++ (Och and Ney, 2000).

Monolingual historical corpora are undoubtedly valuable linguistic resources. It is not uncommon, however, to encounter different spellings and other lexical variations in historical texts. Not knowing an exact spelling or just a simple language barrier may hinder data collection. Parallel corpora can assist in such situations through Historic Document Retrieval (Koolen et al., 2006), which allows researchers to query via the modern translation rather than via the older language. Given the common assumption that "translation equivalents are likely to be inserted in the same or very similar, syntactic, semantic and pragmatic contexts" (Enrique-Arias, 2013, 114), we can assess not only lexical, but also morphological variations. That is, it is possible to a) identify forms that have never been studied and b) find occurrences based on their textual or stylistic conventions. For example, using the parallel Bible corpus of Old Spanish and its English translation, Sánchez López (To Appear) is able to identify a new form, *salvante*, that has never been reported.

Similarly, Enrique-Arias (2012) examines discourse markers, possessive structures and clitics in the Latin Bible and its medieval Spanish translation. In addition, the author is able to observe stylistic variation in choices made by translators depending on Bible sub-genres such as narrative or poetry.

In recent years, there has also been increasing interest in the correspondence between translation and language change. In this view, translation is seen as a "means of tracking change" (Beeching, 2013). Various studies have demonstrated the feasibility of parallel corpora in studies of semantic and (morpho-)syntactic change. For example, Beeching (2013) examines the evolution of the French expression *quand-même* using monolingual and parallel corpora. Similarly, Zeldes (2007) looks at the parallel corpus of Bible translations in two different stages of the same language, Old and Modern Polish. The author is able to detect various changes in nominal affixes. Another interesting approach is suggested by Petrova and Solf (2009), who investigate the influence of Latin in historical documents. When we deal with historical documents that are translations of Latin or other languages, it is hard to assess which phenomena are target language specific or introduced via the translation from the source language. Petrova and Solf (2009) show that this issue can be resolved with a parallel diachronic corpus: They analyze a change in word order in the Old High German translation of the Bible and its original Latin version. Given the assumption that any word order deviation in the translation can be viewed as evidence for Old High German syntax, their investigation is restricted to cases where word order in the translation differs from its original. The results reveal that in contrast to Latin, preverbal objects in subordinate clauses in Old High German convey *given* information (explicitly mentioned in the previous context), whereas postverbal objects carry *new* information.

Finally, linguists and computational linguistics can benefit from parallel corpora in studies of implicit constituents, e.g. zero anaphora. Not all corpora are annotated for implicit occurrences or the omission of certain elements in a sentence. This is a common challenge in the fields, where zero anaphora resolution is necessary, e.g., automatic summarization, machine translation, and studies of syntactic variation. With a parallel corpus, it is possible to search for the explicit form in a translated text and then observe the use or omission of that form in the original text. For instance, in his study of Biblia Medieval, a parallel corpus of Old Spanish Bible translations, Enrique-Arias (2013) analyzes discourse markers and observes instances of zero-marking in Old Spanish by searching for explicit Hebrew markers. Furthermore, such corpora can be used to investigate the convergence universal in machine translation, a correlation between zero anaphora and the degree of text explicitation (Rello and Ilisei, 2009).

We argue that the addition of a translation into a modern language is a simple and intuitive way of giving access to historical texts. This is a useful tool not only for historians and historical linguists but also for a lay audience since the translation provides access to the meaning without introducing additional hurdles such as by a semantic annotation. In section 4, we will present our corpus of choice, the *Romance of Flamenca*, an Old Occitan poem, along with the parallel version that includes a modern English translation. Then, we will present an approach to annotate this corpus for emotions, using non-experts working on the English part and then transferring the annotation to the source language.

3 Using Alignment Methods for Annotating Resource-Poor Languages

Linguistic annotation often involves a great amount of manual labor, which is often not feasible for low-resourced languages. Instead, we can use a method from computational linguistics, namely cross-language transfer, as proposed by Yarowsky and Ngai (2001). This method does not involve any resources in the target language, neither training data, a large lexicon, nor time-consuming manual annotation.

Cross-language transfer has been previously applied to languages with parallel corpora and bilingual lexica (Yarowsky and Ngai, 2001; Hwa et al., 2005). This approach uses parallel text and word alignment to transfer the annotation from one language to the next. Yarowsky and Ngai (2001) show the transfer of a coarse grained POS tagset and base noun phrases from English to French. Yarowsky et al. (2001) extend the approach to Spanish and Czech, and they include named entity tagging. Hwa et al. (2005) use a similar approach to transfer dependency annotations from English to Chinese. Snyder and Barzilay (2008) extend the approach to unsupervised annotation of morphology in Semitic languages via a hierarchical Bayesian network. And Snyder et al. (2009) extend the framework to include multiple source languages.

In previous work (Scrivner and Kübler, 2012), we used another cross-language transfer method, based on the work by Feldman and Hana (2010), to annotate the Flamenca corpus with POS and syntactic annotations. This method does not require parallel texts, it rather uses resources such as lexical or POS taggers from closely related languages. Our annotations were based on resources from Old French (Martineau et al., 2010) and modern Catalan (Civit et al., 2006).

In machine translation, the transfer of sentiment analysis is common in machine translation.Kim et al. (2010) use a machine translation system to map subjectivity lexica from English to other languages. In word sense disambiguation, word alignment has been used as a bridge (Tufis, 2007) based on the assumption that the translated word shares the same sense with the original word. A similar method was used for sentiment transfer from a resource-rich language to a resource-poor language (Mihalcea et al., 2007).

4 Romance of Flamenca

Medieval Provençal literature is well known for its lyric poetry of troubadours. There remains, however, a small number of non-lyric provençal texts, such as *Romance of Flamenca*, *Girart de Rossilho* and *Daurel et Beto*, that have not received much attention. In this project we focus on *Romance of Flamenca*, which can be faithfully described as "the one universally acknowledged masterpiece of Old Occitan narrative" (Fleischmann, 1995). This anonymous romance, written in the 13th century, presents an artistic amalgam of fabliau, courtly romance, troubadours lyrics, and narrative genre. The uniqueness of this "first modern novel" is also seen in its use of setting, adventures, and character portrayal (Blodgett, 1995). The narrator virtuously depicts *Archambaut*'s transmutation from a chivalrous knight to an unbearably jealous husband who locks his beautiful wife *Flamenca* in a tower, as well as *Guilhem*'s ingenious conspiracy to liberate *Flamenca*. Furthermore, this prose in verse played an influential role in the development of French literature. The potential value of this historical resource, however, is limited by the lack of an accessible digital format and linguistic annotation.

There are no known records of *Romance of Flamenca* before the late 18th century, when it was seized from a private collection during the French Revolution and placed later in the library of Carcassonne (Blodgett, 1995). The manuscript came in 139 folios with 8095 octosyllabic verses but missing the beginning and end. It was first edited by Raynouard in 1834. Since then, the manuscript has been edited multiple times (Meyer, 1865, 1901; Gschwind 1976; Huchet, 1982). While Gschwind's edition (1976) remains "the most useful edition", which provides a more accurate interpretation (Blodgett, 1995; Carbonero, 2010), we have chosen the second edition by Meyer for two reasons: a) The edition has no copyright restriction and b) this edition is available in a scanned image format provided by Google[1].

5 Parallel Occitan-English Corpus

The compilation and architecture of the monolingual Old Occitan corpus *Romance of Flamenca* along with the morpho-syntactic and syntactic annotations has been described by Scrivner and Kübler (2012) and Scrivner et al. (2013). In this paper, we augment the monolingual version into the *Romance of Flamenca* corpus with a parallel Old Occitan-English level. As described in section 2, we regard monolingual and parallel corpora as complementary resources. That is, our new corpus conforms to the traditions of a conventional multi-layered monolingual corpus, and at the same time, it offers the research advantages of a parallel bilingual corpus.

In our task, we have made various methodological decisions related to translation and alignment. First, in the selection of a translation of the source, it was important to find the most faithful translation to the original poem. While free translations have their own merits, they pose a great challenge to the alignment task. Our choice fell to the work by Blodgett (1995) for several reasons. Blodgett "endeavored, so far as possible, to respect the loose and often convoluted syntax of the original" (Blodgett, 1995). In addition, the author was able to add lines from the manuscript that were missing in the previous editions. Finally, Blodgett (1995) followed a "conservative approach" and omitted lines that were suggested earlier to replace lacunae in the original. This conservative approach is necessary for ensuring the accurate line alignment of verses.

In a second step, we provided word alignment. This is a challenging task, partly because of the non-standardized spelling in the Old Occitan source, but also because the amount of aligned text is rather small for standard unsupervised approaches. An ad-

[1]https://archive.org/details/leromandeflamen00meyegoog

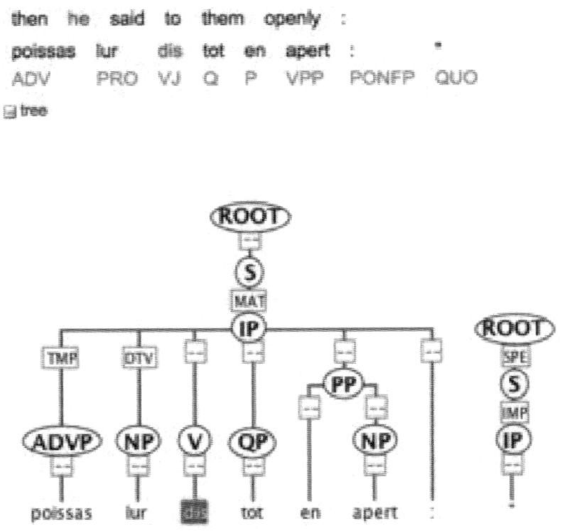

Figure 1: Word alignment: sample of results for the null pronoun in Old Occitan.

ditional challenge results from the verse structure of the poem, which necessitates deviations in the translation. This genre is prone to various stylistic word orders, as compared to political or historical narratives. In addition, sentence boundaries in Occitan do not always correspond to those in the English translation.

If we followed common practice in automatic alignment and chose sentences as the basic text units for the automatic alignment, this very likely would result in many mis-alignments. As a result, we decided to split data by lines, instead of sentences. We performed the line alignment by means of NATools[2]. NATools is a Perl package for processing parallel corpora. This package helps with the alignment of two files on a sentence level and with extracting a probability lexicon.

For word alignment, after some experimentation, we decided to use a fully unsupervised approach since there do not exist any automatic aligners for the Old Occitan-English pair. We chose GIZA++ (Och and Ney, 2000), a freely available automatic aligner, which allows for one-to-one and one-to-many word alignment. In addition, when using GIZA++, we can make use of our extracted probability dictionary. The output of the automatic alignment was then corrected manually. Below, we show an example. In (1), we show the original sentence with the word index as well as the English translation. The GIZA++ output before correction is illustrated in (2), and the corrected version is shown in (3). In both versions, the numbers in parentheses behind a word indicate which word in the original is aligned with this word in the translation.

(1) index: 1 2 3 4 5 6
OO: poissas lur dis tot en apert
ME: then he said to them openly

(2) then (1) he ( ) said (3) to (4) them (2) openly (6)

(3) then (1) he (3) said (3) to (2) them (2) openly (6)

This example shows that in (2), the subject pronoun *he* is not aligned with any word in Old Occitan. This is to be expected since Old Occitan is a pro-drop language, and the pronoun is not expressed overtly. However, during our manual correction, we align the pronoun *he* with the verb *dis*, a standard treatment for null subject pronouns. In a final step, we combine lines with corrected word alignment to form a sentence in order to merge this parallel alignment with our monolingual Old Occitan corpus, as illustrated in Figure 1.

This example also shows that such an alignment can be used to search the Old Occitan corpus via the modern English annotated translation. For example, the query with an explicit English pronoun (PRP)

[2]http://linguateca.di.uminho.pt/natools/

Storm & Storm (1987)	Shaver et al. (1987)	Plutchik (1980)
sadness	sadness	sadness
anger	anger	anger
fear	fear	fear
happiness	happiness	joy
love	affection	disgust
disgust		trust
anxiety		surprise
contentment		anticipation
hostility		
liking		
pride		
shame		

Table 1: Basic emotion models.

aligned to the Occitan verb (VJ) allows to find null occurrences of subject pronouns in Old Occitan.

At present, our parallel corpus contains 14 100 tokens and 1 000 aligned verse lines. Our corpus is further converted to PAULA XML (Dipper, 2005) and imported into the ANNIS search engine (Zeldes et al., 2009), which makes this corpus accessible online[3].

6 Emotion Annotation Transfer

While emotion analysis constitutes an important component in literary analysis, narrative corpora annotated for emotional content are not very common. In contrast, there is a large body of work on emotion and sentiment analysis of non-literary resources, such as blog posts, news and tweets (see (Liu, 2012; Pang and Lee, 2008) for overviews). However, despite the advances in the automatic annotation, the manual annotation of emotions remains a difficult task. On the one hand, the definition of emotion remains a controversial issue as there is still no clear distinction between emotions, attitude, personality, and mood. Various models of emotion clusters have been proposed, as illustrated in Table 1, but no clear standard has emerged so far.

On the other hand, the assignment of emotion is often a subjective decision. While many emotions can be identified through contextual and linguistic cues, e.g., lexical, semantic, or discourse cues, it has been shown that human annotators often assign a different label for the same emotional context (Alm and Sproat, 2005, 670). Finally, available annotated resources are domain specific, e.g., movie reviews and poll opinions, which makes it difficult to adapt to a narrative genre. As Francisco et al. (2011) point out, "the complexity of the emotional information involved in narrative texts is much higher than in those domains".

In recent years, however, with the increasing access to digitized books, such as the Google Books Corpus and Project Gutenberg, there has been growing interest in applying emotion annotation for narrative stories. For example, Alm and Sproat (2005) annotate 22 Grimms' fairy tales and demonstrate the importance of story sequences for emotional story evaluation and Francisco et al. (2011) create a corpus of 18 English folk tales. Both corpora are built using a manual annotation. In contrast, Mohammad (2012) applies a lexicon-based method to the emotion analysis of Google Books. He creates an emotion association lexicon with 14 200 word types, which determines the ratio of emotional terms in text. In addition, Mohammad shows effective visualization methods that trace emotions and compare emotional content in a large collections of texts.

As we have seen, the emotion annotation can be a valuable resource in linguistics and literary studies. However, annotated corpora and emotion lexica exist mainly for resource-rich languages, such as English. Annotating verses in Old Occitan manually for emotional content is a tedious task and requires an expert in the language. Thus neither a manual annotation of the text nor the creation of an emotion lexicon in the source language is viable. However, we can use a resource-poor approach from NLP, namely cross-language transfer (see section 3, which allows us to take advantage of English resources in combination with the word alignment. I.e., we can annotate emotions in English, which is easy enough to do given a lexicon and an undergraduate student. In a second step, we transfer the annotation via the word alignments to the source language.

Below, we will describe our emotion annotation transfer method. First, we compiled a word list from the English version *Flamenca* and removed common function words. We then used the NRC emotion lex-

[3] www.oldoccitancorpus.org

icon[4], which consists of words and their associations with 8 emotions as well as positive or negative sentiment. Mohammad and Yang (2011) created this lexicon by using frequent words from the 1911 *Roget Thesaurus*[5], which were annotated by 5 human annotators. For our application, we focus on the 8 emotion associations: anger, anticipation, disgust, fear, joy, sadness, surprise and trust. Since the emotion annotation is not neutral with regard to context, several emotions can be assigned to the same token in the NRC lexicon, as shown in (4).

	abandon	fear
	abandon	sadness
(4)	lose	anger
	lose	disgust
	lose	fear

As we can see, the word *abandon* has two associations, namely with *fear* and *sadness*, and the word *lose* has three possible associations, namely *anger*, *disgust* and *fear*. During the initial label transfer from the NCR lexicon to the Flamenca lexicon, we kept multiple labels. The tokens with multiple labels were further manually checked, and only one label that would best fit the context to our knowledge was retained. For example, in case of 'abandon', we selected the emotion *sadness*, as the context describes Famenca's father before her marriage. Also the evaluation of 100 randomly selected labels revealed that some associations did not fit our text due to the difference in genre. For example, 'court' in our narrative genre represents a different semantic entity (king's court), whereas in the NCR lexicon, 'court' (a criminal case) is associated with *anger* or *fear*. We decided to leave these cases unannotated.

Finally, the emotion annotation was transferred from the English translated words to their aligned words in Old Occitan. The emotion annotation layer was further added to the main corpus and converted to the ANNIS format.

7 Corpus Query and Visualization

In this section, we will focus on how our parallel corpus can be queried for emotional content. Following the approach from Alm and Sproat (2005), who show the relevance of textual sequencing for emotional analysis, we have segmented the corpus into 10 logical event sequences, namely wedding announcement, preparation for wedding, arrival of Archambaut, marriage, departure, King's arrival, and Queen's jealousy. The corpus consists of different layers of annotations: a) (morpho-)syntactic layer (part-of-speech and constituency annotation for Occitan and part-of-speech for English), b) lemmas, c) discourse layer (speakers classification, e.g., king, queen, Flamenca), d) temporal sequencing (events), e) word alignment (Occitan → English), and f) emotion layer (joy, trust, fear, surprise, sadness, disgust, anger and anticipation). For visualization, we use the search engine ANNIS (Zeldes et al., 2009), which is designed for displaying and querying multi-layered corpora. One advantage of ANNIS consists of its graphical query interface, which allows for user-friendly, graphical queries, instead of traditional textual queries, for which one needs to know the query language. To illustrate the visual query tool, we present a query in Figure 2. In this query, we search for any aligned token that expresses *joy* and is spoken by *Father*.

One example of a query result is illustrated in Figure 3. This example shows the Occitan token *honor* and the aligned English token *honors* that are annotated with *joy* and spoken by *Father*.

Another way of analyzing emotions more generally is to look at the overall emotional content, by querying for any words that have emotion; in other words, they are not annotated as "None" for emotion (query: $emotion! = "None"$). We can then perform a frequency analysis of the results. The frequency distribution is shown in Figure 4, where we see that *trust* and *joy* are the most common emotions.

In recent years, visual and dynamic applications in corpus and literature studies have become more important, thus showing a focus on non-technical users. For example, (Moretti, 2005) advocates the use of maps, trees, and graphs in the literary analysis. Oelke et al. (2012) suggest person network representation, showing relations between characters. In addition, they also use fingerprint plots, which allow to compare the mentioning of various categories, e.g. male, female, across several novels. Hilpert (2011) introduces dynamic motion

[4]http://saifmohammad.com/WebPages/lexicons.html

[5]The words must occur more than 120 000 times in the Google n-gram corpus.

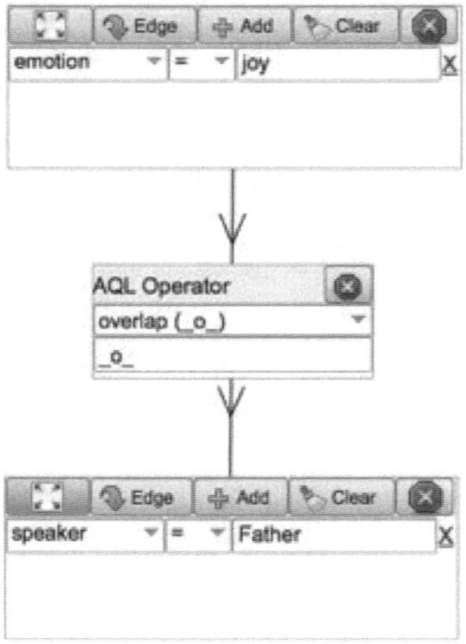

Figure 2: Search for *joy* with the speaker *Father*.

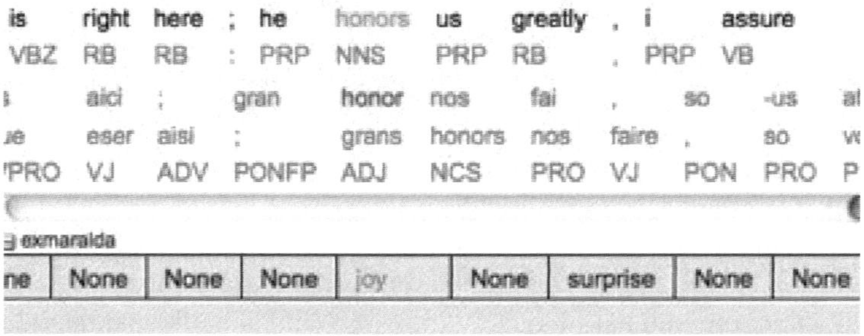

Figure 3: Resulting visualization for the query in Figure 2.

charts as a visualization methodology to the literary and linguistic studies. These charts are common in the socio-economic statistic field and are capable of visualizing in motion the development of a phenomenon in question across time. Hilpert (2011, 436) stresses that "the main purpose of producing linguistic motion charts is to give the analyst an intuitive understanding of complex linguistic development". Following Hilpert's methodology, we converted our data into the R data frame format and produced a motion chart, as shown in Figure 5. At present, our emotion analysis can be assessed as a dynamic motion chart, by using GoogleViz[6], internally interfaced via R (R Development Core Team, 2007). The chart allows for displaying emotion by type, color and size across time sequencing. Thus, the user can access this information in an interactive way without having to extract any information.For the future, we plan on adding discourse and word information.

[6]http://cran.r-project.org/web/packages/googleVis/index.html

8 Conclusion

We have presented an approach to providing access to an Old Occitan text via parallel word alignment with a modern language and cross-language transfer. We regard this project as a case study, showing that we can provide access to many types of information without the user having to learn cumbersome query languages or programming. We have also shown that the use of methods from computational linguistics, namely cross-language transfer, can pro-

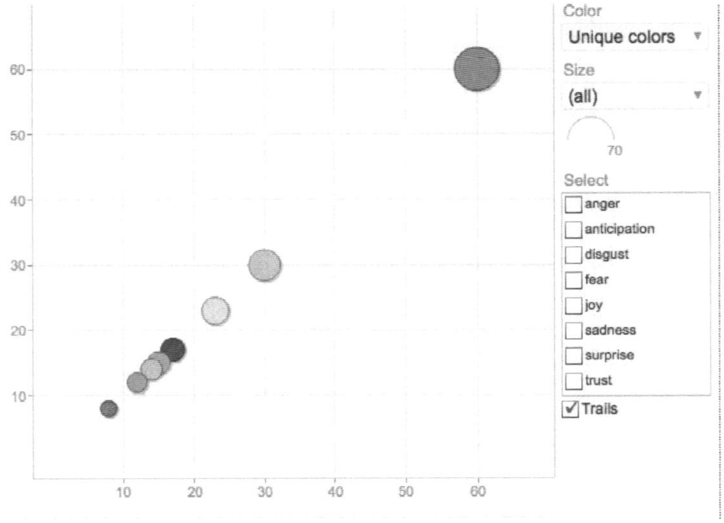

Figure 5: Dynamic emotion analysis with GoogleViz.

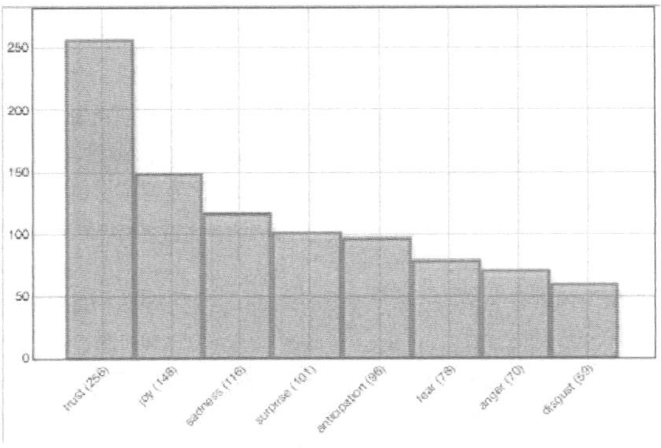

Figure 4: ANNIS frequency analysis.

vide tools for annotating the corpus without having access to an expert in the historical language. Using ANNIS, we showed how a multi-layered corpus can be queried via a user-friendly visual query interface. Finally, we presented a motion chart, which allows the user analyze and trace emotions dynamically without any technical requirements.

This work is part of our on-going project to fully annotate the Romance of Flamenca. Our goal is to provide users with necessary tools allowing for text-mining and visualization of this romance. Given a search query in ANNIS, we plan to develop an R package that will enable users to visualize their individual results exported from ANNIS and processed as motions charts and other statistical plots. Finally, this parallel corpus can be used as a training corpus in machine translation and for parallel dictionary and emotion lexicon building in resource-poor languages, such as Old Occitan.

References

Cecilia Ovesdotter Alm and Richard Sproat. 2005. Emotional sequencing and development in fairy tales. In Jianhua Tao, Tieniu Tan, and Rosalind Picard, editors, *Affective Computing and Intelligent Interaction*, volume 3784 of *Lecture Notes in Computer Science*, pages 668–674. Springer.

Kate Beeching. 2013. A parallel corpus approach to investigating semantic change. In Karin Aijmer and Bengt Altenberg, editors, *Advances in Corpus-Based Contrastive Linguistics: Studies in Honour of Stig Johansson*, pages 103–126. John Benjamins.

E.D. Blodgett. 1995. *The Romance of Flamenca*. Garland, New York.

Monserat Civit, Antònia Martí, and Nuria Bufí. 2006. Cat3LB and Cast3LB: From constituents to dependencies. In *Advances in Natural Language Processing*, pages 141–153. Springer.

Stefanie Dipper. 2005. XML-based stand-off representation and exploitation of multi-level linguistic annotation. In *Proceedings of Berliner XML Tage 2005 (BXML 2005)*, pages 39–50, Berlin, Germany.

Andrés Enrique-Arias. 2012. Parallel texts in diachronic investigations: Insights from a parallel corpus of Spanish medieval Bible translations. In *Exploring Ancient Languages through Corpora (EALC)*, Oslo, Norway.

Andrés Enrique-Arias. 2013. On the usefulness of using parallel texts in diachronic investigations: Insights from a parallel corpus of Spanish medieval Bible translations. In Paul Durrell, Martin Scheible, Silke Whitt, and Richard J. Bennett, editors, *New Methods in Historical Corpora*, pages 105–116. Narr.

Anna Feldman and Jirka Hana. 2010. *A Resource-Light Approach to Morpho-Syntactic Tagging*. Rodopi.

Suzanne Fleischmann. 1995. The non-lyric texts. In F.R.P. Akehurst and Judith M. Davis, editors, *A Handbook of the Troubadours*, pages 176–184. University of California Press.

Virginia Francisco, Raquel Hervás, Federico Peinado, and Pablo Gervás. 2011. Emotales: Creating a corpus of folk tales with emotional annotations. *Language Resources and Evaluation*, 46:341–381.

Martin Hilpert. 2011. Dynamic visualizations of language change: Motion charts on the basis of bivariate and multivariate data from diachronic corpora. *International Journal of Corpus Linguistics*, 16(4):435–461.

Rebecca Hwa, Philip Resnik, Amy Weinberg, Clara Cabezas, and Okan Kolak. 2005. Bootstrapping parsers via syntactic projection across parallel texts. *Natural Language Engineering*, 11(3):311–325.

Jungi Kim, Jin-Ji Li, and Jong-Hyeok Lee. 2010. Evaluating multilanguage-comparability of subjectivity analysis systems. In *Proceedings of the 48th Annual Meeting of the ACL*, pages 595–603, Uppsala, Sweden.

Marijn Koolen, Frans Adriaans, Jaap Kamps, and Maarten de Rijke. 2006. A cross-language approach to historic document retrieval. In M. Lalmas and et al., editors, *Advances in Information Retrieval*, pages 407–419. Springer.

Sandra Kübler and Heike Zinsmeister. 2014. *Corpus Linguistics and Linguistically Annotated Corpora*. Bloomsbury Academic.

Bing Liu. 2012. *Sentiment Analysis and Opinion Mining*. Synthesis Lectures on Human Language Technologies. Morgan & Claypool Publishers.

France Martineau, Paul Hirschbühler, Anthony Kroch, and Yves Charles Morin. 2010. Corpus MCVF (parsed corpus), modéliser le changement: les voies du français. Départment de Français, University of Ottawa.

Anthony McEnery and Zhonghu Xiao. 2007. Parallel and comparable corpora: What is happening? In G. James and G. Anderman, editors, *Incorporating Corpora: Translation and the Linguist*, Translating Europe, pages 18–31. Multilingual Matters.

Rada Mihalcea, Carmen Banea, and Janyce Wiebe. 2007. Learning multilingual subjective language via cross-lingual projections. In *Proceedings of the 45th Annual Meeting of the ACL*, pages 976–983, Prague, Czech Republic.

Saif Mohammad and Tony Yang. 2011. Tracking sentiment in mail: How genders differ on emotional axes. In *Proceedings of the ACL Workshop on Computational Approaches to Subjectivity and Sentiment Analysis (WASSA)*, pages 70–79, Portland, OR.

Saif M. Mohammad. 2012. From once upon a time to happily ever after: Tracking emotions in mail and books. *Decision Support Systems*, 53:730–741.

Franco Moretti. 2005. *Graphs, Maps, Trees: Abstract Models for a Literary History*. Verso.

Franz Josef Och and Hermann Ney. 2000. A comparison of alignment models for statistical machine translation. In *Proceedings of the 18th Conference on Computational Linguistics*, pages 1086–1090, Saarbrücken, Germany.

Daniela Oelke, Dimitrios Kokkinakis, and Mats Malm. 2012. Advanced visual analytics methods for literature analysis. *Proceedings of the 6th EACL Workshop on Language Technology for Cultural Heritage, Social Sciences, and Humanities*, pages 35–44.

Bo Pang and Lillian Lee. 2008. Opinion mining and sentiment analysis. *Foundations and Trends in Information Retrieval*, 2(1-2):1–135.

Svetlana Petrova and Michael Solf. 2009. On the methods of information-structuralanalysis in historical texts: A case study on Old High German. In Roland Hinterhölzl and Svetlana Petrova, editors, *Information structure and language change. New approaches to word order variation in Germanic*, pages 121–160. Walter de Gruyter.

Shaver Philip, Schwartz Judith, Kirson Donald, and O'Connor Cary. 1987. Emotion knowledge: Further exploration of a prototype approach. *Journal of Personality and Social Psychology*, 52(6):1061–1086.

Robert Plutchik. 1980. A general psychoevolutionary theory of emotion. *Emotion: Theory, research, and experience*, 1(3):3–33.

R Development Core Team. 2007. *A language and environment for statistical computing*. R Foundation for Statistical Computing.

Luz Rello and Iustina Ilisei. 2009. Approach to the identification of Spanish zero pronouns. In *Student Research Workshop, RANLP*, pages 60–65, Borovets, Bulgaria.

Cristina Sánchez López, To Appear. *Sintaxis histórica de la lengua española. Tercera parte*, chapter Preposiciones, conjunciones y adverbios derivados de participios. Fondo de Cultura Económica, México.

Olga Scrivner and Sandra Kübler. 2012. Building an Old Occitan corpus via cross-language transfer. In *Proceedings of the First International Workshop on Lan-*

guage Technology for Historical Text(s), pages 392–400, Vienna, Austria.

Olga Scrivner, Sandra Kübler, Barbara Vance, and Eric Beuerlein. 2013. Le Roman de Flamenca : An annotated corpus of old occitan. In *Proceedings of the Third Workshop on Annotation of Corpora for Research in Humanities*, pages 85–96, Sofia, Bulgaria.

Benjamin Snyder and Regina Barzilay. 2008. Unsupervised multilingual learning for morphological segmentation. In *Proceedings of ACL: HTL*, Columbus, OH.

Benjamin Snyder, Tahira Naseem, and Regina Barzilay. 2009. Unsupervised multilingual grammar induction. In *Proceedings of the Joint Conference of the 47th Annual Meeting of the Association for Computational Linguistics and the 4th International Joint Conference on Natural Language Processing of the Asian Federation of Natural Language Processing (ACL-IJCNLP)*, Suntec, Singapore. To appear.

Christine Storm and Tom Storm. 1987. A taxonomic study of the vocabulary of emotions. *Journal of Personality and Social Psychology*, 53(4):805–816.

Dan Tufis. 2007. Exploiting aligned parallel corpora in multilingual studies and applications. In *Proceedings of the 1st International Conference on Intercultural Collaboration*, pages 103–117, Kyoto, Japan.

David Yarowsky and Grace Ngai. 2001. Inducing multilingual POS taggers and NP bracketers via robust projection across aligned corpora. In *Proceedings of the 2nd Meeting of the North American Chapter of the Association for Computational Linguistics (NAACL)*, Pittsburgh, PA.

David Yarowsky, Grace Ngai, and Richard Wicentowski. 2001. Inducing multilingual text analysis tools via robust projection across aligned corpora. In *Proceedings of HLT 2001, First International Conference on Human Language Technology Research*, pages 161–168, San Diego, CA.

Amir Zeldes, J. Ritz, Anke Lüdeling, and Christian Chiarcos. 2009. ANNIS: A search tool for multi-layer annotated corpora. In *Proceedings of Corpus Linguistics*, Liverpool, UK.

Amir Zeldes. 2007. Machine translation between language stages: Extracting historical grammar from a parallel diachronic corpus of Polish. In *Proceedings of the Corpus Linguistics Conference (CL)*, Birmingham, UK.

RhymeDesign: A Tool for Analyzing Sonic Devices in Poetry

Nina McCurdy, Vivek Srikumar, Miriah Meyer
School of Computing
University of Utah
{nina, svivek, miriah}@cs.utah.edu

Abstract

The analysis of sound and sonic devices in poetry is the focus of much poetic scholarship, and poetry scholars are becoming increasingly interested in the role that computation might play in their research. Since the nature of such sonic analysis is unique, the associated tasks are not supported by standard text analysis techniques. We introduce a formalism for analyzing sonic devices in poetry. In addition, we present RhymeDesign, an open-source implementation of our formalism, through which poets and poetry scholars can explore their individual notion of rhyme.

1 Introduction

While the digital humanities have experienced tremendous growth over the last decade (Gold, 2012), the true value of computation to poets and poetry scholars is still very much in question. The reasons for this are complex and multifaceted. We believe that common techniques for reasoning about text, such as topic modeling and analysis of word frequencies, are not directly applicable to poetry, partly due to the unique nature of poetry analysis.

For example, sound is a great source of experimentation and creativity in writing and reading poetry. A poet may exploit a homograph to encode ambiguous meaning, or play with words that look like they should rhyme, but don't, in order to intentionally trip up or excite the reader. Discovering these sonic features is an integral part of a *close reading*, which is the deep and sustained analysis of a poem. While existing tools allow querying for sounds *or* text, close reading requires analyzing both the lexical and acoustic properties.

To investigate the influence that technology can have on the close reading of a poem we collaborated with several poetry scholars over the course of two years. This investigation focused on the computational analysis of complex *sonic devices*, the literary devices involving sound that are used to convey meaning or to influence the close reading experience. Our poetry collaborators identified a broad range of interesting sonic devices, many of which can be characterized as a type of traditional rhyme. To fully capture the range of sonic devices our collaborators described, we adopted a broader definition of rhyme. We found that this broader definition was not only able to capture known instances of sonic devices, but it also uncovered previously unknown instances in poems, providing rich, novel insights for our poetry collaborators.

In this paper, we present two contributions from our work on analyzing sound in poetry. The first is a formalism for analyzing a broad range of sonic devices in poetry. As part of the formalism we identify a language, built on top of regular expressions, for specifying these devices. This language is both highly expressive and designed for use by poets. The second contribution is an open-source implementation of this formalism, called RhymeDesign. RhymeDesign provides both a platform to test and extend the formalism, and a tool through which poets and poetry scholars can explore a broad range of complex sonic devices within a poem.

2 Background

Poetry may be written as formal or free verse: formal verse follows conventional patterns of end rhyme, meter, or some combination thereof, while free verse allows poets more flexibility to experiment with structural features, including variable line and stanza lengths. In poetry analysis, rhyming structure generally focuses on end rhymes, represented as AA BB CC, ABAB CDCD, and so on. Metrical poetry may or may not also incorporate rhyme; blank verse, for example, refers to unrhymed

Proceedings of NAACL-HLT Fourth Workshop on Computational Linguistics for Literature, pages 12–22,
Denver, Colorado, June 4, 2015. ©2015 Association for Computational Linguistics

iambic pentameter. In contrast to such established structures, the more open form of free verse places greater emphasis on sounds and rhythms of speech.

Whether working with sonnets or experimental avant-garde, our poetry collaborators consider a broad and expansive definition of rhyme. To them, the term *rhyme* encompasses all sound patterns and sound-related patterns. We classify these *sonic patterns*, which we define as instances of sonic devices, into four distinct types of rhyme: **sonic rhyme** involves the pronunciations of words; **phonetic rhyme** associates the articulatory properties of speech sound production, such as the location of the tongue in relation to the lips; **visual rhyme** relates words that *look* similar, such as *cough* and *bough*, whether or not they sound alike; and **structural rhyme** links words through their sequence of consonants and vowels. We describe these types of rhyme in more detail in Section 4. For the remainder of this paper, we use the term rhyme in reference to this broader definition.

3 Related Work

Rhyme has been a subject for literary criticism and especially the focus of attention by poets for hundreds of years, and relates to the broader tradition of analyzing and evaluating sound in poetry (Sidney, 1583; Shelley, 1821; Aristotle, 1961; Wesling, 1980; Howe, 1985). More recent literary criticism has tended to focus its attention elsewhere, leaving the discussion of rhyme in literary circles largely to poetry handbooks. Notable exceptions occur in relation to hip-hop poetry and nursery rhymes — perhaps a reflection of the tendency in high-literary circles to treat rhyme as a more simple device than our collaborators see it as being — although other writers share our interest in rhyme's complexities (McGuire, 1987; Stewart, 2009; Caplan, 2014).

Computational research analyzing sound in text stems from multiple fields, from digital humanities to computational linguistics. Our research is grounded in two sources of inquiry: sonic analysis specific to poetry and literature, and formalisms for describing sound. The latter problem of recognizing phonetic units of words is a well studied one; we refer the reader to (Jurafsky and Martin, 2008) for an overview.

A significant body of research, stemming from multiple fields, has been devoted to analyzing poetry. A number of tools and algorithms have been designed for teaching (Tucker, n.d.), analyzing (Plamondon, 2006; Kao and Jurafsky, 2012; Meneses et al., 2013) translating (Byrd and Chodorow, 1985; Genzel et al., 2010; Greene et al., 2010; Reddy and Knight, 2011), and generating (Manurung et al., 2000; Jiang and Zhou, 2010; Greene et al., 2010) poetry, all of which attend, to some degree, to sound and rhyme. While this work inspires our current research, it considers a much more limited, traditional definition of rhyme. As a result, these tools and algorithms disregard many of the sound-related patterns that we seek to reveal.

The growing body of research analyzing rhyme in hip hop and rap lyrics (Kawahara, 2007; Hirjee and Brown, 2009; Hirjee and Brown, 2010; Buda, 2004; Addanki and Wu, 2013; Wu et al., 2013b) considers a broader and more flexible definition of rhyme. Because these lyrics are meant primarily to be heard, the emphasis is placed on rhymes that occur in close proximity, as opposed to rhymes in poetry that can occur anywhere across a poem. Furthermore, rhyme analysis in hip hop and rap is purely sonic, and thus does not include visual rhyme.

Several visualization tools that support the close reading of poetry allow users to interactively explore individual sounds and sonic patterns within text, and consider a broader range of sonic devices (Smolinsky and Sokoloff, 2006; Chaturvedi et al., 2012; Clement, 2012; Abdul-Rahman et al., 2013). For example, PoemViewer (Abdul-Rahman et al., 2013) visualizes various types of sound patterning such as end rhyme, internal rhyme, assonance, consonance and alliteration, and also provides phonetic information across a poem. Enabling a somewhat deeper exploration, ProseVis (Clement, 2012) provides the complete information about the pronunciation of each word within a text and allows users to browse through visual encodings of different patterns related to the pronunciation information. While these tools capture and visualize low-level details about sound, our research goes a step further, building on the sonic information in a poem to detect and query complex sonic patterns.

Our work is most closely related to Pattern-

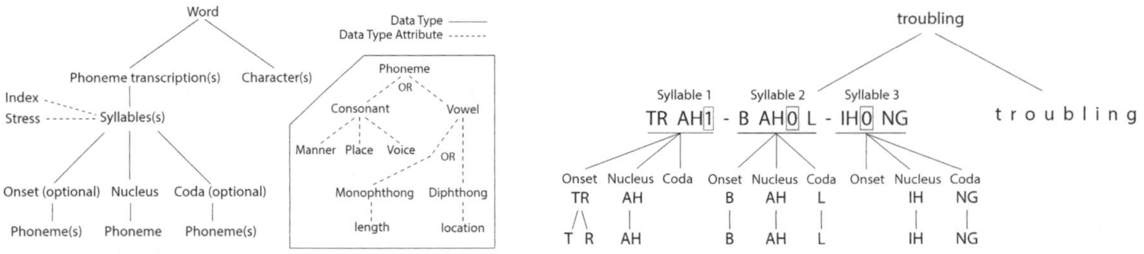

Figure 1: *(left)* The rhyming object data structure, which decomposes a word into several levels of sonic attributes. The subtree to the right captures the various phonetic attributes of a phoneme. *(right)* Decomposition of the word *troubling* into a rhyming object. The phonetic transcription is encoded using the ARPABET.

Finder (Smolinsky and Sokoloff, 2006) which allows users to query patterns involving specific sounds (characterized by one or multiple sonic attributes) within a text. While our work supports this kind of single sound patterning, it further allows users to query complex combinations of both sounds and characters in specified contexts.

4 A Formalism for Analyzing Rhyme

Our formalism for detecting and querying rhyme within a poem is composed of three components: a representation of the sonic and textual structure of a poem; a mechanism for querying complex rhyme; and a query notation designed for poets. We expand on each of these below.

4.1 Rhyming Object Representation

To enable the detection of rhyme, we decompose each word in a poem into its constituent sonic and structural components. We call this decomposition a **rhyming object**, which includes two subrepresentations. The first is a phoneme transcription that captures one or more pronunciations of the word, and the second is a surface form defined by the word's string of characters. We illustrate the rhyming object representation in Figure 1, along with the decomposition of the word *troubling* into its phoneme transcription and surface form. The phoneme transcription is encoded using the ARPABET[1], one of several ASCII phonetic transcription codes. Our rhyme specification strategy, described in Section 4.3, exploits every level of the rhyming object.

[1]The ARPABET was developed by the Advanced Research Projects Agency (ARPA). More information may be found at http://en.wikipedia.org/wiki/Arpabet (accessed 2/28/2015)

Each phoneme transcription is parsed into a sequence of syllables. Syllables are the basic organization of speech sounds and they play a critical role in defining rhyme. An important attribute of the syllable is its articulatory stress. In Figure 1 *(right)*, the stress of each syllable, indicated as either `1` (stressed) or `0` (unstressed), is highlighted with a bounding box. Each syllable is also decomposed into its constituent *onset*, *nucleus*, and *coda*, the leading consonant sound(s), vowel sound, and trailing constant sound(s), respectively. It is important to note that a syllable will always contain a nucleus, whereas the onset and coda are optional — the *troubling* example in Figure 1 illustrates these variations. The onset, nucleus, and coda are further decomposed into one or multiple *phonemes*. Phonemes are the basic linguistic units of speech sound and carry with them a number of attributes describing their physiological production (University of Iowa, 2011).

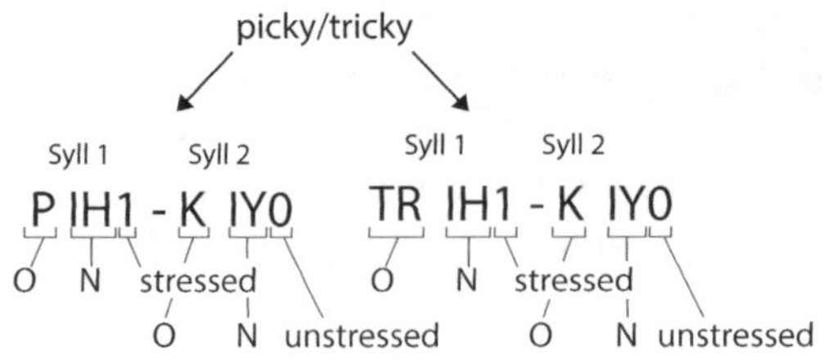

Figure 2: The phoneme transcription of *picky* and *tricky*.

4.2 The Algebra of Rhyme

A broad range of rhymes can be expressed as combinations of rhyming object components. Take for example the rhyme *picky/tricky*. Figure 2 shows the phoneme transcription of each word — we denote onset with O, nucleus with N, and coda with C. This phoneme transcription elucidates that the rhyming segment, *icky*, contains the stressed nucleus of the first syllable, combined with the onset and unstressed nucleus of the second syllable. We can mathematically express this rhyme as:

$$\mathtt{N}^{\text{stressed}}_{\text{syll1}} + (\mathtt{O} + \mathtt{N})^{\text{unstressed}}_{\text{syll2}} \quad (1)$$

Picky/tricky is an instance of a *perfect feminine rhyme*, which is a rhyme defined by an exact match in sound beginning at a stressed nucleus in the penultimate syllable. Equation 1 can also describe other perfect feminine rhymes like *scuba/tuba*.

Neither of these examples, however, includes the optional coda in its syllables. If we generalize Equation 1 to include these codas, and specifically only consider the last two syllables of a word, we can describe *all* instances of perfect feminine rhyme, including complex, multisyllabic rhymes like *synesthesia/amnesia/freesia*:

$$(\mathtt{N} + \mathtt{C})^{\text{stressed}}_{\text{penultimate syll}} + (\mathtt{O} + \mathtt{N} + \mathtt{C})^{\text{unstressed}}_{\text{last syll}} \quad (2)$$

We use expressions like Equation 2 as a rule for defining and detecting instances of a specific rhyme type, in this case perfect feminine rhyme. Such rules, which we call **rhyming templates**, are akin to templates of regular expressions where each template denotes a set of regular expressions.

4.3 ASCII Notation

Table 1 presents our ASCII notation for specifying rhyming templates. Section A lists the general notation applicable to both sonic and textual rhymes. Note that the bracket [] is the fundamental notation for the templates and allows users to specify the rhyming segment as well as the the context in which it appears. Section B lists the notation specific to sonic rhymes, including the symbol indicating a syllable break -, as well as support for phonetic rhymes. Section C lists the notation specific to visual and structural rhymes.

In designing this notation we attempted to balance the competing needs of expressivity versus usability. In particular, to make the notation usable by poets we: limit the symbols to as few as possible; borrow symbols from existing phonetic transcription alphabets, namely the International Phonetic Alphabet (IPA) (IPA, 1999) and the ARPABET; and avoid using symbols which may be overloaded within poetry scholarship. While we appreciate that our notation may cause confusion for regex users, we emphasize that our target users are poets.

Table 2 presents a list of predefined rhyme types deemed interesting by our poetry collaborators, transcribed into our notation. This table serves both as a reference for template building and as an illustration of the expressivity of our notation. Note the transcription of Equation 2 describing perfect feminine rhyme written more succinctly as `...-O[NC' -ONC]`.

We observed our poetry collaborators taking two different approaches when building new rhyming templates. In the first approach they would build a new template based on a generalized instance of a rhyme, analogous to our perfect feminine rhyme example in Section 4.2. The second approach we observed is more exploratory, where the poets would modify and expand a template based on iterative results. Our collaborators told us this approach felt more natural to them as it is similar to practices involved in close reading. We describe one poet's experience with this second approach in Section 6.2.

5 RhymeDesign

We implemented our formalism for analyzing rhyme in an open-source tool called RhymeDesign. RhymeDesign allows users to query for a broad range of rhyme types in a poem of their choosing by selecting from a set of prebuilt rhyming templates, or by building new templates using the ASCII rhyming notation. In this section we describe the major features of RhymeDesign, namely the decomposition of text into rhyming objects, the use of rhyming templates, and the user interface. RhymeDesign is freely available at RhymeDesign.org.

5.1 Text Decomposition

Obtaining the surface form of a word is straightforward, while producing the phoneme transcription is a more complicated task. Within the literature there are three approaches to completing this task: integrating external knowledge using a pronunciation dictionary, using natural language processing

A. General Rhyme Notation	
Notation	Description
[brackets]	indicates the matching portion of the rhyming pair (the rhyming segment)
...	indicates that additional syllables/characters may or may not exist
&	distinguishes between the rhyming pair words (e.g. word1/word2)
|	indicates the occurrence of "one or both"
:	indicates word break (e.g. for cross-word rhymes)
!	indicates no match (must be placed at beginning of rule)

B. Sonic and Phonetic Rhyme Notation	
Notation	Description
O	Onset (leading consonant phonemes)
N	Nucleus (vowel phoneme)
C	Coda (ending consonant phonemes)
C‘	Required coda
O‘	Required onset
-	Syllable break
’	Primary stress
^	Stressed or unstressed
O_{mvp}	Match on onset manner/voice/place
C_{mvp}	Match on coda manner/voice/place
N_{p}	Match on nucleus place

C. Visual and Structural Rhyme Notation	
Notation	Description
A	Vowel
B	Consonant
Y	Vowel or Consonant
*	Mixed character clusters e.g. "est/ets"
char	(lowercase) specific character
A’	First vowel
B’	First consonant
_{s}	Match in structure
	e.g. A_{s} : A/O (vowel/vowel match)

Table 1: The ASCII rhyme notation: *(A)* general rhyme notation applicable to both sonic and visual rhymes; *(B)* notation specific to sonic and phonetic rhymes; and *(C)* notation specific to visual and structural rhymes.

Rhyme Type	**Transcribed Rule**	**Example**
Identical Rhyme	[... - O N C^ - ...]	spruce/spruce;bass/bass;pair/pare/pear
Perfect Masculine	... - O [N C]’	rhyme/sublime
Perfect Feminine	... - O [N C’ - O N C]	picky/tricky
Perfect Dactylic	... - O [N C’ - O N C - O N C]	gravity/depravity
Semirhyme	...- O [N C]’ & ... - O [N C]’ - O N C	end/bending; end/defending
Syllabic Rhyme	... - O [N C]’ & ... - O [N C]	wing/caring
Consonant Slant Rhyme	... - O N [C]’ - ...	years/yours; ant/bent
Vowel Slant Rhyme	...- O [N] C’ -...	eyes/light
Pararhyme	... - [O‘] N [C‘]’ - ...	tell/tail/tall
Syllabic 2 Rhyme	O [N C]’ - ONC - ...	restless/westward
Alliteration	...- [O‘] N C’ - ...	languid/lazy/line/along
Assonance	... - O [N] C^ - ...	blue/estuaries
Consonance	... - [O‘] | [C‘]^ - ...	shell/chiffon; shell/wash;
Eye rhyme	!O[NC^-...] and ...[A’...]	cough/bough ; daughter/laughter
Forced rhyme	...-O[NC‘_{mv}]’-...	one/thumb; shot/top/sock
Mixed 3-character cluster	...[YYY]*...	restless/inlets
Structural rhyme	[B_{s}A_{s}B_{s}B_{s}]	fend/last

Table 2: A range of example rhyme types represented using the ASCII rhyme notation.

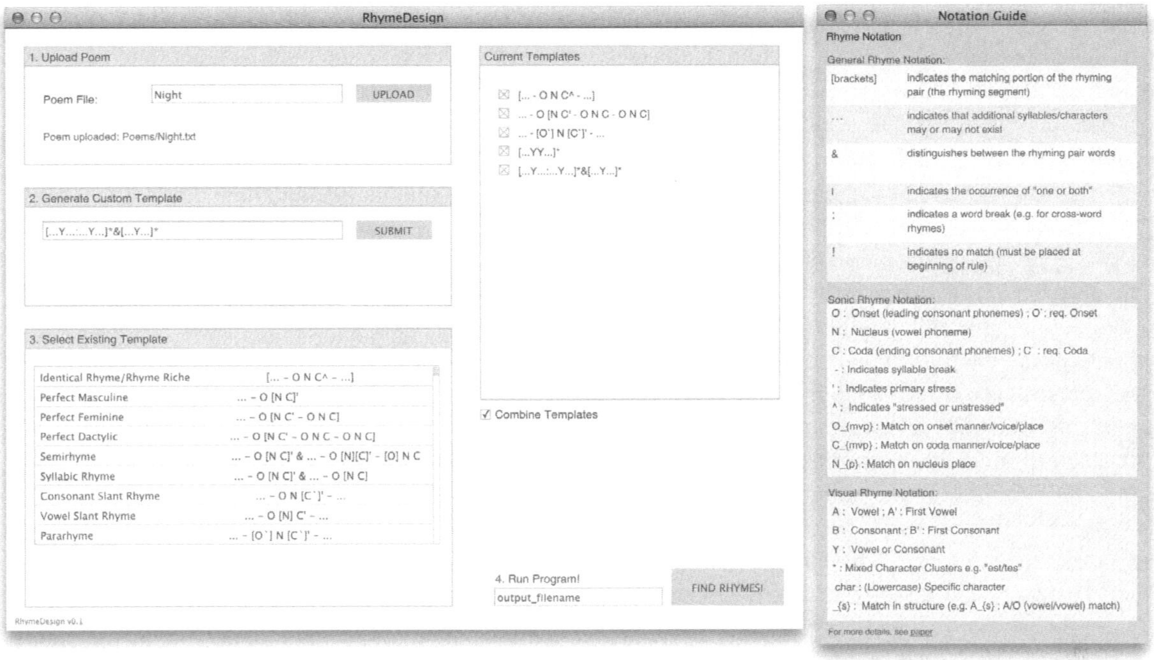

Figure 3: The RhymeDesign interface comprises two browser windows, the main RhymeDesign interface and a notation guide that provides a quick reference for rhyme specification. In the main interface, a user can upload a poem of his/her choosing, generate custom rhyming templates or choose from existing ones, and extract sets of rhyming words based on chosen templates. An option to *Combine Templates* allows users to query rhymes combining patterns in sounds and characters.

tools, or using some combination of the two. In RhymeDesign we use the hybrid approach.

For external knowledge we rely on the Carnegie Mellon University (CMU) pronunciation dictionary (CMU, 1998). The CMU dictionary provides the phoneme transcriptions of over 125K words in the North American English lexicon. Words are mapped to anywhere from one to three transcriptions, taking into account differing pronunciations as well as instances of homographs. Syllable boundaries are not provided in the original CMU transcriptions; however, the syllabified CMU dictionary (Bartlett et al., 2009) addresses this problem by training a classifier to identify syllable boundaries.

When relying on any dictionary there is a high likelihood, particularly in the domain of poetry, that a given text will have one or multiple out-of-dictionary words. To address this, we've integrated existing letter-to-sound (LTS) rules (Black et al., 1998) and syllable segmentation algorithms (Bartlett et al., 2009) to predict the phoneme transcriptions of out-of-dictionary words. Adapted from CMU's Festivox voice building tools (Black, n.d.), the LTS system was trained on the CMU dictionary in order to generate the most consistent results.

It is important to note that each of these phoneme transcription methods introduces a different element of uncertainty into our analysis. For in-dictionary words there is a possibility that the CMU dictionary will return the wrong homograph, while for out-of-dictionary words there is a chance the LTS system will simply predict a mispronunciation. Our poetry collaborators find this uncertainty incredibly interesting as it reveals possible sonic devices that experienced readers have been hard-wired to neglect. We therefore expose this uncertainty in RhymeDesign and allow users to address it as they wish.

To summarize the decomposition process, raw text is split into words by tokenizing on whitespace. For each word, we first check to see if it exists in our pronunciation dictionary. If it does, it is tagged as an in-dictionary word and its phoneme transcription(s) are retrieved directly. If not, it is tagged as an out-of-dictionary word and its phoneme transcription is predicted using our LTS methods. Transcriptions are then parsed down to the phoneme level, and a look-up table is used to retrieve phonetic properties.

5.2 Rhyme Detection

Given a rhyming template, our detection engine iterates through every pair of words in the poem, extracting all possible rhyme segments for each word, and comparing them to find all instances of rhyme. Each new instance of rhyme is then either added to an existing rhyme set or initiates a new rhyme set.

Our detection engine is similar to a typical regex engine, but with a few important differences. First, our engine performs on a pairwise basis and attempts to establish a match based on a generic template. The process of extracting rhyme segments is also similar to that of regex engines, in which the engine marches through both the expression and the subject string, advancing only if a match is found on the current token. However, for expressions with multiple permutations, rather than only returning the leftmost match, as is the case for regex engines, our engine returns all matches to ensure that all existing patterns are revealed.

5.3 User Interface

As shown in Figure 3, RhymeDesign is composed of two browser windows, the main RhymeDesign interface and a notation guide that provides a quick reference for rhyme specification. In the main interface a user can upload a poem of his/her choosing, generate novel rhyming templates or choose from existing ones, and extract sets of rhyming words based on chosen templates. An option to *Combine Templates* allows users to query rhymes combining patterns in sounds and characters. The resulting sets of words are specified in a *results* file, organized by rhyming template. This file also includes alternative pronunciation options for in-dictionary words, and the predicted pronunciation for out-of-dictionary words. Pronunciation modifications are made in an *uncertainty* file, where users may specify alternative pronunciations for in-dictionary words, or enter custom pronunciations for both in- and out-of-dictionary words. For more details on the use of RhymeDesign and the formats of the resulting files, please see the user documentation at `RhymeDesign.org`.

6 Validation

Our validation takes two forms: the first is an experiment that tests our formalism and the expressivity of our rhyming language; the second is a qualitative evaluation of RhymeDesign which includes a description of how two of our collaborators used RhymeDesign in a close reading.

6.1 Formalism

To validate our formalism we designed an experiment to test the expressivity of the rhyming language. For this experiment we requested examples of interesting rhyme types from our collaborators, along with a brief description of the rhyming characteristics. For each example we asked for two different instances of the same rhyme type. One member of the research team then manually composed a rhyming template for each of the examples based on the example's description and first instance (the prototype). The rhyming templates were then run against the second instances (the test prototypes). This allowed us to check that the new rhyming templates were in fact detecting their associated second instances, and that any other instances detected were indeed suitable.

Gathering the examples turned out to be more challenging than we anticipated. We soon realized that coming up with new rhyme types was a very involved research task for our poetry collaborators. The end result was a smaller set of 17 examples than our initial goal of 20-30. Some of the examples we received were incomplete, requiring us to iterate with our collaborators on the descriptions; generate second instances ourselves (by someone other than the template builder); or in some cases to proceed with only one instance. Our results from this experiment are summarized in Table 3, however we highlight our favorite example here, the cross-word anagram *Britney Spears/Presbyterians*, which can be represented using the rhyming template `[...Y... : ...Y...]* & [...Y...]`.

While we were able to express the majority (14/17) of examples, we found at least one opportunity to improve our notation in a way that allowed us to express certain rhyme types more succinctly.

Prototype	Description	Template	T.P.
1. blessed/blast	pararhyme	...-[O‘]N[C‘]’-...	Y
2. orchard/tortured	ear rhyme	...-O[NC’-...] and !...[A’...]	Y
3. bard/drab/brad	anagram	[...Y...]*	Y
4. Britney Spears/presbyterians	cross word anagram	[...Y... : ...Y...]* & [...Y...]*	Y
5. paws/players	character pararhyme	[Y]...[Y]	Y
6. span/his pan	cross word rhyme	[...Y...] & ...[Y]:[...Y...]	Y
7. ethereal/blow	flipped vowel+L/L+vowel	...[Al]*...	Y
8. brittle/fumble	match on final coda and character cluster	...-ON[C]^ and ...[..YY]	Y
9. soul/on	near assonance (shared place on nucleus)	...-O[N_{p}]C’-... and !...-O[N]C’-...	Y
10. dress/wantonness	perfect rhyme, mono/polysyllable words	O[NC]’ & ...-ONC^-O[NC]^	Y
11. stone/home/unknown	Matching vowel, final consonants differ by one phonetic attribute	...-O[NC_{mv}]^	N
12. paws/still	last character of first word matches with first character of second word	...[Y]&[Y]...	Y
13. blushing crow/crushing blow	spoonerism	[O‘]NC^-...:ONC^-... & ONC^-...:[O‘]NC^-... and ONC^-...:[O‘]NC^-... & [O‘]NC^-...:ONC^-... and O[NC^-...]:O[NC^-...]	Y (1:2)
14. nevermore/raven	reversed consonant sounds	[B]ABAB...& BABA[B]... and BABA[B]...& [B]ABAB... and BA[B]AB...	NA
15. separation/kevin bacon	match in all vowel sounds		
16. crystal text/tristal crest	chiastic rhyme		
17. whack-a-mole/guacamole	hybrid ear-eye rhyme		

Table 3: The results of our expressivity experiment. Examples 1- 14 could be expressed using our language. Of the 3 that we failed to express (15-17), 2 of them (16,17) could not be precisely defined by our collaborators. Y/N in the rightmost column indicates whether test prototypes were detected. We note that the test prototype for example 11 did not follow the same pattern as the original example prototype. We have since modified our notation to express examples 13 and 14 more succinctly.

Of the 3 examples that we failed to express using our language (items 15-17 in Table 3), 2 of them (16,17) could not be precisely defined by our collaborators. Incidentally, a few other instances of indefinable rhyme were encountered earlier in the example collection process. The question of how to capture patterns that cannot be precisely defined is something that we are very interested in exploring in our future work.

Of the examples that we were able to express, all but two of the test prototypes were detected. One example provided two test prototypes, of which only one was detected, and the other test prototype that we failed to detect did not follow the same pattern as the original example prototype.

6.2 RhymeDesign

Validation for RhymeDesign came in the form of informal user feedback. We conducted interviews with two of our poetry collaborators, each of whom were asked to bring a poem with interesting sonic patterns. Interviews began with an introduction to the formalism, followed by a tour of the RhymeDesign interface. Each poet was then given time to experiment with querying different kinds of rhyme.

We conducted the first interview with a poet who brought the poem "Night" by Louise Bogan. Taking an exploratory approach to template building, she began by querying rhymes involving a vowel followed by two consonants `...[ABB]...`. This turned up several different rhyming sets, one of which connected the words *partial* and *heart* via the *art* character cluster. Shifting her attention from *art* to *ear* in *heart*, she then queried rhymes involving mixed *ear* clusters `...[ear]*...`. This revealed a new pattern connecting *heart* with *breathes* and *clear*. This is illustrated in Figure 4. She told us that she suspected she would have connected *clear* and *heart* on her own, but she said she thought it unlikely she would have noticed the words' shared link with *breathes*. This connection, and especially the fact that it was found by way of the *ear* cluster was thrilling to this poet, as it prompted her to reconsider roles and interrelations of the ear, heart, and breath in the context of writing poetry as set forth in Charles Olson's seminal 1950 poetics essay, "Projective Verse" — she is pursuing the ramifications of this potential theoretical reframing in ongoing research. In reflection, she commented that this exploratory approach was very similar to how close readings were conducted, and that RhymeDesign naturally facilitated it.

The cold remote islands
And the blue estuaries
Where what **breathes**, **breathes**
...
And the **clear** nights of stars
...
Than blood in the **heart**

Figure 4: Excerpt from the poem "Night" by Louise Bogan, with the detected ...[ear]*... rhyming set shown in bold. Ellipses indicate skipped lines.

We conducted the second interview with a poet who brought "Platin" by Peter Inman, which is a poem composed almost entirely of non-words. Using RhymeDesign she was able to query a range of patterns involving character clusters as well as different kinds of structural rhymes. Exploring sonic patterns proved to be very interesting as well. Given a non-word, it is the natural tendency of a reader to predict its pronunciation. This is similar to the prediction made by the automated LTS system. Comparing the predicted pronunciations of the reader with that of the computer revealed new paths of exploration and potential sources of experimentation on the part of Peter Inman. This poet commented that using RhymeDesign was the perfect way to research language poetry, and that it was a great way to gain entrance into a complicated and possibly intimidating text. Furthermore, she noted that *"using Rhyme Design has had the delightful side effect of deepening my understanding of language structures, sound, rhyme, rhythm, and overall facture of words both written and spoken...which can only make me a better, more sophisticated poet"*. Finally, she said that RhymeDesign affirmed previous observations made in her own close readings of the same poem.

7 Conclusions & Future Work

This paper presents two contributions. The first is a formalism for analyzing sonic devices in poetry. As part of this formalism we identify a language for specifying new types of complex rhymes, and we design a corresponding ASCII notation for poets. While both our language and notation may not be complete, we present a first iteration which we will continue to develop and improve based on extensive user feedback. Our second contribution is an open-source implementation of the formalism called RhymeDesign. We validated both the formalism and RhymeDesign with our poetry collaborators.

One of the biggest challenges that we encounter in this research stems from our grapheme-to-phoneme (g2p) conversion. Our use of the CMU pronunciation dictionary restricts our analysis to one very specific lexicon and dialect. This restriction is problematic for poetry, where pronunciations span a vast number of dialects, both geographically and temporally, and where reaching across dialects can be a sonic device within itself. While automated g2p techniques have come along way, we suspect that even an ideal g2p converter would fail to support the complex tasks outlined in this paper. One interesting approach that we would like to explore would be to integrate speech and phone recognition software, thereby allowing a user to perform the sonic analysis based on his/her own reading of the poem.

Other future work we plan to explore includes the automation of rhyme template generation using machine learning techniques. This could allow users to select words sharing some sonic resemblance, and extract additional sets of words connected through similar sonic themes. We will also work towards building a visualization tool on top of RhymeDesign that would permit users to explore the interaction of sonic devices in the space of the poem.

Acknowledgments

We are deeply grateful for the participation of our poetry collaborators, Professor Katherine Coles and Dr. Julie Lein, throughout this project. Thanks to Jules Penham who helped us test the RhymeDesign interface and gathered test data for the evaluation. This work was funded in part by NSF grant IIS-1350896 and NEH grant HD-229002.

References

Alfie Abdul-Rahman, Julie Lein, Katharine Coles, Eamonn Maguire, Miriah Meyer, and Martin Wynne, Chris Johnson, Anne E. Trefethen, Min Chen. 2013. *Rule-based Visual Mappings - with a Case Study on Poetry Visualization.* In Computer Graphics Forum, 32(3):381-390.

Aristotle 1961 *Poetics.* Trans. S. H. Butcher. Hill and Wang. pages 95-104.

Karteek Addanki and Dekai Wu. 2013. *Unsupervised Rhyme Scheme Identification in Hip Hop Lyrics using Hidden Markov Models.* Proceedings of the 1st International Conference on Statistical Language and Speech Processing (SLSP - 2013), Tarragona, Spain.

Susan Bartlett, Grzegorz Kondrak, and Colin Cherry. 2009. *On the syllabification of phonemes.* In Proceedings of Human Language Technologies: The 2009 Annual Conference of the North American Chapter of the Association for Computational Linguistics (NAACL '09). Association for Computational Linguistics, Stroudsburg, PA, USA, 308316.

Alan W. Black, Kevin Lenzo and Vincent Pagel. 1998. *Issues in building general letter to sound rules.* International Speech Communication Association. ESCA Workshop in Speech Synthesis, Australia. pages 7780.

Bradley Buda. 2004. *A System for the Automatic Identification of Rhymes in English Text.* University of Michigan.

Roy J. Byrd and Martin S. Chodorow. 1985. *Using an on-line dictionary to find rhyming words and pronunciations for unknown words.* In Proceedings of the 23rd annual meeting on Association for Computational Linguistics (ACL '85). Association for Computational Linguistics, Stroudsburg, PA, USA, 277-283. DOI=10.3115/981210.981244 http://dx.doi.org/10.3115/981210.981244

Manish Chaturvedi, Gerald Gannod, Laura Mandell, Helen Armstrong, Eric Hodgson. 2012. *Rhyme's Challenge: Hip Hop, Poetry, and Contemporary Rhyming Culture.* Oxford University Press, 2014 - Literary Criticism - 178 pages.

Manish Chaturvedi, Gerald Gannod, Laura Mandell, Helen Armstrong, Eric Hodgson. 2012. *Myopia: A Visualization Tool in Support of Close Reading.* Digital Humanities 2012.

Tanya Clement. 2012. *Distant Listening or Playing Visualizations Pleasantly with the Eyes and Ears.* Digital Studies / Le champ numrique. 3.2.

CMU. 1998. *Carnegie Mellon Pronouncing Dictionary.* Carnegie MellonUniversity: http://www. speech. cs. cmu. edu/cgi-bin/cmudict.

Alan W. Black n.d. *Carnegie Mellon Pronouncing Dictionary.* [computer software] available from http://www.festvox.org

Dmitriy Genzel and Jakob Uszkoreit and Franz Och. 2010. *"Poetic" Statistical Machine Translation: Rhyme and Meter.* Proceedings of the 2010 Conference on Empirical Methods in Natural Language Processing, pages 158-166.

Matthew K. Gold, ed. 2012 *Debates in the Digital Humanities.* Minneapolis, MN, USA: University of Minnesota Press. Retrieved from http://www.ebrary.com

Erica Greene , Tugba Bodrumlu and Kevin Knight. 2010. *Automatic Analysis of Rhythmic Poetry with Applications to Generation and Translation.* Proceedings of the 2010 Conference on Empirical Methods in Natural Language Processing, pages 524533

Hussein Hirjee and Daniel Brown. 2010. *Using automated rhyme detection to characterize rhyming style in rap music.* Empirical Musicology Review.

Hussein Hirjee and Daniel Brown. 2009. *Automatic Detection of Internal and Imperfect Rhymes in Rap Lyrics.* In Proceedings of the 10th International Society for Music Information Retrieval Conference. pages 711-716.

Susan Howe. 1985. *My Emily Dickinson.* New Directions.

International Phonetic Association. 1999. *Handbook of the International Phonetic Association: A Guide to the Use of the International Phonetic Alphabet.* Cambridge University Press.

Long Jiang and Ming Zhou. 2010. *Generating Chinese Couplets Using a Statistical MT Approach.* Proceedings of the 22nd International Conference on Computational Linguistics, COLING 2008, vol. 1, pages 377-384.

Daniel Jurafsky and James H. Martin. 2008 *Speech and language processing: An introduction to speech recognition. Computational Linguistics and Natural Language Processing. 2nd Edn.* Prentice Hall, ISBN, 10(0131873210), 794-800.

Justine Kao and Dan Jurafsky. 2012. *A computational analysis of style, affect, and imagery in contemporary poetry.* Proceedings of NAACL 2012 Workshop on Computational Linguistics for Literature.

Shigeto Kawahara. 2007. *Half rhymes in Japanese rap lyrics and knowledge of similarity* Journal of East Asian Linguistics, 16(2), pages 113-144.

Hisar M Manurung, Graeme Ritchie, and Henry Thompson. 2000. *Towards A Computational Model of Poetry Generation.* In Proceedings of AISB Symposium on Creative and Cultural Aspects and Applications of AI and Cognitive Science. pages 7986.

Philip C. McGuire. 2006 *"Shakespeare's Non-Shakespearean Sonnets."* Shakespeare Quarterly. 38:3, pages 304-319.

Luis Meneses, Richard Furuta, Laura Mandell. 2006. *Ambiances: A Framework to Write and Visualize Poetry.* Digital Humanities 2013: URL: http://dh2013.unl.edu/abstracts/ab-365.html

Marc R. Plamondon. 2006 *Virtual verse analysis: Analysing patterns in poetry.* Literary and Linguistic Computing 21, suppl 1 (2006), 127–141. 2

Percy Bysshe Shelley. 1821. *A Defence of Poetry.* The Poetry Foundation. URL: http://www.poetryfoundation.org/learning/poetics-essay/237844

Sravana Reddy and Kevin Knight. 2011. *Unsupervised Discovery of Rhyme Schemes.* Proceedings of the 49th Annual Meeting of the Association for Computational Linguistics: Human Language Technologies. pages 7782.

Sir Philip Sidney. 1583. *The Defence of Poesy.* The Poetry Foundation. URL: http://www.poetryfoundation.org/learning/poetics-essay/237818

Stephanie Smolinsky and Constantine Sokoloff. 2006. *Introducing the Pattern-Finder* Conference abstract: Digital Humanities 2006.

Susan Stewart. 2009. *"Rhyme and Freedom."* The Sound of Poetry / The Poetry of Sound. Ed. Marjorie Perloff and Craig Dworkin. University of Chicago Press, pages 29-48.

Herbert Tucker. n.d. *For Better For Verse* University of Virginia, Department of English.

The University of Iowa. 2011. *Phonetics: The Sounds of English and Spanish - The University of Iowa." Phonetics: The Sounds of English and Spanish.* The University of Iowa. N.p., n.d. Web. 22 Nov. 2013. http://www.uiowa.edu/ acadtech/phonetics/#

Donald Wesling 1980. *The Chances of Rhyme: Device and Modernity.* Berkeley: University of California Press, c1980 1980. http://ark.cdlib.org/ark:/13030/ft0f59n71x/.

Dekai Wu and Karteek Addanki. 2013. *Modeling hip hop challenge-response lyrics as machine translation.* 4th Machine Translation Summit (MT Summit XIV).

Rhetorical Figure Detection: the Case of Chiasmus

Marie Dubremetz
Uppsala University
Dept. of Linguistics and Philology
Uppsala, Sweden
marie.dubremetz@lingfil.uu.se

Joakim Nivre
Uppsala University
Dept. of Linguistics and Philology
Uppsala, Sweden
joakim.nivre@lingfil.uu.se

Abstract

We propose an approach to detecting the rhetorical figure called chiasmus, which involves the repetition of a pair of words in reverse order, as in "**all** for **one**, **one** for **all**". Although repetitions of words are common in natural language, true instances of chiasmus are rare, and the question is therefore whether a computer can effectively distinguish a chiasmus from a random criss-cross pattern. We argue that chiasmus should be treated as a graded phenomenon, which leads to the design of an engine that extracts all criss-cross patterns and ranks them on a scale from prototypical chiasmi to less and less likely instances. Using an evaluation inspired by information retrieval, we demonstrate that our system achieves an average precision of 61%. As a by-product of the evaluation we also construct the first annotated corpus of chiasmi.

1 Introduction

Natural language processing (NLP) automates different tasks: translation, information retrieval, genre classification. Today, these technologies definitely provide valuable assistance for humans even if they are not perfect. But the automatic tools become inappropriate to use when we need to generate, translate or evaluate texts with stylistic quality, such as great political discourse, novels, or pleadings. Indeed, one is reluctant to trust computer assistance when it comes to judging the rhetoric of a text. As expressed by Harris and DiMarco (2009):

> Too much attention has been placed on semantics at the expense of rhetoric (including stylistics, pragmatics, and sentiment). While computational approaches to language have occasionally deployed the word 'rhetoric', even in quite central ways (such as Mann and Thompsons Rhetorical Structure Theory (1988)), the deep resources of the millenia-long research tradition of rhetoric have only been tapped to a vanishingly small degree.

Even though the situation has improved slightly during the last years (see Section 2), the gap underlined by Harris and DiMarco in the treatment of traditional rhetoric is still important. This study is a contribution aimed at filling this gap. We will focus on the task of automatically identifying a rhetorical device already studied in the first century before Christ by Quintilian (Greene, 2012, art. antimetabole), but rarely studied in computational linguistics: the chiasmus.

Chiasmi are a family of figures that consist in repeating linguistic elements in reverse order. It is named by the classics after the Greek letter χ because of the cross this letter symbolises (see Figure 1). If the name 'chiasmus' seems specific to rhetorical studies, the figure in itself is known to everybody through proverbs like (1) or quotations like (2).

(1) **Live** not to **eat**, but **eat** to **live**.

(2) Ask not what your **country** can do for **you**; ask what **you** can do for your **country**.

One can talk about chiasmus of letters, sounds, concepts or even syntactic structures as in (3).

Proceedings of NAACL-HLT Fourth Workshop on Computational Linguistics for Literature, pages 23–31,
Denver, Colorado, June 4, 2015.

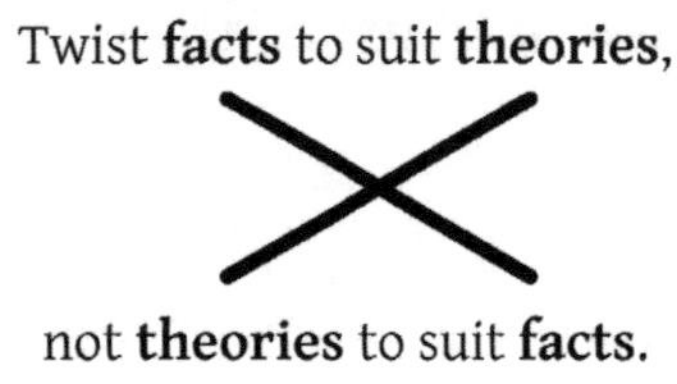

Figure 1: Schema of a chiasmus.

(3) Each **throat** was **parched**, and **glazed** each **eye**.

Strictly speaking, we will only be concerned with one type of chiasmus: the chiasmus of identical words (also called antimetabole) or of identical lemmas, as exemplified in (4) and (5), respectively.

(4) A comedian does **funny things**,
a good comedian does **things funny**.

(5) A **wit** with **dunces** and a **dunce** with **wits**

From now on, for the sake of simplicity, we will restrict the term 'chiasmus' to exclusively chiasmus of words that share identity of lemma.

We see different reasons why NLP should pay attention to chiasmi. First, it may be useful for a literary analysis: tools for supporting studies of literature exist but mostly belong to textometry. Thus, they mainly identify word frequency and some syntactic patterns, not figures of speech. Second, the chiasmus has interesting linguistic properties: it expresses semantic inversion thanks to syntax inversion, as in (2) above. Horvei (1985, p.49) points out that chiasmus can be used to emphasize antagonism as in (6) as well as reciprocity as in (7).

(6) **Portugal** has no rivers that flow into **Spain**, but **Spain** does have rivers that flow into **Portugal**.

(7) Hippocrates said that **food** should be our **medicine** and **medicine** our **food**.

To see whether we can detect such interplay of semantics and syntax is an interesting test case for computational linguistics.

Chiasmus is extremely rare. To see this, one can read a book like *River War* by Winston Churchill. Indeed, despite the fact that this book comes from a politician recognized for his high rhetorical abilities and despite the length of the text (more than one hundred thousand words) we could find only one chiasmus:

(8) **Ambition** stirs **imagination** nearly as much as **imagination** excites **ambition**.

Such rareness is a challenge for our discipline. NLP is accustomed to treating common linguistic phenomena (multiword expressions, anaphora, named entities), for which statistical models work well.We will see that chiasmus is a needle in the haystack problem. For the case of chiasmus, we have a double-fold challenge: we must not only perform well at classifying the majority of wrong instances but above all perform well in finding the infrequent phenomenon.

This paper will promote a new approach to chiasmus detection that takes chiasmus as a graded phenomenon. According to our evaluation, inspired from information retrieval methodology, our system gets up to 61% average precision. At the end of this paper the reader will have a list of precise features that can be used in order to rank chiasmus. As a side effect we provide a partially annotated tuning set with 1200 extracts manually annotated as true or false chiasmus instances.

2 Related Work

The identification of chiasmus is not very common in computational linguistics, although it has sometimes been included in the task of detecting figure of repetition (Gawryjolek, 2009; Harris and DiMarco, 2009; Hromada, 2011). Gawryjolek (2009) proposes to extract every pair of words repeated in reverse order in the text, but this method quickly becomes impractical with big corpora. When we try it on a book (*River War* by Churchill, 130,000 words) it outputs 66,000 inversions: as we shall see later, we have strong reason to believe that only one of them is a real chiasmus.

At the opposite end of the spectrum, Hromada (2011) makes a highly precise detection by detecting three pairs of words repeated in reverse order without any variation in the intervening material as illustrated in (9), but thus he limits the variety of chiasmus pattern that can be found and limits the recall (Dubremetz, 2013).

(9) You don't need [**intelligence**] [to have] [**luck**], but you do need [**luck**] [to have] [**intelligence**].

In our example, *River War*, the only chiasmus of the book (Sentence (8)) does not follow this pattern of three identical words. Thus, with Hromada's algorithm we obtain no false positive but no true positive either: we have got an empty output. Finally, Dubremetz (2013) proposes an algorithm in between, based on a stopword filter and the occurrence of punctuation, but this algorithm still has low precision. With this method we found one true instance in *River War* but only after the manual annotation of 300 instances. Thus the question is: can we build a system for chiasmus detection that has a better trade-off between recall and precision?

3 A New Approach to Chiasmus Detection

To make progress, we need to move beyond the binary definition of chiasmus as simply a pair of inverted words, which is oversimplistic. The repetition of words is an extremely common phenomenon. Defining a figure of speech by just the position of word repetitions is not enough (Gawryjolek, 2009; Dubremetz, 2013). To become a real rhetorical device, the repetition of words must be "a use of language that creates a literary effect".[1] This element of the definition requires us to distinguish between the false positives, or accidental inversions of words, and the (true) chiasmi, that is, when the inversion of words explicitly provokes a figure of speech. Sentence (10) is an example of false positive (here with 'the' and 'application'). It contrasts with Sentence (11) which is a true positive.

(10) My government respects the **application** of **the** European directive and **the application** of the 35-hour law.

(11) **One** for **all**, **all** for **one**.

However, the distinction between chiasmus and accidental inversion is not trivial to draw. Some cases are obvious for every reader, some are not. For instance, it is easy to say that there is chiasmus when the figure constitutes all the sentence and shows a perfect symmetry in the syntax:

(12) Chuck **Norris** does not fear **death**, **death** fears Chuck **Norris**.

But how about cases where the chiasmus is just one clause in a sentence or is not as symmetric as our canonical examples:

(13) We are all **European citizens** and we are all **citizens** of a **European** Union which is underpinned.

The existence of borderline cases indicates the need for a detector that does not only eliminate the most flagrant false positives, but above all establishes a ranking from prototypical chiasmi to less and less likely instances. In this way, the tool becomes a real help for the human because it selects interesting cases of repetitions and leaves it to the human to evaluate unclear cases.

A serious bottleneck in the creation of a system for ranking chiasmus candidates is the lack of annotated data. Chiasmus is not a frequent rhetorical figure. Such rareness is the first reason why there is no huge corpus of annotated chiasmi. It would require annotators to read millions of words in order to arrive at a decent sample. Another difficulty comes from the requirement for qualified annotators when it comes to literature-specific devices. Hammond et al. (2013), for example, do not rely on crowd sourcing when it comes to annotating changing voices. They use first year literature students. Annotating chiasmi is likely to require the same kind of annotators which are not the most easy to hire on crowdsourcing platforms. If we want to create annotations we have to face the following problem: most of the inversions made in natural language are not chiasmi (see the example of *River War*, Section 2). Thus, the annotation of every inversion in a corpus would be a massive, repetitive and expensive task for human annotators.

This also explains why there is no large scale evaluation of the performance of the chiasmus detectors through literature. To overcome this problem we can seek inspiration from another field of computational linguistics: information retrieval targeted at

[1]Definition of 'rhetorical device' given by Princeton wordnet: https://wordnet.princeton.edu/

the world wide web, because the web cannot be fully annotated and a very small percentage of the web pages is relevant to a given request. As described already fifteen years ago by Chowdhury (1999, p.213), in such a situation calculating the absolute recall is impossible. However, we can get a rough estimate of the recall by comparing different search engines. For instance Clarke and Willett (1997, p.186), working with Altavista, Lycos and Excite, made a pool of relevant documents for a particular query by merging the outputs of the three engines. We will base our evaluation system on the same principle: through our experiments our different "chiasmus retrieval engines" will return different hits. We annotate manually the top hundreds of those hits and obtain a pool of relevant (and irrelevant) inversions. In this way both precision and recall can be estimated without a massive work of annotation effort. In addition, we will produce a corpus of annotated (true and false) instances that can later be used as training data.

The definition of chiasmus (any pair of inversion that provokes literary effect) is rather floating (Rabatel, 2008, p.21). No clear discriminative test has been stated by linguists. This forces us to rely our annotation on human intuition. However, we keep transparency of our annotation and evaluation by publishing all the chiasmi we consider positive as well as samples of false and borderline cases (see Appendix).

4 A Ranking Model for Chiasmus

A mathematical model should be defined for our ranking system. The way we compute the chiasmus score is the following. We define a standard linear model by the function:

$$f(r) = \sum_{i=1}^{n} x_i \cdot w_i$$

Where r is a string containing a pair of inverted words, x_i is a set of feature values, and w_i is the weight associated with each features. Given two inversions r_1 and r_2, $f(r_1) > f(r_2)$ means that the inversion r_1 is more likely to be a chiasmus than r_2.

4.1 Features

We experiment with four different categories of features that can be easily encoded. Rabatel (2008), Horvei (1985), García-Page (1991), Nordahl (1971), and Diderot and D'Alembert (1782) deliver examples of canonical chiasmi as well as useful observations. Our features are inspired by them.

1. Basic features: stopwords and punctuation
2. Size-related features
3. N-gram features
4. Lexical clues

We group in a first category what has been tested in previous research (Dubremetz, 2013). They are indeed expected and not hard to motivate. For instance, following the Zipf law, we can expect that most of the false positives are caused by the grammatical words ('a', 'the', etc.) which justifies the use of a stopword list. As well, even if nothing forbids an author to make chiasmi that cross sentences, we hypothesize that punctuation, parentheses, quotation marks are definitely a clue that characterises some false positives, for instance in the false positive (14).

(14) They could **use** the format : 'Such-and-such **assurance** , reliable ' , so that the citizens will know that the **assurance** undertaking **uses** its funds well .

We see in (14) that the inversion 'use/assurance' is interrupted by quotation marks, commas and colon.

The second feature type is the one related to size or the number of words. We can expect that a too long distance between main terms or a huge size difference between clauses is an easy-to-compute false positive characteristic as in this false positive:

(15) It is strange that other **committees** <u>can apparently acquire</u> **secretariats** and well-equipped **secretariats** <u>with many staff, but that this is not possible for the Women' s</u> **Committee**.

In 15, indeed, the too long distance between 'secretariats' and 'Committee' in the second clause breaks the axial symmetry prescribed by Morier (1961, p.113)

The third category of features follows the intuition of Hromada (2011) when he looks for three pairs of inverted words instead of two: we will not just check if there are two pairs of similar words but as well if some other words are repeated. As we see in (16), similar contexts are a characteristic pattern of chiasmi (Fontanier, 1827, p.381). We will evaluate the similarity by looking at the overlapping N-grams.

(16) *In* peace, **sons** *bury their* **fathers**; *in* war, **fathers** *bury their* **sons**.

The last group consists of the lexical clues. These are language specific and, in contrast to stopwords in basic features, this is a category of positive features. We can expect from this category to encode features like conjunction (Rabatel, 2008, p.28) because they underline the axial symmetry (Morier, 1961) as in (17).

(17) **Evidence** of **absence** *or* **absence** of **evidence**?

We capture negations as well. Indeed, Fontanier (1827, p.160) stresses that prototypical chiasmi are used to underline opposition. As well Horvei (1985) concludes that chiasmi often appear in general atmosphere of antagonism. We can observe such negations in (1), (6), (9), and (12).

4.2 Setting the Weights

As observed in Section 3, there is no existing set of annotated data. This excludes traditional supervised machine learning to set the weights. So, we proceeded empirically, by observation of our successive results on our tuning set. We make available on the web the results of our trainings.

5 Experiments

5.1 Corpus

We perform experiments on English. We choose a corpus of politics often used in NLP: Europarl.[2] From this corpus, we take two extracts of two million words each. One is used as a tuning corpus to test our hypotheses on weigths and features. The other one is the test corpus which is only used for the final evaluation. In Section 5.3 we only present results based on this test corpus.

[2]Europarl English to Swedish corpus 01/1997-11/2011

5.2 Implementation

Our program[3] takes as an input a text file and gives as output the chiasmus candidates with a score that allows us to rank them: higher scores at the top, lower scores at the bottom. To do so, it tokenises and lemmatises the text with TreeTagger (Schmid, 1994). Once this basic processing is done it extracts every pair of repeated and inverted lemmas within a window of 30 tokens and passes them to the scoring function.

In our experiments we implemented twenty features. They are grouped into the four categories described in Section 4.1. We present all the features and weights in Table 1 using the notation from Figure 2.

5.3 Evaluation

In order to evaluate our features we perform four experiments. We start with only the basic features. Then, for each new experiment, we add the next group of features in the same order as in Table 1 (size, similarity and lexical clues). Thus the fourth and last experiment (called '+Lexical clues') accumulates all the features. Each time we run an experiment on the test set, we manually annotate as True or False the top 200 hits given by the machine. Thanks to this manual annotation, we present the evaluation in a precision-recall graph (Figure 3).

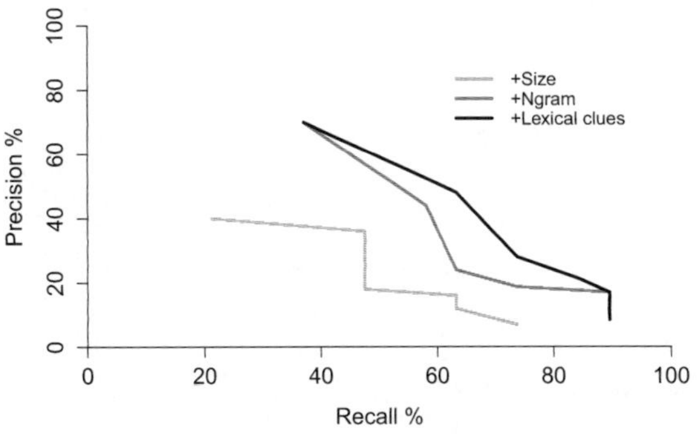

Figure 3: Precision-Recall graphs for the top two hundred candidates in each experiment. (The 'basic' experiment is not included because of too low precision.)

[3]Available at http://stp.lingfil.uu.se/~marie/chiasme.htm.

$$\underbrace{\text{In prehistoric times}}_{C_{\text{Left}}}\ \underbrace{\textbf{women}}_{W_a}\ \underbrace{\text{resembled}}_{C_{ab}}\ \underbrace{\textbf{men}}_{W_b}\ \underbrace{\text{, and}}_{C_{bb}}\ \underbrace{\textbf{men}}_{W'_b}\ \underbrace{\text{resembled}}_{C_{ba}}\ \underbrace{\textbf{women}}_{W'_a}.$$

Figure 2: Schematic representation of chiasmus, C stands for context, W for word.

Feature	**Description**	**Weight**
	Basic	
#punct	Number of hard punctuation marks and parentheses in C_{ab} and C_{ba}	−10
#softPunct	Number of commas in C_{ab} and C_{ba}	−10
#centralPunct	Number of hard punctuation marks and parentheses in C_{bb}	−5
isInStopListA	W_a is a stopword	−10
isInStopListB	W_b is a stopword	−10
#mainRep	Number of additional repetitions of W_a or W_b	−5
	Size	
#diffSize	Difference in number of tokens between C_{ab} and C_{ba}	−1
#toksInBC	Position of W'_a minus position of W_b	−1
	Similarity	
exactMatch	True if C_{ab} and C_{ba} are identical	5
#sameTok	Number of identical lemmatized tokens in C_{ab} and in C_{ba}	1
simScore	#sameTok but normalised	10
#sameBigram	Number of bigrams that are identical in C_{ab} and C_{ba}	2
#sameTrigram	Number of trigrams that are identical in C_{ab} and C_{ba}	4
#sameCont	Number of tokens that are identical in C_{Left} and C_{bb}	1
	Lexical clues	
hasConj	True if C_{bb} contains one of the conjunctions 'and', 'as', 'because', 'for', 'yet', 'nor', 'so', 'or', 'but'	2
hasNeg	True if the chiasmus candidate contains one of the negative words 'no', 'not', 'never', 'nothing'	2
hasTo	True if the expression "from ... to" appears in the chiasmus candidate or 'to' or 'into' are repeated in C_{ab} and C_{ba}	2

Table 1: The four groups of features used to rank chiasmus candidates

Precision at candidate	+Size	+Ngram	+Lex. clues
10	40	70	70
50	18	24	28
100	12	17	17
200	7	9	9
Ave. P.	34	52	61

Table 2: Average precision, and precision at a given top rank, for each experiment.

In Figure 3, recall is based on 19 true positives. They were found through the annotation of the 200 top hits of our 4 different experiments. On this graph the curves end when the position 200 is reach. For instance, the curve of '+Size' experiment stops at 7% precision because at candidates number 200 only 14 chiasmi were found. The 'basic' experiment is not present because of too low precision. Indeed, 16 out of the 19 true positives were ranked by the 'basic' features as first but within a tie of 1180 other criss-cross patterns (less than 2% precision).

When we add size features, the algorithm outputs the majority of the chiasmi within 200 hits (14 out of 19, or a recall of 74%), but the average precision is below 35%(Table 2). The recall can get significantly better. We notice, indeed, a significant progression of the number of chiasmi if we use N-gram similarity features (17 out of 19 chiasmi). Finally the lexical clues do not permit us to find more chiasmi (the maximum recall is still 90% for both the third and the fourth experiment) but the precision improves slightly (plus 9% for '+Lexical clues' experiment Table 2).

We never reach 100% recall. This means that 2 of the 19 chiasmi we found were not identifiable by the best algorithm ('+Lexical clues'). They are ranked more highly by the non-optimal algorithms. It can be that our features are too shallow, but it can be as well that the current weights are not optimal. Since our tuning is manual, we have not tried every combination of weights possible.

Chiasmus is a graded phenomenon, our manual annotation ranks three levels of chiasmi: true, borderline, and false cases. Borderline cases are by definition controversial, thus we do not count them in our table of results.[4] Duplicates are not counted either.[5]

Comparing our model to previous research is not straightforward. Our output is ranked, unlike Gawryjolek (2009) and Hromada (2011). We know already that Gawryjolek (2009) extracts every criss-cross pattern with no exception and thus obtains 100% recall but for a precision close to 0% (see Section 2). We run the experiment of Hromada (2011) on our test set.[6] It outputs 6 true positives for a total of only 9 candidates. In order to give a fair comparison with Hromada (2011), the 3 systems will be compared only for the nine first candidates (Table 3).

	+Lex. clues	Gawryjolek (2009)	Hromada (2011)
Precision	78	0	67
Recall	37	0	32
F_1-Score	59	0	43

Table 3: Precision, recall, and F-measure at candidate number 9. Comparison with previous works.

Finally, the efficiency: our algorithm takes less than three minutes and a half for one million words (214 seconds). It is three times more than Hromada (2011) (78 seconds per million words) but still reasonable.

6 Conclusion

The aim of this research is to detect a rare linguistic phenomenon called chiasmus. For that task, we have no annotated corpus and thus no possibility of supervised machine learning, and no possibility to evaluate the absolute recall of our system. Our first contribution is to redefine the task itself. Based on linguistic observations, we propose to rank the chiasmi instead of classifying them as true or false. Our second contribution was to offer an evaluation scheme and carry it out. Our third and main contribution was to propose a basic linear model with four categories of features that can solve the problem. At the moment, because of the small amount of positive examples in our data set, only tentative conclusions can be drawn. The results might not be statistically significant. Nevertheless, on this data set, this model gives the best F-score ever obtained. We kept track of all annotations and thus our fourth contribution is a set of 1200 criss-cross patterns manually annotated as true, false and borderline cases, which can be used for training or evaluation or both.

Future work could aim at gathering more data. This would allow the use of machine learning techniques in order to set the weights. There are still linguistic choices to make as well. Syntactic patterns seem to emerge in our examples. Identifying those patterns would allow the addition of structural features in our algorithm such as the symmetrical swap of syntactic roles.

A Chiasmi Annotated as True

1. Hippocrates said that **food** should be our **medicine** and **medicine** our **food**.
2. It is much better to bring **work** to **people** than to take **people** to **work**.
3. The annual reports and the promised follow-up report in January 2004 may well prove that this report, this agreement, is not the **beginning** of the **end** but the **end** of the **beginning**.

[4] We invite our reader to read them in Appendix B and at http://stp.lingfil.uu.se/~marie/chiasme.htm

[5] For example, if the machine extracts both: "**All for** one, one **for all**", "**All** for **one**, **one** for **all**" we take into account only the second case even if both extracts belong to a chiasmus.

[6] Program furnished by D. Hromada in the email of the 10th of February. We provide this regex at http://stp.lingfil.uu.se/~marie/chiasme.htm.

4. The basic problem is and remains: social State or liberal State? More **State** and less **market** or more **market** and less **State** ?

5. She wants to feed **chickens** to **pigs** and **pigs** to **chickens**.

6. There is no doubt that **doping** is changing **sport** and that **sport** will be changed due to **doping**, which means it will become absolutely ludicrous if we do nothing to prevent it.

7. Portugal and Spain are in quite unequal positions, given that we are a downstream country, in other words, **Portugal** has no rivers that flow into **Spain**, but **Spain** does have rivers that flow into **Portugal**.

8. Mr President, some **Eurosceptics** are in favour of the Treaty of Nice because **federalists** protest against it. **federalists** are in favour of it because **Eurosceptics** are opposed to it.

9. Companies must be enabled to find a solution to sending their products from the **company** to the **railway** and once the destination is reached, from the **railway** to the **company**.

10. That is the first difficulty in this exercise, since each of the camps expects first of all that we side with it against its enemy, following the old adage that my enemy 's **enemy** is my **friend**, but my enemy 's **friend** is my **enemy**.

11. It is high time that **animals** were no longer adapted to suit their **environment**, but the **environment** to suit the **animals**.

12. That is, it must not be a matter of **Europe** following the **Member** States or of **Member** States following **Europe**.

13. I would like to say once again that the European **Research** Area is not simply the European **Framework** Programme. The European **Framework** Programme is an aspect of the European **Research** Area.

14. We also need to clarify another point, i.e. that we are calling for an international **solution** because this is an international **problem** and international **problems** require international **solutions**.

15. Finally, I would like to discuss this commitment from all in the sense that, as Bertrand Russell said, in order to be happy we need three things: the courage to accept the **things** that we cannot **change**, enough determination to **change** the **things** that we can change and the wisdom to know the difference between the two.

16. Perhaps we should adapt the Community **policies** to these **regions** instead of expecting the **regions** to adapt to an elitist European **policy**.

17. What is to prevent **national** parliamentarians appearing more regularly in the **European** Parliament and **European** parliamentarians more regularly in the **national** parliaments ?

18. In my opinion, it would be appropriate if the **European** political parties took part in **national** elections, rather than having **national** political parties take part in **European** elections.

19. The directive entrenches a situation in which **protected** companies can take over **unprotected** ones, yet **unprotected** companies cannot take over **protected** ones.

B Chiasmi Annotated as Borderline Cases

Random sample out of a total of 10 borderline cases.

1. also ensure that beef and **veal** are safer than ever for **consumers** and that **consumer** confidence is restored in beef and **veal**.

2. If all this is not **helped** by a **fund** , the **fund** is no **help** at all.

3. Both men and **women** can be **victims** , but the main **victims** are **women** [...].

4. The **Commission** should **monitor** the agency and we should **monitor** the **Commission**.

5. The more harmless **questions** have been **answered** , but the evasive or inadequate **answers** to other **questions** are unacceptable.

C Chiasmi Annotated as False

Random sample out of 390 negative instances.

1. the charging of environmental and **resource** costs associated with water **use** are aimed at those Member States that still make excessive **use** of and pollute their water **resources** , and therefore not

2. at 3 p.m.) Council **priorities** for the meeting of the United Nations Human Rights Commission in Geneva The next item is the **Council** and Commission statements on the **Council priorities** for the meeting of

3. President , the two basic **issues** are whether we intend to harmonise social **policy** and whether the power of the Commission will be extended to cover social **policy issues** . I will start

4. of us within the Union **agree** on every **issue** , but on this **issue** we are **agreed** . When we are

5. appear that the reference to **regulation** 2082/ 90 may be a departure from the **directive** and that the **directive** and the **regulation** could be considered to

References

Gobinda Chowdhury. 1999. The internet and information retrieval research: a brief review. *Journal of Documentation*, 55(2):209–225.

Sarah J. Clarke and Peter Willett. 1997. Estimating the recall performance of Web search engines. *Proceedings of Aslib*, 49(7):184–189.

Denis Diderot and Jean le Rond D'Alembert. 1782. *Encyclopédie méthodique: ou par ordre de matières, volume 66*. Panckoucke.

Marie Dubremetz. 2013. Vers une identification automatique du chiasme de mots. In *Actes de la 15e Rencontres des Étudiants Chercheurs en Informatique pour le Traitement Automatique des Langues (RECITAL'2013)*, pages 150–163, Les Sables d'Olonne, France.

Pierre Fontanier. 1827. *Les Figures du discours*. Flammarion, 1977 edition.

Mario García-Page. 1991. El "retruécano léxico" y sus límites. *Archivum: Revista de la Facultad de Filología de Oviedo*, 41-42:173–203.

Jakub J. Gawryjolek. 2009. *Automated Annotation and Visualization of Rhetorical Figures*. Master thesis, Universty of Waterloo.

Roland Greene. 2012. *The Princeton Encyclopedia of Poetry and Poetics: Fourth Edition*. Princeton University Press.

Adam Hammond, Julian Brooke, and Graeme Hirst. 2013. A Tale of Two Cultures: Bringing Literary Analysis and Computational Linguistics Together. In *Proceedings of the Workshop on Computational Linguistics for Literature*, pages 1–8, Atlanta, Georgia, June. Association for Computational Linguistics.

Randy Harris and Chrysanne DiMarco. 2009. Constructing a Rhetorical Figuration Ontology. In *Persuasive Technology and Digital Behaviour Intervention Symposium*, pages 47–52, Edinburgh, Scotland.

Harald Horvei. 1985. *The Changing Fortunes of a Rhetorical Term: The History of the Chiasmus*. The Author.

Daniel Devatman Hromada. 2011. Initial Experiments with Multilingual Extraction of Rhetoric Figures by means of PERL-compatible Regular Expressions. In *Proceedings of the Second Student Research Workshop associated with RANLP 2011*, pages 85–90, Hissar, Bulgaria.

William C. Mann and Sandra A. Thompson. 1988. Rhetorical structure theory: Toward a functional theory of text organization. *Text*, 8(3):243–281.

Henri Morier. 1961. *Dictionnaire de poétique et de rhétorique*. Presses Universitaires de France.

Helge Nordahl. 1971. Variantes chiasmiques. Essai de description formelle. *Revue Romane*, 6:219–232.

Alain Rabatel. 2008. Points de vue en confrontation dans les antimétaboles PLUS et MOINS. *Langue française*, 160(4):21–36.

Helmut Schmid. 1994. Probabilistic Part-of-Speech Tagging Using Decision Trees. In *Proceedings of International Conference on New Methods in Language Processing*, pages 44–49, Manchester, Great Britain.

Validating Literary Theories Using Automatic Social Network Extraction

Prashant Arun Jayannavar
Department of Computer Science
Columbia University
NY, USA
pj2271@columbia.edu

Apoorv Agarwal
Department of Computer Science
Columbia University
NY, USA
apoorv@cs.columbia.edu

Melody Ju
Columbia College
Columbia University
NY, USA
mj2558@columbia.edu

Owen Rambow
Center for Computational Learning Systems
Columbia University
NY, USA
rambow@ccls.columbia.edu

Abstract

In this paper, we investigate whether long-standing literary theories about nineteenth-century British novels can be verified using computational techniques. Elson et al. (2010) previously introduced the task of computationally validating such theories, extracting conversational networks from literary texts. Revisiting their work, we conduct a closer reading of the theories themselves, present a revised and expanded set of hypotheses based on a divergent interpretation of the theories, and widen the scope of networks for validating this expanded set of hypotheses.

1 Introduction

In his book *Graphs, Maps, Trees: Abstract Models for Literary History*, literary scholar Franco Moretti proposes a radical transformation in the study of literature (Moretti, 2005). Advocating a shift from the close reading of individual texts in a traditionally selective literary canon, to the construction of abstract models charting the aesthetic form of entire genres, Moretti imports quantitative tools to the humanities in order to inform what he calls "a more rational literary history." While Moretti's work has inspired both support and controversy, this reimagined mode of reading opens a fresh direction from which to approach literary analysis and historiography.

By enabling the "distant reading" of texts on significantly larger scales, advances in Natural Language Processing and applied Machine Learning can be employed to empirically evaluate existing claims or make new observations over vast bodies of literature. In a seminal example of this undertaking, Elson et al. (2010) attempted to validate an assumption of structural difference between the social worlds of rural and urban novels using social networks extracted from nineteenth-century British novels. Extrapolating from the work of various literary theorists, Elson et al. (2010) hypothesized that nineteenth-century British novels set in urban environments feature numerous characters who share little conversation, while rural novels have fewer characters with more conversations. Using quoted speech attribution, the authors extracted *conversation networks* from 60 novels, which had been manually classified by a scholar of literature as either rural or urban. Elson et al. (2010) concluded that the results of their analysis of conversation networks, which indicated no difference between the social networks of rural and urban novels, invalidated literary hypotheses. However, we believe that Elson et al. (2010) misrepresented the original theories, and that their results actually support rather than contradict the original theories in question.

In this paper, we revisit the work of Elson et al. (2010), presenting a nuanced interpretation of their results through a closer reading of the original theories cited. We propose that Elson et al. (2010)'s results actually align with these theories. We then employ a more powerful tool for extracting social networks from texts, which allows us to examine a wider set of hypotheses and thus provide deeper insights into the original theories. Our findings confirm that the setting (rural versus urban) of a novel

Proceedings of NAACL-HLT Fourth Workshop on Computational Linguistics for Literature, pages 32–41,
Denver, Colorado, June 4, 2015.

in Elson et al. (2010)'s corpus has no effect on its social structure, even when one goes beyond conversations to more general and different notions of interactions. Specifically, we extend the work of Elson et al. (2010) in four significant ways: (1) we extract *interaction networks*, a conceptual generalization of conversation networks; (2) we extract *observation networks*, a new type of network with directed links; (3) we consider unweighted networks in addition to weighted networks; and (4) we investigate the number and size of communities in the extracted networks.

For extracting interaction and observation networks, we use our existing system called SINNET (Agarwal et al., 2010; Agarwal et al., 2013b; Agarwal et al., 2014). In addition to validating a richer set of hypotheses using SINNET, we present an evaluation of the system on the task of automatic social network extraction from literary texts. Our results show that SINNET is effective in extracting interaction networks from a genre quite different from the genre it was trained on, namely news articles.

The paper is organized as follows. In section 2 we revisit the theories postulated by various literary theorists and critics. In Section 3, we present an expanded set of literary hypotheses. Section 4 presents the methodology used by Elson et al. (2010) for validating their literary hypothesis. We use the same methodology for validating our expanded set of literary hypotheses. In Section 5, we give details on the difference between conversation, observation, and interaction networks. We then evaluate SINNET on the data set provided by Elson et al. (2010) (Section 6). We test our hypotheses against the data in Section 7 and conclude with future directions of research in Section 8.

2 Literary Theories

In section 3 of their paper, Elson et al. (2010) present a synthesis of quotations from literary theorists Mikhail Bakhtin (Bakhtin, 1937), Raymond Williams (Williams, 1975), Franco Moretti (Moretti, 1999; Moretti, 2005) and Terry Eagleton (Eagleton, 1996; Eagleton, 2013). Elson et al. (2010) simplify the quotations to derive the following hypotheses:

- EDM1: There is an inverse correlation between the number of dialogues and the number of characters.
- EDM2: In novels set in urban environments, numerous characters share little conversational interactions. Rural novels, on the other hand, have fewer characters with more conversations.

We argue that the theories themselves are misconstrued and that the results of Elson et al. (2010)'s experiments actually support what theorists imply about the distinction between rural and urban novels as sub-genres of 19th century realist fiction. For instance, Elson et al. (2010) quote Williams (1975) as follows:

> Raymond Williams used the term "knowable communities" to describe this [rural] world, in which face-to-face relations of a restricted set of characters are the primary mode of social interaction (Williams, 1975, 166). By contrast, the urban world, in this traditional account, is both larger and more complex.

On re-visiting this quotation in a larger and original context, we note that Williams (1975) actually apply the term "knowable communities" to novels in general, not to settings, and specifically not – as Elson et al. (2010) presume – to any particular setting (rural in this case). Williams (1975) states that "most novels are in some sense knowable communities", meaning that the novelist "offers to show people and their relationships in essentially knowable and communicable ways." However, the need or desire to portray some setting in a realistic ("knowable") way does not automatically entail the ability to do so: evolutions in real-world social milieu may occur independently of the evolutions in novelistic technique that specifically allow such evolutions to be captured in literature.

In the same vein, Robert Alter asserts that "there may [at any point in social history] be inherent limits on the access of the novelistic imagination to objective, collective realities" (Alter, 2008, p. x). And Moretti's central point is that a shortage of linguistic resources for reproducing the experience of an urban community persisted as literature shifted its focus toward the portrayal of urban realities in the nineteenth century. Moretti asks, "given the over-complication of the nineteenth-century urban setting - how did novels 'read' cities? By what narrative mechanisms did they make them 'legible', and turn urban noise into information?" (Moretti, 1999, p. 79). To answer this question, Moretti points to the reductive rendering techniques of the urban genre's first wave; these novels "don't show 'London', only a small, monochrome portion of it" (Moretti, 1999, p. 79). In order to make London legible, nineteenth century British novelists, including Austen and Dickens, reduce its complexity and its randomness, thereby amputating the richer, more unpredictable interactions that could occur in a more complex city (Moretti, 1999, p. 86). Moretti compares Dickens's London with Balzac's Paris; unlike Dickens, Balzac allows the complications of his urban subject to flourish and inform narrative possibility. The following quote presented by Elson et al. (2010) is actually used by Moretti to describe Balzac's Paris specifically, not urban settings in general, and specifically not Dickens's London:

> As the number of characters increases, Moretti argues (following Bakhtin in his logic), social interactions of different kinds and durations multiply, displacing the family-centered and conversational logic of village or rural fictions. "The narrative system becomes complicated, unstable: the city turns into a gigantic roulette table, where helpers and antagonists mix in unpredictable combinations" (Moretti, 1999).

In summary, the simple fact that a novel is set in an urban environment (and the evocation of the urban setting by name or choice of props) does not equate with the creation of a truly urban *space*. The latter is the key that renders possible an urban story with an urban social world; "without a certain kind of space," Moretti declares, "a certain kind of story is simply impossible" (Moretti, 1999, p. 100).

Moretti exposes another reductive rendering technique used by Dickens: the narrative crux of the family romance. This technique, he asserts, "is a further instance of the tentative, contradictory path followed by urban novels: as London's random and unrelated enclaves increase the 'noise', the 'dissonance', the complexity of the plot – the family romance tries to reduce it, turning London into a coherent whole" (Moretti, 1999, p. 130). Alter agrees, arguing that in Dickens' *London*, "representation of human solidarity characteristically sequesters it in protected little enclaves within the larger urban scene" (Alter, 2008, p. 55) and that "in these elaborately plotted books of Dickens's, almost no character is allowed to go to waste; each somehow is linked with the others as the writer deftly brings all the strands together in the complication and resolution of the story" (Alter, 2008, p. 67). In terms of the "perception of the fundamental categories of time and space, the boundaries of the self, and the autonomy of the individual" (Alter, 2008, p. xi), Dickens essentially writes a rural fiction, but in an urban setting.

To summarize these arguments: when novelists – like Dickens – employ narrative techniques not originally evolved for the portrayal of urban areas in novels with an urban *setting*, they fail to create in the novel the type of urban *space* in which an urban story with an urban social world is possible. Setting is sociological (it exists outside of novels), but space is literary (it exists only in novels): it is only the development of new practices in writing that are able to create truly urban spaces, those which reflect the fundamental transformations in the nature of human experience by the city: "Urban crowds and urban dwellings may reinforce a sense of isolation in individuals which, pushed to the extreme, becomes an incipient solipsism or paranoia. This feeling of being cut off from meaningful human connections finds a congenial medium in modes of narration – pioneered by Flaubert – that are rigorously centered in the consciousness of the character" Alter (2008, p. 107).

We now turn to Elson et al. (2010)'s presentation of the literary theories. They muddy the difference between setting and space, a serious flaw in interpreting Bakhtin. Urban setting does not equal urban space, and space – not setting – is what concerns Bakhtin's chronotope. The nature of the space of a novel, not its explicit setting, defines what can happen in it, including its social relationships. Each text in Elson et al. (2010)'s corpus of 60 novels is classified as either rural or urban by the following definitions. They define urban to mean set in a metropolitan zone, characterized by multiple forms of labor (not just agricultural), where social relations are largely financial or commercial in character. Conversely, rural is defined to mean set in a country or village zone, where agriculture is the primary activity, and where land-owning, non-productive, rent-collecting gentry are socially predominant. Thus, the distinction between rural and urban for Elson et al. (2010) is clearly one of setting, not one of space. Hypothesis EDM2 of Elson et al. (2010) is therefore *not* a correct representation of the theories they cite.

Interestingly, Elson et al. (2010) cannot validate their own hypothesis EDM2: their results suggest that the "urban" novels within the corpus do *not* belong to a fundamentally separate class of novels, insofar as basic frameworks of time and space inform the essential experience of the characters. They conclude:

> We would propose that this suggests that the form of a given novel – the standpoint of the narrative voice, whether the voice is "omniscient" or not – is far more determinative of the kind of social network described in the novel than where it is set or even the number of characters involved.

Put differently, differences in novels' social networks are more related to *literary* differences (space) than to non-literary differences (setting).

3 Expanded Set of Literary Hypotheses

In light of the analysis in the previous section, we propose that Elson et al. (2010)'s results, though they invalidate hypotheses EDM1 and EDM2, actually align with the parent theories from which they are derived. In direct opposition to EDM1 and EDM2, we expect our analysis to confirm the absence of correlation between setting and social network within our corpus of novels. While Elson et al. (2010)'s approach is constricted to examining social networks from the perspective of conversation, we obtain deeper insight into the novels by exploring an expanded set of hypotheses which takes general interaction and observation into account. If a comprehensive look at the social networks in our corpus confirms a lack of structural difference between the social worlds of rural- and urban-set novels, we confirm the need to look beyond setting in order to pinpoint facets of novelistic form that do determine social networks.

Similar to the approach of Elson et al. (2010), our hypotheses concern (a) the implications of an increase in the number of characters, and (b) the implications of the dichotomy between rural and urban settings. However, unlike Elson et al. (2010), we do not claim any hypothesized relation between the increase in number of characters and the social structure. We formulate our own hypotheses (H1.1, H1.2, H3.1, H3.2, H5) concerning the increase in number of characters and study them out of curiosity and as an exploratory exercise. Furthermore, unlike Elson et al. (2010), we claim that literary theorists did not posit a relation between setting and social structure. Following is the set of hypotheses we validate in this paper:

- H0: As setting changes from rural to urban, there is no change in the number of characters. The number of characters is given by the formula 1 in table 1.
- H1.1: There is a positive correlation between the number of interactions and the number of characters. The number of interactions is given by the formula 3 in table 1.
- H1.2: There is a negative correlation between the number of characters and the number of other characters a character interacts with (unweighted version of H1.1, formula 4).
- H2.1: As setting changes from rural to urban, there is no change in the total number of interactions that occur. The number of interactions is given by the formula 3 in table 1.
- H2.2: As setting changes from rural to urban, there is no change in the average number of characters each character interacts with.
- H3.1: There is a positive correlation between the number of observations and the number of characters. The number of observations is given by the formula 3 in table 1.

- H3.2: There is a negative correlation between the number of characters a character observes (formula 4), and the number of characters.

- H4.1: As setting changes from rural to urban, there is no change in the total number of observations that occur. The number of observations is given by the formula 3 in table 1.

- H4.2: As setting changes from rural to urban, there is no change in the average number of observations performed by each character. (This hypothesis is the unweighted version of H4.1, formula 4, and the OBS counterpart of H2.2).

- H5: As the number of characters increases, the number of communities increases, but the average size of communities decreases.

- H6: As setting changes from rural to urban, there is no change in the number nor the average size of communities.

4 Methodology for Validating Hypotheses

Elson et al. (2010) provide evidence to invalidate EDM1. They report a positive Pearson's correlation coefficient (**PCC**) between the number of characters and the number of dialogues to show that the two quantities are not inversely correlated. We use the same methodology to examine our hypotheses related to the number of characters.

Elson et al. (2010) provide evidence to invalidate EDM2. They extract various features from the social networks of rural and urban novels and show that these features are not statistically significantly different. They use the **homoscedastic t-test** to measure statistical significance (with $p < .05 \implies$ statistical significance). We employ the same methodology to examine our hypotheses related to the rural/urban dichotomy.

The features that Elson et al. (2010) use to invalidate EDM2 are as follows: (a) average degree, (b) rate of cliques, (c) density, and (d) rate of characters' mentions of other characters. EDM2 posits that the number of characters in urban settings share lesser conversation as compared to the rural settings. The average degree (count of the number of conversations normalized by the number of characters, see formula 4 in Table 1) seems to be the metric that is relevant for (in)validating EDM2. It is unclear why Elson et al. (2010) report the correlation between other features to invalidate EDM2. We therefore, validate our formulation of the theory (similar to EDM2) using only the average degree metric.

5 Types of Networks

This section provides definitions for the three different types of networks we consider in our study.

5.1 Conversation Network

Elson et al. (2010) defined a conversation network as a network in which nodes are characters and links are conversations. The authors defined a conversation as a continuous span of narrative time in which a set of characters exchange dialogues. Since dialogues are denoted in text by quotation marks, Elson et al. (2010) used simple regular expressions for dialogue detection. However, associating dialogues with their speakers (a task known as *quoted speech attribution*) turned out to be non-trivial (Elson and McKeown, 2010; He et al., 2013). In a separate work, Elson and McKeown (2010) presented a feature-based, supervised machine learning system for performing quoted speech attribution. Using this system, Elson et al. (2010) successfully extracted conversation networks from the novels in their corpus. We refer to the system as **EDM2010** throughout this paper.

5.2 Observation and Interaction Networks

In our past work (Agarwal et al., 2010), we defined a social network as a network in which nodes are characters and links are *social events*. We defined two broad categories of social events: observations (OBS) and interactions (INR). Observations are defined as unidirectional social events in which *only one* entity is cognitively aware of the other. Interactions are defined as bidirectional social events in which *both* entities are cognitively aware of each other *and* of their mutual awareness.

In Example 1, Mr. Woodhouse is *talking about* Emma. He is therefore cognitively aware of Emma. However, there is no evidence that Emma is also aware of Mr. Woodhouse. Since only one character is aware of the other, this is an observation event directed from Mr. Woodhouse to Emma.

No	Name	Formula	Weighted?	Remark
1	# of characters	$\|V\|$		
2	# of interaction pairs	$\|E\|$	unw.	
3	# of interactions	$W := \Sigma_{i=1}^{\|E\|} w_i$	weighted	
4	average degree	$\frac{\Sigma_{v \in V} \|E_v\|}{\|V\|} = \frac{2\|E\|}{\|V\|}$	unw.	number of characters a character interacts with on average
5	average weighted degree	$\frac{\Sigma_{u \in V} \Sigma_{v \in E_u} w_{u,v}}{\|V\|} = \frac{2W}{\|V\|}$	weighted	number of interactions a character has on average

Table 1: Table connecting the social network terminology to the natural language interpretation, along with the formulae. Interactions may be replaced with observations to obtain the corresponding formula.

(1) "[Emma] never thinks of herself, if she can do good to others," {rejoined} [Mr. Woodhouse] **OBS**

In Example 2, Mr. Micawber is talking about going home with Uriah. Since Mr. Micawber is talking about Uriah, there is a directed OBS link from Mr. Micawber to Uriah. Since he went home with Uriah, they must both have been aware of each other and of their mutual awareness. Thus, there is a bidirectional INR link between the two characters.

(2) [Mr. Micawber] $\{\text{said}\}_{OBS}$, that [he] had $\{\text{gone home with}\}_{INR}$ [Uriah] **OBS** and **INR**

In Example 3, the author (Jane Austen) states a fact about three characters (Elton, Mr. Knightley, and Mr. Weston). However, the author does not tell us about the characters' cognitive states, and thus there is no social event between the characters.

(3) [Elton]'s manners are superior to [Mr. Knightley]'s or [Mr. Weston]'s. **NoEvent**

As these examples demonstrate, the definition of a social event is quite broad. While quoted speech (detected by Elson et al. (2010)) represents only a strict sub-set of interactions, social events may be linguistically expressed using other types of speech as well, such as reported speech.

In our subsequent work (Agarwal and Rambow, 2010; Agarwal et al., 2013b; Agarwal et al., 2014), we leveraged and extended ideas from the relation extraction literature (Zelenko et al., 2003; Kambhatla, 2004; Zhao and Grishman, 2005; GuoDong et al., 2005; Harabagiu et al., 2005; Nguyen et al., 2009) to build a tree kernel-based supervised system for automatically detecting and classifying social events. We used this system for extracting observation and interaction networks from novels. We will refer to it as **SINNET** throughout this paper.

5.3 Terminology Regarding Networks

A network (or graph), $G = (V, E)$, is a set of vertices (V) and edges (E). The set of edges incident on vertex v is written E_v. In weighted networks, each edge between nodes u and v is associated with a weight, denoted by $w_{u,v}$. In the networks we consider, weight represents the frequency with which two people interact or observe one another. An edge may be directed or undirected. Interactions (INR) are undirected edges and observations (OBS) are directed edges. Table 1 presents the name and the mathematical formula for social network analysis metrics we use to validate the theories.

Edges in a network are typed. We consider four types of networks in this work: networks with undirected interaction edges (INR), with directed observation edges (OBS), with a combination of interaction and observation edges (INR + OBS), and with a combination of interaction, observation, and undirected conversational edges (CON). We denote these networks by $G_{INR} = (V, E_{INR})$, G_{OBS}, $G_{INR+OBS}$, and $G_{INR+OBS+CON}$ respectively. Each of these networks may be weighted or unweighted.

6 Evaluation of SINNET

In our previous work, we showed that SINNET adeptly extracts the social network from one work of fiction, *Alice in Wonderland* (Agarwal et al., 2013b).

Novel Excerpt	CONV-GOLD		INT-GOLD					
	EDM2010	SINNET	EDM2010			SINNET		
	R	R	P	R	F1	P	R	F1
Emma	0.40	**0.70**	1.0	0.13	0.22	0.86	0.48	**0.61**
Study in Scarlet	0.50	0.50	1.0	0.18	0.31	0.69	0.41	**0.51**
David Copperfield	0.70	**0.80**	1.0	0.22	0.36	0.80	0.63	**0.70**
Portrait of a Lady	0.66	0.66	1.0	0.22	0.36	0.73	0.44	**0.55**
Micro-Average	0.56	**0.68**	1.0	0.18	0.30	0.79	0.50	**0.61**

Table 3: Performance of the two systems on the two gold standards.

Novel Excerpt	# of char. pairs	# of links CG	# of links IG
Emma	91	10	40
Study in Scarlet	55	8	22
David Copperfield	120	10	32
Portrait of a Lady	55	6	18

Table 2: A comparison of the number of links in the two gold standards; CG is CONV-GOLD and IG is INT-GOLD

In this paper, we determine the effectiveness of SINNET on an expanded collection of literary texts. Elson et al. (2010) presented a gold standard for measuring the performance of EDM2010, which we call CONV-GOLD. This gold standard is not suitable for measuring the performance of SINNET because SINNET extracts a larger set of interactions beyond conversations. We therefore created another gold standard more suitable for evaluating SINNET, and refer to it as INT-GOLD.

6.1 Gold standards: CONV-GOLD and INT-GOLD

Elson et al. (2010) created their gold standard for evaluating the performance of EDM2010 using excerpts from four novels: Austen's *Emma*, Conan Doyle's *A Study in Scarlet*, Dickens' *David Copperfield*, and James' *The Portrait of a Lady*. The authors enumerated all pairs of characters for each novel excerpt. If a novel features n characters, its corresponding list contains $\frac{n*(n-1)}{2}$ elements. For each pair of characters, annotators were asked to mark "1" if the characters *converse* (defined in Section 5) and "0" otherwise. Annotators were asked to identify conversations framed with both direct (quoted) and indirect (unquoted) speech.

As explained in previous sections, *conversations* are a strict subset of general *interactions*. Since SINNET aims to extract the entire set of observations and interactions, the gold standard we created records all forms of observation and interaction between characters. For each pair of characters, annotators were asked to mark "1" if the characters *observe* or *interact* and "0" otherwise.

Table 2 presents the number of character pairs in each novel excerpt, the number of character pairs that converse according to CONV-GOLD and the number of character pairs that observe or interact according to INT-GOLD. The difference in the number of links between CONV-GOLD and INT-GOLD suggests that the observation and interaction of many more pairs of characters is expressed through reported speech in comparison to conversational speech. For example, the number of conversational links identified in the excerpt from *Emma by Jane Austen* was 10, while the number of interaction links identified was 40.

6.2 Evaluation and Results

Table 3 presents the results for the performance of EDM2010 and SINNET on the two gold standards (CONV-GOLD and INT-GOLD). The recall of SINNET is significantly better than that of EDM2010 on CONV-GOLD (columns 2 and 3), suggesting that most of the links expressed as quoted conversations are also expressed as interactions via reported speech. Note that, because SINNET extracts a larger set of interactions, we do not report the precision and F1-measure of SINNET on CONV-GOLD. By definition, SINNET will predict links between characters that may not be linked in CONV-GOLD; therefore the precision (and thus

Hypothesis	As # of characters ↑ ...		As settings go from rural to urban ...	
	PCC	Valid?	t-test	Valid?
[H0] ... # of characters $\sim$			$p > 0.05$	✓
[H1.1] ... # of interactions ↑	0.83	✓		
[H1.2] ... # of characters interacted with ↓	-0.36	✓		
[H2.1] ... # of interactions $\sim$			$p > 0.05$	✓
[H2.2] ...# of characters interacted with $\sim$			$p > 0.05$	✓
[H3.1] ... # of observations ↑	0.77	✓		
[H3.2]... # of characters observed ↓	-0.36	✓		
[H4.1] ... # of observations $\sim$			$p > 0.05$	✓
[H4.2] ... # of characters observed $\sim$			$p > 0.05$	✓
[H5] ... # of communities ↑	0.98	✓		
[H5] ...average size of communities ↓	-0.26	✓		
[H6] ...# of communities $\sim$			$p > 0.05$	✓
[H6] ... average size of communities $\sim$			$p > 0.05$	✓

Table 4: Hypotheses and results. All correlations are statistically significant. $\sim$ denotes no significant change. As an example, hypothesis H0 may be read as: As settings go from rural to urban ... the number of characters does not change significantly.

F1-measure) of SINNET will be low (and uninterpretable) on CONV-GOLD.

Table 3 additionally presents the performance of the two systems on INT-GOLD (the last six columns). These results show that EDM2010 achieves perfect precision, but significantly lower recall than SINNET (0.18 versus 0.50). This is expected, as EDM2010 was not trained (or designed) to extract any interactions besides conversation.

6.3 Discussion of Results

If there are any conversational links that EDM2010 detects but SINNET misses, then the two systems should be treated as complementary. To determine whether or not this is the case, we counted the number of links in all four excerpts that are detected by EDM2010 and missed by SINNET. For Austen's *Emma*, SINNET missed two links that EDM2010 detected (with respect to INT-GOLD). For the other three novels, the counts were SINNET two, zero, and one, respectively. In total, the number of links that SINNET missed and EDM2010 detected is five out of 112. Since the precision of EDM2010 is perfect, it seems advantageous to combine the output of the two systems.

7 Results for Testing Literary Hypotheses

Table 4 presents the results for all hypotheses (H0-H6) formulated in this paper. There are two broad categories of hypotheses: (1) ones that comment on social network analysis metrics (the rows) based on the increase in the number of characters (columns 2 and 3), and (2) ones that comment on the social network analysis metrics based on the type of setting (rural versus urban, columns 4 and 5).

The results show that as settings change from rural to urban, there is no significant change in the number of characters (row H0, column t-test). Furthermore, as the number of characters increases, the number of interactions also increases with a high Pearson correlation coefficient of 0.83 (row H1.1, column PCC). Similarly, for all other hypotheses, the relation between the number of characters and the setting of novels behaves as expected in terms of various types of networks and social network analysis metrics. Our results thus provide support for the cogency of the original theories.

These results highlight one of the critical findings of this paper: while network metrics are significantly correlated with the number of characters, there is **no correlation at all between setting and number of characters** within our corpus (hypothesis H0 is valid). If H0 were invalid, then all hypotheses concerning the effects of setting would be false. However, since H0 is true, we may conclude that setting (as defined by our rural/urban classification) has **no predictive effect** on any of the aspects of social networks that we investigate.

We also consider whether examining different network types (interaction, observation, and combination) in conjunction produces the same results as examining each individually. The results indeed align with those in Table 4, but with slightly different correlation numbers. We give one example: we find that the correlation between number of characters and number of interactions (hypothesis H1.1) increases from 0.83 for G_{INR} alone (as shown in Table 4) to 0.85 for $G_{INR+OBS}$ and also 0.85 for $G_{INR+OBS+CONV}$. This pattern is observed for all hypotheses.

8 Conclusion and Future Work

In this paper, we investigated whether social network extraction confirms long-standing assumptions about the social worlds of nineteenth-century British novels. Namely, we set out to verify whether the social networks of novels explicitly located in urban settings exhibit structural differences from those of rural novels. Elson et al. (2010) had previously proposed a hypothesis of difference as an interpretation of several literary theories, and provided evidence to invalidate this hypothesis on the basis of conversational networks. Following a closer reading of the theories cited by Elson et al. (2010), we suggested that their results, far from invalidating the theories themselves, actually support their cogency. To extend Elson et al. (2010)'s findings with a more comprehensive look at social interactions, we explored the application of another methodology for extracting social networks from text (called SINNET) which had previously not been applied to fiction. Using this methodology, we were able to extract a rich set of observation and interaction relations from novels, enabling us to build meaningfully on previous work. We found that the rural/urban distinction proposed by Elson et al. (2010) indeed has no effect on the structure of the social networks, while the number of characters does.

As our findings support our literary hypothesis that the urban novels within Elson et al. (2010)'s original corpus do not belong to a fundamentally separate class of novels, insofar as the essential experience of the characters is concerned possible directions for future research include expanding our corpus in order to identify novelistic features that do determine social worlds. We are particularly interested in studying novels which exhibit innovations in narrative technique, or which occur historically in and around periods of technological innovation. Lastly, we would like to add a temporal dimension to our social network extraction, in order to capture information about how networks transform throughout different novels.

Acknowledgments

We would like to thank anonymous reviewers for their insightful comments. We would also like to thank David Elson for providing the gold standard the data set used in their previous work. This paper is based upon work supported in part by the DARPA DEFT Program. The views expressed are those of the authors and do not reflect the official policy or position of the Department of Defense or the U.S. Government.

References

Apoorv Agarwal and Owen Rambow. 2010. Automatic detection and classification of social events. In *Proceedings of the 2010 Conference on Empirical Methods in Natural Language Processing*, pages 1024–1034, Cambridge, MA, October. Association for Computational Linguistics.

Apoorv Agarwal, Owen C. Rambow, and Rebecca J. Passonneau. 2010. Annotation scheme for social network extraction from text. In *Proceedings of the Fourth Linguistic Annotation Workshop*.

Apoorv Agarwal, Anup Kotalwar, and Owen Rambow. 2013a. Automatic extraction of social networks from literary text: A case study on alice in wonderland. *In the Proceedings of the 6th International Joint Conference on Natural Language Processing (IJCNLP 2013)*.

Apoorv Agarwal, Anup Kotalwar, Jiehan Zheng, and Owen Rambow. 2013b. Sinnet: Social interaction network extractor from text. In *Sixth International Joint Conference on Natural Language Processing*, page 33.

Apoorv Agarwal, Sriramkumar Balasubramanian, Anup Kotalwar, Jiehan Zheng, and Owen Rambow. 2014. Frame semantic tree kernels for social network extraction from text. *14th Conference of the European Chapter of the Association for Computational Linguistics*.

Robert Alter. 2008. *Imagined cities: urban experience and the language of the novel*. Yale University Press.

Mikhail M Bakhtin. 1937. Forms of time and of the chronotope in the novel: Notes toward a historical poetics. *Narrative dynamics: Essays on time, plot, closure, and frames*, pages 15–24.

Terry Eagleton. 1996. *Literary theory: An introduction*. U of Minnesota Press.

Terry Eagleton. 2013. *The English novel: an introduction*. John Wiley & Sons.

David K Elson and Kathleen McKeown. 2010. Automatic attribution of quoted speech in literary narrative. In *AAAI*.

David K. Elson, Nicholas Dames, and Kathleen R. McKeown. 2010. Extracting social networks from literary fiction. *Proceedings of the 48th Annual Meeting of the Association for Computational Linguistics*, pages 138–147.

Zhou GuoDong, Su Jian, Zhang Jie, and Zhang Min. 2005. Exploring various knowledge in relation extraction. In *Proceedings of 43th Annual Meeting of the Association for Computational Linguistics*.

Sanda Harabagiu, Cosmin Adrian Bejan, and Paul Morarescu. 2005. Shallow semantics for relation extraction. In *International Joint Conference On Artificial Intelligence*.

Hua He, Denilson Barbosa, and Grzegorz Kondrak. 2013. Identification of speakers in novels. In *ACL (1)*, pages 1312–1320.

Nanda Kambhatla. 2004. Combining lexical, syntactic, and semantic features with maximum entropy models for extracting relations. In *Proceedings of the ACL 2004 on Interactive poster and demonstration sessions*, page 22. Association for Computational Linguistics.

Franco Moretti. 1999. *Atlas of the European novel, 1800-1900*. Verso.

Franco Moretti. 2005. *Graphs, Maps, Trees: Abstract Models for a Literary History*. Verso.

Truc-Vien T. Nguyen, Alessandro Moschitti, and Giuseppe Riccardi. 2009. Convolution kernels on constituent, dependency and sequential structures for relation extraction. *Conference on Empirical Methods in Natural Language Processing*.

Raymond Williams. 1975. *The country and the city*. Oxford University Press.

Dmitry Zelenko, Chinatsu Aone, and Anthony Richardella. 2003. Kernel methods for relation extraction. *The Journal of Machine Learning Research*, 3:1083–1106.

Shubin Zhao and Ralph Grishman. 2005. Extracting relations with integrated information using kernel methods. In *Proceedings of the 43rd Meeting of the ACL*.

GutenTag: An NLP-driven Tool for Digital Humanities Research in the Project Gutenberg Corpus

Julian Brooke
Dept of Computer Science
University of Toronto
jbrooke@cs.toronto.edu

Adam Hammond
School of English and Theatre
University of Guelph
adam.hammond@uoguelph.ca

Graeme Hirst
Dept of Computer Science
University of Toronto
gh@cs.toronto.edu

Abstract

This paper introduces a software tool, GutenTag, which is aimed at giving literary researchers direct access to NLP techniques for the analysis of texts in the Project Gutenberg corpus. We discuss several facets of the tool, including the handling of formatting and structure, the use and expansion of metadata which is used to identify relevant subcorpora of interest, and a general tagging framework which is intended to cover a wide variety of future NLP modules. Our hope that the shared ground created by this tool will help create new kinds of interaction between the computational linguistics and digital humanities communities, to the benefit of both.

1 Introduction

The emerging field of digital literary studies has embraced not only statistical analysis of literary texts in the corpus linguistics tradition, but even more complex methods such as principal components analysis (Burrows, 1987), clustering (Rybicki, 2006), and topic modeling (Goldstone and Underwood, 2012; Jockers, 2013). At the same time, there is sustained interest in computational linguistics in tackling problems that are specific to literature, as evidenced by an annual dedicated workshop as well as various papers at major conferences (Elson et al., 2010; Wallace, 2012; He et al., 2013; Bamman et al., 2014). Though some work in the shared ground between these two fields is explicitly cross-disciplinary, this is still fairly atypical, reflecting a deep cultural barrier (Hammond et al., 2013): in most cases, digital humanists are using off-the-shelf statistical tools with little or no interaction with computer scientists, and computational linguists are developing literature-specific techniques which are unavailable or unknown to the digital humanist community. The high-level goal of the project proposed here is to create an on-going two-way flow of resources between these groups, allowing computational linguists to identify pressing problems in the large-scale analysis of literary texts, and to give digital humanists access to a wider variety of NLP tools for exploring literary phenomena. The context for this exchange of ideas and resources is a tool, GutenTag[1], aimed at facilitating literary analysis of the Project Gutenberg (PG) corpus, a large collection of plain-text, publicly-available literature.

At its simplest level, GutenTag is a corpus reader; given the various eccentricities of the texts in Project Gutenberg (which reflects the diversity of the source texts and the rather haphazard nature of their collection), this application alone serves to justify its existence. A second facet of the tool is a corpus filter: it uses the information contained explicitly within the PG database and/or derived automatically from other sources to allow researchers to build subcorpora of interest reflecting their exact analytic needs. Another feature gives GutenTag its name: the tool has access to tagging models which represent the intersection of literary analysis needs and existing NLP methods. The output of GutenTag is either an XML corpus with tags (at both text and metatextual levels) based on the TEI-encoding standard; or, if desired, direct statistical analysis of the distribution of tags across different subcorpora. None of the features of GutenTag mentioned above are intended to be static: GutenTag is a tool that will grow and improve with feedback from the digital human-

[1] GutenTag is available at http://www.cs.toronto.edu/~jbrooke/gutentag/

Proceedings of NAACL-HLT Fourth Workshop on Computational Linguistics for Literature, pages 42–47,
Denver, Colorado, June 4, 2015. ©2015 Association for Computational Linguistics

ities community and new methods from the computational linguistics community.

2 Project Gutenberg

Project Gutenberg is a web-based collection of texts (mostly literary fiction such as novels, plays, and collections of poetry and short stories, but also nonfiction titles such as biographies, histories, cookbooks, reference works, and periodicals) which have fallen out of copyright in the United States. There are versions of Project Gutenberg in various countries around the world, but the development of GutenTag has been based on the US version.[2] The entire contents of the current archive is almost fifty thousand documents, though the work here is based on the most recently released (2010) DVD image, which has 29,557 documents. Nearly all major canonical works of English literature (and many from other languages) published before 1923 (the limit of US copyright) are included in the collection. The English portion of the corpus consists of approximately 1.7 billion tokens. Although it is orders of magnitude smaller than other public domain collections such as HathiTrust, the Internet Archive, and Google Books, PG has some obvious advantages over those collections: all major modern digitization efforts use OCR technology, but the texts in Project Gutenberg have also been at least proofread by a human (some are hand-typed), and the entire corpus remains sufficiently small that it can be conveniently downloaded as a single package;[3] this last is an important property relative to our interests here, since the tool assumes a complete copy of the PG corpus is present.

3 Reader

The standard format for texts in the PG corpus is plain text, most commonly the Latin-1 character set though some are UTF-8 Unicode. Generally speaking, the actual content is bookended by information about creation of the corpus and the copyright. The first challenge is removing this information–not a trivial task, given that the exact formatting is extremely inconsistent across texts in the corpus. GutenTag employs a fairly complex heuristic involving regular expressions; this handles some of the more troublesome cases by making sure that large sections of the text are not being tossed out. Other common extra-textual elements that we remove during this stage include references to illustrations and notes that are clearly not part of the text (e.g. transcriber's notes).

Most texts are structured to some degree, and this structure is reflected inconsistently in the raw Gutenberg texts by implicit indicators such as extra spacing, capitalized headings, and indentations. The structure depends on the type of literature, which may or may not be indicated in the datafile (see Section 4). Most books contain at least a title and chapter/section/part headings (which may be represented by a number, a phrase, or both); other common elements include tables of contents, introductions, prefaces, dedications, or initial quotations. Plays have an almost entirely different set of elements, including character lists, act/scene breaks, stage directions, and speaker tags. GutenTag attempts to identify common elements when they appear; these can be removed from the text under analysis if desired and/or used to provide structure to the text in the final output (as special tags, see Section 5). Note that this step generally has to occur before tokenization, since many markers of structure are destroyed in the tokenization process.

GutenTag is written in Python and built on top of the Natural Language Toolkit (Bird et al., 2009): for sentence and word tokenization, we use the NLTK regex tokenizer, with several pre- and post-processing tweaks to deal with specific properties of the corpus and to prevent sentence breaks after common English abbreviations. We are careful to preserve within-word hyphenation, contractions, and the direction of quotation marks.

4 Subcorpus Filter

Taken as a whole, the Gutenberg corpus is generally too diverse to be of use to researchers in particular fields. Relevant digital humanities projects are far more likely to target particular subsections of the corpus, e.g. English female novelists of the late 19th century. Fortunately, in addition to the raw texts, each document in the PG corpus has a correspond-

[2] http://www.gutenberg.org

[3] http://www.gutenberg.org/wiki/Gutenberg:The_CD_and_DVD_Project

ing XML data file which provides a bibliographic record, including the title, the name of the author, the years of the author's birth and death, the language in which the text is written, the Library of Congress classification (sometimes multiple), and the subject (often multiple). GutenTag provides a complete list of each of the non-numerical tags for reference and allows the user to perform an exact or partial string match to narrow down subcorpora of interest or to combine lists of independently defined subcorpora into a single subcorpus.

Although they are extremely useful, there are numerous problems with the built-in PG annotations. While Library of Congress classification is generally reliable for distinguishing literature from other books, for instance, it does not reliably distinguish between genres of literature. Therefore, GutenTag distinguishes prose fiction from drama and poetry by (at present) simple classification based on the typical properties of these genres. For drama, it looks to see if there are significant numbers of speaker tags (which unfortunately appear in numerous distinct forms in the corpus); to distinguish poetry from prose fiction, it uses line numbers and/or the location of punctuation (in poetry, punctuation often appears at the end of lines of verse); collections of short stories can often be distinguished from novels by their titles (e.g. *and other stories*). We make these automatic annotations available as a "genre" tag to help users create a more-exact subcorpus definition.

Other useful information missing from the PG database includes the text's publication date and place and information about the author such as their gender, nationality, place of birth, education, marital status, and membership in particular literary schools. When possible, we collect additional information about texts and their authors from other structured resources such as Open Library, which has most of the same texts but with additional publication information and metadata, and Wikipedia, which only references a small subset of titles/author, but usually in more detail. A more speculative idea for future work is to derive information about less-popular texts and authors from unstructured text.

We did not carry out a full independent evaluation of the (non-trival) subcorpus filtering and reader features of GutenTag, but we nevertheless took steps to ensure basic functionality: after developing some initial heuristics, we sampled 30 prose texts, 10 poetry texts, and 10 plays randomly from the PG corpus based on our automatic classification, resampling and improving our classification heuristics until we reached perfect performance. Then, using those 50 correctly-classified texts, we improved our heuristics for removing non-textual elements and identifying basic text structure until we had perfect performance in all 50 texts (as judged by one of the authors). Needless to say, we avoided including heuristics that had no possibility of generalization across multiple texts (for instance, hand-coding the titles of books). We also used these texts to confirm that sub-corpus filtering was working as expected. GutenTag comes with a list of the texts that were focused on during development, with the idea they could be pulled out using sub-corpus filtering and used as training or testing examples for more-sophisticated statistical techniques.

5 Tagging

Once a text has been tokenized, a tag can be defined as a string identifier, possibly with nominal or numerical attributes, which is associated with a span of tokens. Tags of the same type can be counted together, and their attributes can be counted (for nominal attributes) or summed or averaged (for numerical attributes) across a text, or across a subcorpus of texts. The particular tags desired in a run of GutenTag are specified by the user in advance. The simplest tag for each token is the token itself, or a lemmatized version of the token. Another tag of length one is the part-of-speech tag, which, in GutenTag, is currently provided by the NLTK part-of-speech tagger. GutenTag also supports simple named entity recognition to identify the major characters in a literary work, by looking at repeated proper names which appear in contexts which indicate personhood. Any collection of words or phrases can be grouped under a single tag using user-defined lexicons, which can be nominal or numerical; as examples of this, the GutenTag includes word properties from the MRC psycholinguistic database (Coltheart, 1980), the General Inquirer Dictionary (Stone et al., 1966) and high-coverage stylistic and polarity lexicons (Brooke and Hirst, 2013; Brooke and Hirst, 2014) which were built automatically using the variation within the PG corpus itself.

Tags above the word level include, most prominently, structural elements such as chapters identified in the corpus-reader step. Another tag supported in GutenTag is the TEI "said" tag which is used to identify quoted speech and assign it to a specific character. The current version of "said" identification first detects the quotation convention being used in the text (i.e. single or double quotes), matches right and left quotes to create quote spans, and then looks in the immediate vicinity around the quotes to identify a character (as identified using the character module) to whom to assign the quotation. Though currently functional, this is the first module in line to be upgraded to a fully statistical approach, for instance based on the work of He et al. (2013).

As far as GutenTag is concerned, a tagger is simply a function which takes in a tokenized text and (optionally) other tags which have been identified earlier in the pipeline, and then outputs a new set of tags. Even complex statistical models are often complex only in the process of training, and classification is often matter of simple linear combinations of features; adding new tagging modules should therefore be simple and seamless from both a user's and a developer's perspective. To conclude this section, we will discuss some of the ideas for kinds of tagging that might be useful from a digital humanities perspective as well as interesting for computational linguists. Some have been addressed already, and some have not. The following is intended not as an exhaustive list but rather as a starting point for further discussion.

At the simpler end of the spectrum, we can imagine taggers which identify some of the classic poetic elements such as rhyme scheme, meter, anaphora, alliteration, onomatopoeia, and the use of foreign languages (along with identification of the specific language being used). Metaphor detection is of growing interest in NLP (Tsvetkov et al., 2014), and would undoubtedly be useful for literary analysis (as would simile detection, a somewhat simpler task). Another challenging but important task is the identification of literary allusions: we envision not only the identification of allusions, but also the establishment of direct connections between alluding and alluded works with the PG corpus, which we could then employ to derive metrics of influence and canonicity within the corpus. We are also interested, where appropriate, in identifying features relevant to narratives: when analyzing a novel, for example, it would be interesting to be able to tag entire scenes with a physical location, a time of day, and a list of participants; for an entire narrative, it would be useful to identify particular points in the plot structure such as climax and dénouement, and other kinds of variation such as topic (Kazantseva and Szpakowicz, 2014) and narrator viewpoint (Wiebe, 1994).

6 Interfaces

GutenTag is intended for users with no programming background. The potential options are sufficiently complex that a run of GutenTag is defined within a single configuration file, including any number of defined subcorpora, the desired tag sets (including various built-in tagging options and user-defined lexicons), and options for output. We also offer a web interface for small-scale, limited analysis for those who do not want to download the entire corpus.

Given our interest in serving the digital humanities community, it is important that the output options reflect their needs. For those looking only for a tagged corpus, the Text Encoding Initiative (TEI) XML standard[4] is the obvious choice for corpus output format. The only potential incompatibility is with overlapping but non-nested tags (which are supported by our tag schema but not by XML), which are handled by splitting up the tags over the smaller span and linking them using an identifier and "next" and "prev" attributes. Numerical attributes for lexicons are handled using a "value" attribute. Again, users can choose whether they want to include structural elements that are not part of the main text, and whether they want to include these as part of the text, or as XML tags, or both.

For those who want numerical output, the default option is a count of all the desired tags for all the defined subcorpora. The counts can be normalized by token counts and/or divided up into scores for individual texts. We also allow counts of tags occurring only inside other tags, so that, for instance, different sub-genres within the same texts can be compared. GutenTag is not intended to provide more-

[4]http://www.tei-c.org/Guidelines/

sophisticated statistical analysis, but we can include it in the form of interfaces to the Numpy/Scipy Python modules if there is interest. We will include support for direct passing of subcorpora and the portions of subcorpora with a particular tag to MALLET (McCallum, 2002) for the purposes of building topic models, given the growing interest in their use among digital humanists.

7 Comparison with other tools

GutenTag differs from existing digital humanities text-analysis offerings in its focus on large-scale analysis using NLP techniques. Popular text-analysis suites such as Voyant[5] and TAPoR[6] present numerous useful and user-friendly options for literary scholars, but their focus on individual texts or small groups of texts as well as output which consists mostly of simple statistical measures or visualizations of surface phenomena means that they are unable to take advantage of the new insights that larger corpora and modern NLP methods can (potentially) provide. As digital humanists become increasingly interested in statistical approaches, the limiting factor is not so much the availability of accessible statistical software packages for doing analysis but rather the ability to identify interesting subsets of the data (including text spans *within* texts) on which to run these tools; GutenTag supplements these tools with the goal of producing more diverse, meaningful, and generalizable results.

GutenTag also has some overlap in functionality with literary corpus tools such as PhiloLogic[7], but such tools are generally based on manual annotations of structure and again offer only surface treatment of linguistic phenomena (e.g. identification of keywords) for text retrieval. We also note that there is a simple Python corpus reader for Gutenberg available[8], but it is intended for individual text retrevial via the web, and the only obvious overlap with GutenTag is the deletion of copyright header and footers; in this regard GutenTag is noticeably more advanced since the existing reader relies only on presence or absence of keyphrases in the offending spans.

[5]http://voyant-tools.org/

[6]http://tapor.ca/

[7]https://sites.google.com/site/philologic3/

[8]https://pypi.python.org/pypi/Gutenberg/0.4.0

There are of course many software toolkits that offer off-the-shelf solutions to a variety of general computational linguistics tasks: GutenTag makes direct use of NLTK (Bird et al., 2009), but there numerous other popular options–our choice of NLTK mostly reflects our preference for using Python, which we believe will allow for quicker and more flexible development in the long run. What is more important is that GutenTag is intended to make only modest use of off-the-shelf techniques, because we strongly believe that using NLP for literary analysis will require building literature-specific modules, even for tasks that are otherwise well-addressed in the field. In numerous ways, literary texts are simply too different from the newswire and web texts that have been the subject of the vast majority of work in the field, and there are many tasks fundamental to literary study that would be only a footnote in other contexts. Our intent is that GutenTag will become a growing repository for NLP solutions to tasks relevant to literary analysis, and as such we hope those working in digital humanities or computational linguistics will bring to our attention new modules for us to include. It is this inherently cross-disciplinary focus that is the clearest difference between GutenTag and other tools.

8 Conclusion

In the context of computational analysis of literature, digital humanists and computational linguists are natural symbionts: while increasing numbers of literary scholars are becoming interested in the insights that large-scale computational analysis can provide, they are often limited by their lack of technical expertise. GutenTag meets the needs of such scholars by providing an accessible tool for building large, highly customizable literary subcorpora from the PG corpus and for performing pertinent advanced NLP tasks in a user-appropriate manner. By thus drawing increasing numbers of literary scholars into the realm of computational linguistics, GutenTag promises to enrich the latter field by supplying it with new problems, new questions, and new applications. As the overlap between the spheres of digital humanities and computational linguistics grows larger, both fields stand to benefit.

Acknowledgements

This work was supported by the Natural Sciences and Engineering Research Council of Canada, the MITACS Elevate program, and the University of Guelph.

References

David Bamman, Ted Underwood, and Noah A. Smith. 2014. A bayesian mixed effects model of literary character. In *Proceedings of the 52st Annual Meeting of the Association for Computational Linguistics (ACL '14)*.

Steven Bird, Ewan Klein, and Edward Loper. 2009. *Natural Language Processing with Python*. O'Reilly Media Inc.

Julian Brooke and Graeme Hirst. 2013. Hybrid models for lexical acquisition of correlated styles. In *Proceedings of the 6th International Joint Conference on Natural Language Processing (IJCNLP '13)*.

Julian Brooke and Graeme Hirst. 2014. Supervised ranking of co-occurrence profiles for acquisition of continuous lexical attributes. In *Proceedings of The 25th International Conference on Computational Linguistics (COLING 2014)*.

John F. Burrows. 1987. *Computation into Criticism: A Study of Jane Austen's Novels and an Experiment in Method*. Clarendon Press, Oxford.

Max Coltheart. 1980. *MRC Psycholinguistic Database User Manual: Version 1*. Birkbeck College.

David K. Elson, Nicholas Dames, and Kathleen R. McKeown. 2010. Extracting social networks from literary fiction. In *Proceedings of the 48th Annual Meeting of the Association for Computational Linguistics (ACL '10)*.

Andrew Goldstone and Ted Underwood. 2012. What can topic models of PMLA teach us about the history of literary scholarship? *Journal of Digital Humanities*, 2.

Adam Hammond, Julian Brooke, and Graeme Hirst. 2013. A tale of two cultures: Bringing literary analysis and computational linguistics together. In *Proceedings of the 2nd Workshop on Computational Literature for Literature (CLFL '13)*.

Hua He, Denilson Barbosa, and Grzegorz Kondrak. 2013. Identification of speakers in novels. In *Proceedings of the 51st Annual Meeting of the Association for Computational Linguistics (ACL '13)*.

Matthew Jockers. 2013. *Macroanalysis: Digital Methods and Literary History*. University of Illinois Press, Champaign, IL.

Anna Kazantseva and Stan Szpakowicz. 2014. Hierarchical topical segmentation with affinity propagation. In *Proceedings of the 25th International Conference on Computational Linguistics (COLING 2014)*.

Andrew Kachites McCallum. 2002. Mallet: A machine learning for language toolkit. http://mallet.cs.umass.edu.

Jan Rybicki. 2006. Burrowing into translation: Character idiolects in Henryk Sienkiewicz's trilogy and its two English translations. *Literary and Linguistic Computing*, 21:91–103.

Philip J. Stone, Dexter C. Dunphy, Marshall S. Smith, and Daniel M. Ogilivie. 1966. *The General Inquirer: A Computer Approach to Content Analysis*. MIT Press.

Yulia Tsvetkov, Leonid Boytsov, Anatole Gershman, Eric Nyberg, and Chris Dyer. 2014. Metaphor detection with cross-lingual model transfer. In *Proceedings of the 52nd Annual Meeting of the Association for Computational Linguistics (ACL '14)*.

Byron C. Wallace. 2012. Multiple narrative disentanglement: Unraveling *Infinite Jest*. In *Proceedings of the 2012 Conference of the North American Chapter of the Association for Computational Linguistics: Human Language Technologies (NAACL-HLT '12)*.

Janyce M. Wiebe. 1994. Tracking point of view in narrative. *Computational Linguistics*, 20(2):233–287, June.

A Pilot Experiment on Exploiting Translations for Literary Studies on Kafka's "Verwandlung"

Fabienne Cap, Ina Rösiger and Jonas Kuhn
Institute for Natural Language Processing
University of Stuttgart
Germany
[cap|roesigia|kuhn]@ims.uni-stuttgart.de

Abstract

We present a manually annotated word alignment of Franz Kafka's *"Verwandlung"* and use this as a controlled test case to assess the principled usefulness of word alignment as an additional information source for the (monolingually motivated) identification of literary characters, focusing on the technically well-explored task of co-reference resolution. This pilot set-up allows us to illustrate a number of methodological components interacting in a modular architecture. In general, co-reference resolution is a relatively hard task, but the availability of word-aligned translations can provide additional indications, as there is a tendency for translations to *explicate* underspecified or vague passages.

1 Introduction

We present a pilot study for a methodological approach starting out with combinations of fairly canonical computational linguistics models but aiming to bootstrap a modular architecture of text-analytical tools that is more and more adequate from the point of view of literary studies. The core modeling component around which our pilot study is arranged is word-by-word alignment of a text and its translation, in our case Franz Kafka's *"Verwandlung"* (= *Metamorphosis*) and its translation to English. As research in the field of statistical machine translation has shown, word alignments of surprisingly good quality can be induced automatically exploiting co-occurrence statistics, given a sufficient amount of parallel text (from a reasonably homogeneous corpus of translated texts). In this pilot study, we present a manually annotated reference word alignment and use this to assess the principled usefulness of word alignment as an additional information source for the (monolingually motivated) task of identifying mentions of the same literary character in texts ((Bamman et al., 2014)). This is a very important analytical sub-step for further analysis (e.g., network analysis, event recognition for narratological analysis, stylistic analysis of character speech etc.). Literary character identification is related to, but not identical to named entity recognition, as is pointed out in Jannidis et al. (2015). In addition, co-reference resolution is required to map pronominal and other anaphoric references to full mentions of the character, using his or her name or other characteristic descriptions. In our present study we focus on the technically well-explored task of co-reference resolution.[1] This pilot set-up allows us to illustrate a number of methodological components interacting in a modular architecture.

2 Background

Whenever computational linguists exchange thoughts with scholars from literary studies who are open-minded towards "the Digital Humanities", the feeling arises that the machinery that computational linguistics (CL)/Natural Language Processing (NLP) has in their toolbox should *in principle* open up a variety of analytical approaches to literary studies – if only the tools and models were

[1] In their large-scale analysis of >15,000 English novels, Bamman et al. (2014) adopt a simpler co-reference resolution strategy for character clustering. Our work explores the potential for a more fine-grained analysis.

Proceedings of NAACL-HLT Fourth Workshop on Computational Linguistics for Literature, pages 48–57,
Denver, Colorado, June 4, 2015. ©2015 Association for Computational Linguistics

appropriately adjusted to the underlying research questions and characteristics of the targeted texts. At a technical level, important analytical steps for such studies are often closely related to "classical" tasks in CL and NLP. Possible applications include the identification of characters in narrative texts, extraction of interactions among them as they are depicted in the text, and possibly more advanced analytical categories such as the focalization of characters in the narrative perspective. Based on preprocessing steps that extract important feature information from formal properties of the text, algorithmic models that are both theoretically informed and empirically "trained" using reference data, should lead to automatic predictions that will at least support exploration of larger collections of literary texts and ideally also the testing of quantitative hypotheses.

Of course, the qualifying remark that the tools and models would first need to be adjusted to the higher-level questions and the characteristics of the texts under consideration weighs quite heavily: despite the structural similarity with established NLP analysis chains, the *actual* analytical questions are different, and NLP tools optimized for the standard domains (mostly newspaper text and parliamentary debates) may require considerable adjustment to yield satisfactory performance on literary texts.

2.1 Methodological Considerations

The large-scale solution to these challenges would be to overhaul the entire chain of standard NLP processing steps, adjusting it to characteristics of literary texts and then add new components that address analytical questions beyond the canonical NLP offerings. This would however presuppose a master plan, which presumably requires insights that can only come about during a process of stepwise adjustments. So, a more realistic approach is to bootstrap a more adaquate (modular) system architecture, starting from some initial set-up building on existing machinery combined in a pragmatic fashion. Everyone working with such an approach should be aware of the limited adequacy of many components used – but this may be a "healthy" methodological training: no analytical model chain should be relied on without critical reflection; so an imperfect initial architecture may increase this awareness and help adopting to meta-level analysis tools for visualization and stepwise evaluation. Ideally, it should also make it clear that the literary scholars' insights into the texts and the higher-level questions are instrumental in improving the system at hand, moving to more appropriate complex models (taking a view on modeling in the sense of McCarty (2005) as an iterative cycle of constructing, testing, analyzing, and reconstructing intermediate-stage models, viewed as tools to advance our understanding of the modeled object).[2]

2.2 Pilot Character of Word-aligned Text

This paper tries to make a contribution in this spirit, addressing a methodological modular "building block" which (i) has received enormous attention in technically oriented NLP work, and (ii) intuitively seems to bear considerable potential as an analytical tool for literary studies – both for in-depth analysis of a small selection of texts and for scalable analysis tasks on large corpora – and for which (iii) a realistic assessment leads one to expect the need for some systematic adjustments in the methods and machinery to make the established NLP approach fruitful in literary studies. We are talking about the use of translations of literary works into other languages and techniques from NLP research on statistical machine translation and related fields. Literature translations exist in abundance (relatively speaking), often in multiple variants for a given target language, and multiple target languages can be put side by side. Such translation corpora ("parallel corpora") are a natural resource for translational studies, but research in various subfields of NLP has shown that beyond this, the interpretive work that a translator performs as a by-product of translating a text, can often be exploited for analytical questions that are not *per se* taking a cross-linguistic perspective: Tentative word-by-word correspondences in a parallel corpus can be induced automatically, taking advantage of co-occurrence statistics from a large collection, with surprising reliability. These "word alignment" links can then be used to map concepts that are sufficiently invariant across languages. The so-called paradigm of "annotation projection" (pio-

[2]For a more extensive discussion of our methodological considerations, see also Kuhn and Reiter (2015 to appear).

neered by Yarowsky et al. (2001)) has been enormously successful, even for concepts that one would not consider particularly invariant (such as grammatical categories of words): here, strong statistical tendencies can be exploited.

Since the statistical induction of word alignments requires no knowledge-based preprocessing (the required sentence alignment can also be calculated automatically), it can in principle be applied to any collection of parallel texts. Hence, it is possible to test quite easily for which analytical categories that are of interest to literary scholars the translator's interpretive guidance could be exploited.

As pointed out in the introduction, we pick literary character identification as an analytical target category that is very central to literary studies of narrative text, focusing on the task of building chains of co-referent mentions of the same character. Co-reference resolution is a relatively hard task, but the availability of word-aligned translations can provide additional indications: surprisingly often, translators tend to use a different type of referential phrase in a particular position: pronouns are translated as more descriptive phrases, and vice versa. A hypothesis that is broadly adapted in translational studies states there is a tendency for translations to *explicate* underspecified or vague passages (Blum-Kulka, 1986). An example of "explication" that affects character mentions is found in the second sentence of the English translation of Kafka's *"Der Prozess"*:[3] the apposition *seiner Zimmervermieterin* ("his landlady"), whose attachment is structurally ambiguous, is translated with a parenthetical that makes the attachment to *Mrs. Grubach* explicit:

(DE) Die Köchin der Frau Grubach, seiner Zimmervermieterin, die ihm jeden Tag gegen acht Uhr früh das Frühstück brachte, kam diesmal nicht.

(EN) Every day at eight in the morning he was brought his breakfast by Mrs. Grubach's cook – Mrs. Grubach was his landlady – but today she didn't come.

As the example also illustrates, potential referential ambiguity is however only one aspect translators deal with. Here, the translation avoids the long relative clause (*die … brachte*) from the original after the initial subject, at the cost of using a completely different sentence structure. As a side effect, an additional referential chain (*Mrs. Grubach's cook – she*) is introduced in the English translation. So, it is an open question how effective it is in practice to use translational information in co-reference resolution of the original.[4]

For the purposes of this paper, which are predominantly methodological, aiming to exemplify the modular bootstrapping scenario we addressed above, the combination of word-alignment and coreference is a convenient playing ground: we can readily make use of existing NLP tool chains to reach analytical goals that are structurally not far from categories of serious interest. At the same time, the off-the-shelf machinery is clearly in a stage of limited adequacy, so we can point out the need for careful critical reflection of the system results.

2.3 Reference Data and Task-based Evaluation

To go beyond an impressionistic subjective assessment of some analytical tool's performance (which can be highly misleading since there are just too many factors that will escape attention), it is crucial to rely on a controlled scenario for assessing some modular component. It is indeed not too hard to arrive at a manually annotated reference dataset, and this can be very helpful to verify some of the working assumptions. In our case, working with translated literary texts, we made various assumptions: automatic word alignment will be helpful for accessing larger amounts of text; standard techniques from machine translation are applicable to this; word alignment can be used to "project" invariant analytical categories for text segments etc.

A manual word alignment gives us a reference dataset that can give us a clearer picture about many of these assumptions: we can compare an automatic alignment obtained by various techniques with the reference alignment; we can check how "projection" works in the ideal case that the alignment is correct

[3] www.farkastranslations.com/books/Kafka_Franz-Prozess-en-de.html

[4] An additional advantage of literary texts that we are not going into here is that often multiple translations (to the same or different languages) are available, which a robust automatic approach could exploit, hence multiplying the chance to find a disambiguating translation (see also (Zhekova et al., 2014)).

etc. With Kafka's *"Verwandlung"* we chose a literary text that has some convenient properties at a superficial level. At the same time, Kafka's extremely internalized narrative monoperspective makes this text highly marked. So, in a future study that goes deeper into narrative perspectives, this reference text may be complemented with other examples.

3 Manual Word Alignment

The basis for a good word alignment is a reliable sentence alignment. However, the latter is a challenging task on its own – especially when it comes to literature translations – and is thus beyond the scope of this paper. We start from a freely available version of Franz Kafka's *"Verwandlung"* which has been carefully sentence-aligned and provided for download[5]. We selected *"Verwandlung"* for two reasons: the first has to do with the original language of the work, here: German. Usually, human translators tend to *explicate* ambiguities in their translations. We thus assume that the word alignment will be useful for German co-reference resolution. The other has to do with the limitation of this work, both in terms of quantity (the parallel text to be manually aligned consisted of only 675 lines), and in terms of the low number of characters involved. It is fairly simple to resolve ambiguities occurring in this limited set of characters for a human annotator, but that does not neccessarily apply to an automatic co-reference resolver.For this pilot study, manual word alignments were established by a German native speaker with a computational linguistics background. The annotator was asked to mark translational correspondences. In lack of suitable correspondences, words are to be left unaligned.

3.1 Results

In the following, we quantitatively summarize the alignments we established for *"Verwandlung"*, focussing on personal pronouns and their respective translations. Let us first consider the translations for the pronouns of the original, German, language in Table 1 (a): it can be seen that indeed there are a few cases where a German pronoun is translated into a more specified person in English (see highlighted markup of the respective table cells). An ex-

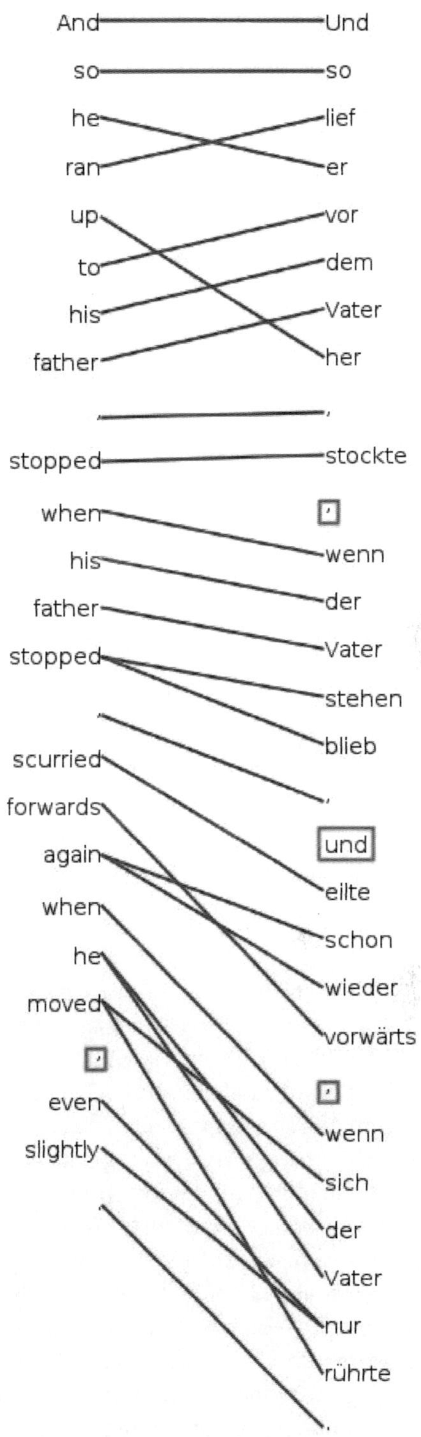

Figure 1: Screenshot of manual word alignment tool. It can be seen how the alignment from the second **he** to **der Vater** helps disambiguate the co-reference.

[5]http://opus.lingfil.uu.se/Books.php

(a) German pronouns together with their English translations

German	English translation					all
er	he	his	himself	him	Gregor's father	
	315	12	9	2	1	339
ihn	him	it	he	his		
	50	17	9	2		78
ihm	him	he	his	it		
	42	11	4	2		59
sein/seine[nmrs]	his	he	the	him	Gregor's	
	142	5	5	4	1	157
sie *(sg)*	she	her	his sister			
	107	24	1			132
ihr/ihre[nmrs] *(sg)*	her	she	the	his sister's		
	57	10	4	1		72
sie *(pl)*	they	their/them	the food	the pain	Gregor's father and mother	
	52	8	1	1	1	63
ihr/ihre[nmrs] *(pl)*	their	they	them			
	25	1	1			15

(b) English pronouns together with their alignment to the original German text

English	German original text							all
he	er	ihm	ihn	Gregor	man	sein/sein[er]	der Vater	
	349	12	9	10	5	5	2	390
him	ihn	ihm	Gregor	er	sein/sein[emrs]	sich	Vater	
	51	43	15	11	7	6	1	134
his	die	sein/sein[emrs]	de[nmrs]	ihm	Gregors	eine[nr]	des Vaters	
	140	140	111	4	4	4	2	380
she	sie	ihr/ihre[rm]	die	die Schwester	die Bedienerin	die Mutter	Grete	
	115	11	2	2	2	1	1	134
her	ihr/ihre[nmr]	de[mnr]	sie	die	(die) Mutter	die Schwester	das	
	51	24	22	17	2	2	2	120

Table 1: Overview of how German (a) and English (b) pronouns have been translated. The translations are obtained through manual alignment of the parallel German and English editions of the work. Highlighting indicates pronouns where the translations might actually help co-reference resolution.

ample is *"er"* (= "he"), which in one case is translated as "Gregor's father". In case of the plural pronoun *"sie"* (= "they") we can see that it is translated as "Gregor's father and mother" in one case and into the more abstract entities "the food" and "the pain". Even though not denoting personal entities, the latter can still help resolving the other pronouns that might occur in the close context. In Table 1 (b), we give results for the opposite direction, namely we show the German original words from which the English pronouns have been translated. Comparing these two tables, we can see that in general, more English pronouns are used than German ones (cf. last column "all" indicating the frequency with which the pronoun has occurred overall in the text). Be it a consequence thereof or not, we also find more resolved co-referential ambiguities in this translation direction. While "he" has been translated 10 times from *"Gregor"* and two times from *"der Vater"* (= "the father"), we find a more diverse distribution when looking at the female counterpart *"she"*, which has amongst others been translated from *"die Schwester"* (= "the sister"), *"die Bedienerin"* (= "the charwoman"), *"die Mutter"* (= "the mother") or *"Grete"*. In the next section, we will run a state-of-the-art co-reference resolver on both the German original and the English translation of the novel. For a subset of pronouns, we will then manually compare the outcome of the resolver with the translation to see in which of the cases highlighted in Table 1 (where access to a translation might help co-reference resolution), the access to the translation actually can improve co-reference resolution.

4 Automatic Coreference Resolution

Noun phrase coreference resolution is the task of determining which noun phrases (NPs) in a text or dialogue refer to the same real-world entities (Ng, 2010). Coreference resolution has been extensively addressed in NLP research, e.g. in the CoNLL shared task 2011 and 2012 (Pradhan et al., 2011; Pradhan et al., 2012)[6] or in the SemEval shared task 2010 (Recasens et al., 2010)[7]. State-of-the-art tools that take into account a variety of linguistic rules and features, most of the time in a machine learning setting, achieve promising results. However, when applying co-reference resolution tools on out-of-domain texts, i.e. texts that the system has not been trained on, performance typically decreases. Thus, co-reference resolution on literature text is even more challenging as most state-of-the-art co-reference resolver are trained on newspaper text. For a system that has been trained on newspaper articles, it is difficult to resolve the longer literary texts that typically revolve around a fixed set of characters. In our experiments, we for example observe a tendency of the resolver to create several co-reference chains for one character. Domain-adaptation is time-consuming, as it often requires manually designed gold data to increase performance. Moreover, recall that Kafka's *"Verwandlung"* has been written 100 years ago and that German language has been changing in this time period. This might lead to additional sparsities.

Apart from that, there are even some more general difficulties an automatic co-reference resolver has to deal with: First, it is difficult for a system to resolve an NP that has more than one potential antecedent candidates that match morpho-syntactically, i.e. that agree, for example, in number and gender. Second, often background or world knowledge is required to find the right antecedent. Consider the following examples taken from *"Verwandlung"* showing gold co-reference annotations through different colour markup: **Gregor** and **the father**.

(1) And so **he** ran up to **his father**, stopped when **his father** stopped, scurried forwards again when **he** moved, even slightly.

(2) **He** had thought that nothing at all remained from **his father's** business, at least **he** had never told **him** anything different, and **Gregor** had never asked **him** about it anyway.

For an automatic system, it is easy to confuse the two male persons present in the sentence, as they are both singular and masculine. Interestingly, humans can easily resolve these cases.

Due to the above mentioned reasons, it is particularly important to exploit given resources in a certain domain. In the literature area, translations into many languages are typically available. In the following, we will explain the benefits of using such translations by showing examples of how manual word alignment can help co-reference resolution, here in the case of *"Verwandlung"*. We will also talk about the prospects of automatic word alignment.

4.1 Experimental Setup

For English, we perform our experiments using the IMS HotCoref co-reference resolver (Björkelund and Kuhn, 2014) as a state-of-the-art co-reference resolution system that obtains the best results published to date on the English CoNLL 2012 Shared Task data[8]. It models co-reference as a directed rooted tree, making it possible to use non-local features that go beyond pair-based information. We use the English non-local model[9] that comprises the training and development datasets from the CoNLL 2012 shared task. These datasets, as common in most NLP tasks, mainly consists of news text and dialogue.

For German, our experiments are also based on the IMS HotCoref system, but as German is not a language that is featured in the standard resolver, we first had to adapt it to it. These adaptations include gender and number agreement, lemma-based (sub)string match and a feature that addresses German compounds, to name only a few. Again, the training data consists of newspaper texts as we base our experiments on the Tueba-D/Z SemEval data[10] (version 8).

[6] http://conll.cemantix.org/2012

[7] http://stel.ub.edu/semeval2010-coref/

[8] www.ims.uni-stuttgart.de/forschung/ressourcen/werkzeuge/HOTCoref.en.html

[9] www2.ims.uni-stuttgart.de/cgi-bin/anders/dl?hotcorefEngNonLocalModel

[10] http://www.sfs.uni-tuebingen.de/de/ascl/ressourcen/corpora/tueba-dz.html

4.2 Using Alignments

In order to assess the usefulness of word alignments in co-reference resolution, we ran IMS-HotCoref on both the German original text and its English translation. Then, we had a closer look at the sentences in which having access to the translation of a pronoun presumably helps its resolution. In Table 2, we show how the co-reference resolver performs for each of the German translations being highlighted in Table 1(a). It can be seen that in 3 out of 7 cases, the word alignment would indeed improve the resolution.

German	English	IMS-HotCoref	correct?
er	Gregor's father	der	NO
seiner	Gregor's	der Zug	NO
sie *(sg)*	his sister	Schwester	YES
ihre	his sister's	Schwester	YES
sie *(pl)*	the food	Herren	NO
	the pain	Schmerzen	YES
	Gregor's mother and father	Eltern	YES

Table 2: Results of the German co-reference resolver.

For the opposite direction, where the German original text is assumed to help resolve coreferential ambiguities, Table 3 contains the results of the co-reference resolver for all crucial occurrences of the pronoun "he", as highlighted in Table 1(b).

English	German	IMS-HotCoref	correct?
he	Gregor	one of the trainees	NO
	Gregor	Gregor	YES
	Gregor	Gregor	YES
	Gregor	(one after) another	NO
	Gregor	Gregor	YES
	Gregor	Gregor	YES
	Gregor	father	NO
	Gregor	Gregor	YES
	Gregor	Gregor	YES
	Gregor	Gregor	YES
	der Vater	Gregor	NO
	der Vater	Gregor	NO

Table 3: Results of the English co-reference resolver.

And even here, we find evidence in 5 of 12 cases that the alignment to the original language would help co-reference resolution. Thereof, the latter two cases are particularly challenging. In fact, we have already introduced them as Examples (1) and (2) above. For Example (1), Figure 2 (a) shows the proposed co-reference annotations by the DE and EN co-reference resolver on the right hand side while gold annotations are shown on the left hand side.

The German sentence is much easier to process for an automatic system, as it contains fewer pronouns and many identical definite descriptions, and so unsurprisingly, the output of the German tool is correct. The English system, however, wrongly links the second pronoun *he* (marked with a box) to Gregor (=the first *he*), as there are two potential antecedents in the sentence that both agree in number and gender with the anaphor.

If we have word alignments, as shown in Figure 1, we can see that the second *he* is aligned with *der Vater* (again, marked with a box), and therefore we now know that the tool's assignment was wrong.

For Example (2), the word alignment again helps predict the right co-reference links. The output of the tool and the right gold annotation is shown in Figure 2 (b). The English co-reference resolver wrongly puts the second *he* (marked by a box) in the co-reference chain describing Gregor, but the word alignment (not shown for Example (2)) tells us that this is not the case: it actually refers to the father.

We also experimented with a second EN co-reference resolver, the Stanford co-reference system as part of the Stanford Core NLP tools[11], but the results were similar to the IMS HotCoref system. When comparing two system outputs or gold annotations with the output predicted by the system, the ICARUS Coreference Explorer[12] (Gärtner et al., 2014) is a useful tool to browse and search co-reference-annotated data. It can display co-reference annotations as a tree, as an entity grid, or in a standard text-based display mode. Particularly useful in our case is the fact that the tool can compare two different annotations on the same document. In the differential view, the tool analyses discrepancies between the predicted and the gold annotation (or two predicted annotations, respectively) and marks different types of errors with different colors. Figure 3 shows an exemplary differential view between the Stanford and the HotCoref system for Kafka's *"Verwandlung"*.

[11] `nlp.stanford.edu/software/corenlp.shtml`

[12] `www.ims.uni-stuttgart.de/forschung/ressourcen/werkzeuge/icarus.html`

	gold co-reference annotations	output of IMS-HotCoref
EN	And so he ran up to his father, stopped when his father stopped, scurried forwards again when he moved, even slightly.	And so he ran up to his father, stopped when his father stopped, scurried forwards again when he moved, even slightly.
DE	Und so lief er vor dem Vater her, stockte, wenn der Vater stehen blieb, und eilte schon wieder vorwärts, wenn sich der Vater nur rührte.	Und so lief er vor dem Vater her, stockte, wenn der Vater stehen blieb, und eilte schon wieder vorwärts, wenn sich der Vater nur rührte.

(a) Example (1)

	gold co-reference annotations	output of IMS-HotCoref
EN	He had thought that nothing at all remained from his father's business, at least he had never told him anything different, and Gregor had never asked him about it anyway.	He had thought that nothing at all remained from his father's business, at least he had never told him anything different, and Gregor had never asked him about it anyway.
DE	Er war der Meinung gewesen , daß dem Vater von jenem Geschäft her nicht das Geringste übriggeblieben war , zumindest hatte ihm der Vater nichts Gegenteiliges gesagt , und Gregor allerdings hatte ihn auch nicht darum gefragt .	Er war der Meinung gewesen , daß dem Vater von jenem Geschäft her nicht das Geringste übriggeblieben war , zumindest hatte ihm der Vater nichts Gegenteiliges gesagt , und Gregor allerdings hatte ihn auch nicht darum gefragt .

(b) Example (2)

Figure 2: Illustration of gold co-reference annotations and tool outputs for Examples (1)+(2).

5 Related Work

As mentioned earlier, the "annotation projection" paradigm was first described by Yarowsky et al. (2001) in order to improve POS-tagging. However, it has proven useful for a number of other applications, e.g. for multilingual co-reference resolution. Most approaches aim at projecting co-references which are available for one (usually well-resourced) language to another (less-resourced) language for which no tools or not even annotated training data are available. The degree of automatic processing ranges from using manually annotated co-references and hand-crafted translations (e.g. Harabagiu and Maiorano (2000)) to automatically obtained word alignments and combined with a manual post-editing of the obtained co-references (e.g. (Postolache et al., 2006)). Finally, some approaches make use of automatic word alignment, but instead of manual post-editing, they access the quality of the projection through training an own co-reference resolver for the under-resourced language based on the projected data (e.g. de Souza and Orăsan (2011) and Rahman and Ng (2012)). Zhekova et al. (2014) were to our knowledge the first ones who projected co-reference annotations in the literature domain, in contrast to general language texts. In lack of a reasonable amount of parallel training data to train an automatic word alignment of the language pair Russian to German, they developed an alignment tool which facilitates manual alignment. In contrast to previous works, they used not only one translation but different German translations of a Russian novel. Mikhaylova (2014) applied automatic word alignment to the same Russian novel and its German translations, trained on the novel itself. In order to improve word alignment performance on such a comparably small training corpus, she made use of simple generalisation techniques (e.g. lemmatisation). Most previous works on multilingual co-reference resolution focus on using co-referential annotations in one language to obtain the same kind of annotations in another language. In our work, we want to improve co-reference resolution in one (sufficiently well resourced) language by using translations from or into another language. This underlying concept has already been described by Harabagiu and Maiorano (2000). However, they rely on manual projections instead of automatic word alignment and moreover, they apply their approach to general language text and not to literature.

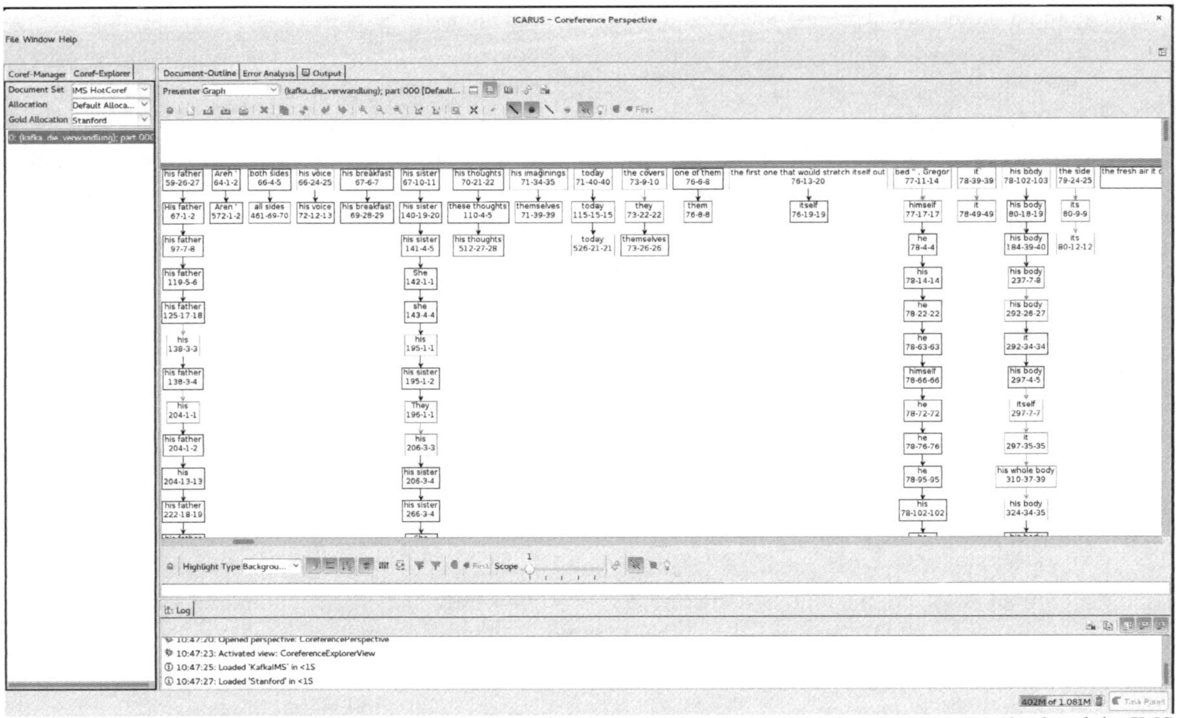

Figure 3: The ICARUS differential error analysis explorer illustrates the differences between the Stanford and the IMS HotCoref system using colour markup.

6 Conclusion and Future Work

We presented a pilot study in which we show how computational linguistic tools and resources can help to improve the identification of character/persona references in literary texts. Our test case is fairly controlled, which enables us to assess the modular components on their own. Based on a manual gold standard word alignment of Franz Kafka's *"Verwandlung"* we show numerous examples for which the translation of a pronominal referent can help to resolve coreferential ambiguites which otherwise may not be resolved accordingly. Having shown that, we will in the near future focus on substituting the manual alignment with an automatic word alignment approach. Due to the limited training data, we will examine different possibilities to improve automatic word alignment of literature text. As German is a morphologically rich language, lemmatisation should definitely be considered. Moreover, the training text for automatic word alignment might be enriched with general language data. In order to enhance the positive matching of personal pronouns to names used in the underlying novel, we will use a POS-tagger to identify proper nouns and then either replace them with names used in the literature or leave them underspecified. The manual gold standard alignment we presented for *"Verwandlung"* is useful in at least two respects for future works: on the one hand it serves us as an upper bound for annotation projection beyond standard co-reference resolution (e.g. distinguishing canonical stative present tense usage and historical/scenic present tense usage), on the other hand we can use it to approximate the quality of different automatic word alignment approaches on literary texts. In the future, we will adopt our automatic co-reference resolver to use the word alignment of pronominal referents, which should lead to an improved performance. While our pilot study is on literary texts, word alignments can be used for co-reference resolution even for texts from other genres, as long as parallel translations are available.

Acknowledgements

This work was supported by the Deutsche Forschungsgemeinschaft (DFG) grants for the projects D2 and A6 of the SFB 732.

References

David Bamman, Ted Underwood, and Noah A. Smith. 2014. A Bayesian Mixed Effects Model of Literary Character. In *Proceedings of the 52nd Annual Meeting of the Association for Computational Linguistics*, pages 370–379, Baltimore, Maryland.

Anders Björkelund and Jonas Kuhn. 2014. Learning Structured Perceptrons for Coreference Resolution with Latent Antecedents and Non-local Features. In *ACL'14: Proceedings of the 52nd Annual Meeting of the Association for Computational Linguistics*, Baltimore, Maryland.

Shoshana Blum-Kulka. 1986. Shifts of Cohesion and Coherence in Translation. In J. House and S. Blum-Kulka, editors, *Interlingual and Intercultural Communication*, pages 17–35. Gunter Narr Verlag, Tübingen, Germany.

José Guilherme Camargo de Souza and Constantin Orăsan. 2011. Can Projected Chains in Parallel Corpora Help Coreference Resolution? In *Anaphora Processing and Applications*, pages 59–69. Springer.

Markus Gärtner, Gregor Thiele, Wolfgang Seeker, Anders Björkelund, and Jonas Kuhn. 2014. ICARUS – An Extensible Graphical Search Tool for Dependency Treebanks. In *ACL'13: Proceedings of the 51nd Annual Meeting of the Association for Computational Linguistics: Systems Demonstrations.*, Sofia, Bulgaria.

Sanda M Harabagiu and Steven J Maiorano. 2000. Multilingual Coreference Resolution. In *Proceedings of the 6th Conference on Applied Natural Language Processing*, pages 142–149.

Fotis Jannidis, Markus Krug, Isabella Reger, Martin Toepfer, Lukas Weimer, and Frank Puppe. 2015. Automatische Erkennung von Figuren in deutschsprachigen Romanen. Conference Presentation at "Digital Humanities im deutschsprachigen Raum".

Jonas Kuhn and Nils Reiter. 2015, to appear. A Plea for a Method-Driven Agenda in the Digital Humanities. In *Proceedings of Digital Humanities 2015: Global Digital Humanities*, Sydney.

Willard McCarty. 2005. *Humanities Computing*. Palgrave Macmillan.

Alena Mikhaylova. 2014. Koreferenzresolution in mehreren Sprachen. Master's thesis, Ludwig Maximilians Universität München.

Vincent Ng. 2010. Supervised Noun Phrase Coreference Research: The First Fifteen Years. In *ACL'10: Proceedings of the 48th Annual Meeting of the Association for Computational Linguistics*, pages 1396–1411.

Oana Postolache, Dan Cristea, and Constantin Orasan. 2006. Transferring Coreference Chains Through Word Alignment. In *LREC'06: Proceedings of the 5th International Conference on Language Ressources and Evaluation*.

Sameer Pradhan, Lance Ramshaw, Mitchell Marcus, Martha Palmer, Ralph Weischedel, and Nianwen Xue. 2011. CoNLL-2011 Shared Task: Modeling Unrestricted Coreference in OntoNotes. In *CoNLL'11: Proceedings of the 15th Conference on Computational Natural Language Learning: Shared Task*, pages 1–27.

Sameer Pradhan, Alessandro Moschitti, Nianwen Xue, Olga Uryupina, and Yuchen Zhang. 2012. CoNLL-2012 Shared Task: Modeling Multilingual Unrestricted Coreference in OntoNotes. In *Proceedings of the Joint Conference on Empirical Methods in Natural Language Processing (EMNLP) and the Conference on Computational Natural Language Learning (CoNLL): Shared Task*, pages 1–40.

Altaf Rahman and Vincent Ng. 2012. Translation-based Projection for Multilingual Coreference Resolution. In *Proceedings of the 2012 Conference of the North American Chapter of the Association for Computational Linguistics: Human Language Technologies*, pages 720–730.

Marta Recasens, Lluís Màrquez, Emili Sapena, M Antònia Martí, Mariona Taulé, Véronique Hoste, Massimo Poesio, and Yannick Versley. 2010. Semeval-2010 Task 1: Coreference Resolution in Multiple Languages. In *Semeval'10: Proceedings of the 5th International Workshop on Semantic Evaluation*, pages 1–8. Association for Computational Linguistics.

David Yarowsky, Grace Ngai, and Richard Wicentowski. 2001. Inducing Multilingual Text Analysis Tools via Robust Projection across Aligned Corpora. In *HLT'01: Proceedings of the 1st International Conference on Human Language Technology research*, pages 1–8. Association for Computational Linguistics.

Desislava Zhekova, Robert Zangenfeind, Alena Mikhaylova, and Tetiana Nikolaienko. 2014. Alignment of Multiple Translations for Linguistic Analysis. In *Proceedings of the The 3rd Annual International Conference on Language, Literature and Linguistics (L3)*, pages 9–10.

Identifying Literary Texts with Bigrams

Andreas van Cranenburgh[*†]
[*]Huygens ING
Royal Dutch Academy of Sciences
The Hague, The Netherlands
Andreas.van.Cranenburgh@huygens.knaw.nl

Corina Koolen[†]
[†]Institute for Logic, Language and Computation
University of Amsterdam
The Netherlands
C.W.Koolen@uva.nl

Abstract

We study perceptions of literariness in a set of contemporary Dutch novels. Experiments with machine learning models show that it is possible to automatically distinguish novels that are seen as highly literary from those that are seen as less literary, using surprisingly simple textual features. The most discriminating features of our classification model indicate that genre might be a confounding factor, but a regression model shows that we can also explain variation between highly literary novels from less literary ones within genre.

1 Introduction

> The prose, plot, [the] characters, the sequence of the events, the thoughts that run in Tony Websters mind, big revelation in the end . . . They are all part of the big beautiful ensemble that delivers an exceptionally nice written novella. — (from a review on Goodreads of Julian Barnes, *A Sense of an Ending*)

However much debated the topic of literary quality is, one thing we do know: we cannot readily pinpoint what 'literary' means. Literary theory has insisted for a number of years that it lies mostly outside of the text itself (cf. Bourdieu, 1996), but this claim is at odds with the intuitions of readers, of which the quote above is a case in point. Publishers, critics, and literary theorists all influence the opinions of readers, but nevertheless, in explaining the sense of rapture or awe they experience, they will choose textual elements to refer to. In our project,[1] we try to find whether novels that are seen as literary have certain textual characteristics in common, and if so, what meaning we can assign to such commonalities. In other words, we try to answer the following question: are there particular textual conventions in literary novels that contribute to readers judging them to be literary?

In this paper, we show that there are indeed textual characteristics that contribute to perceived literariness. We use data from a large survey conducted in the Netherlands in 2013, in which readers were asked to rate novels that they had read on a scale of literariness and of general quality (cf. section 2). We show that using only simple bigram features (cf. section 3), models based on Support Vector Machines can successfully separate novels that are seen as highly literary from less literary ones (cf. section 4). This works with both content and style related features of the text. Interestingly, general quality proves harder to predict. Interpretation of features shows that genre plays a role in literariness (cf. section 5), but results from regression models indicate that the textual features also explain differences within genres.

2 Survey Data and Novels

During the summer of 2013, the Dutch reading public was asked to give their opinion on 401 novels published between 2007 and 2012 that were most often sold or borrowed between 2009 and 2012. This list was chosen to gather as many ratings as possible

[1]The Riddle of Literary Quality, cf. http://literaryquality.huygens.knaw.nl

Proceedings of NAACL-HLT Fourth Workshop on Computational Linguistics for Literature, pages 58–67,
Denver, Colorado, June 4, 2015.

	Original	Translated
Thrillers	0	31
Literary thrillers	26	29
Literary fiction	27	33

Table 1: The number of books in each category. These categories were assigned by the publishers.

(less popular novels might receive too few ratings for empirical analysis), and to ensure that readers were not influenced too much by common knowledge on their canonisation (this is less likely for more recent books). About 13,000 people participated in the survey. Participation was open to anyone. Participants were asked, among other things, to select novels that they had read and to rate them on two scales from 1–7: literariness (not very literary–very literary) and general quality (bad–good). These two were distinguished because a book that is not literary can still be considered to be a good book, because it is suspenseful or funny for instance; conversely, a novel that is seen as literary can still be considered to be bad (for instance if a reader does not find it engaging), although we found no examples of this in our results. No definition was given for either of the two dimensions, in order not to influence the intuitive judgments of participants. The notion of literariness in this work is therefore a pretheoretical one, directly reflecting the perceptions of the participants. In this work we use the mean of the ratings of each book.

The dataset used in this paper contains a selection of 146 books from the 401 included in the survey; see Table 1 and 2. Both translated and original (Dutch) novels are included. It contains three genres, as indicated by the publisher: literary novels, literary thrillers and thrillers. There are no Dutch thrillers in the corpus. Note that these labels are ones that the publishers have assigned to the novels. We will not be using these labels in our experiments—save for one where we interpret genre differences—we base ourselves on reader judgements. In other words: when we talk about highly literary texts, they (in theory) could be part of any of these genres, as long as readers judged them to be highly literary.

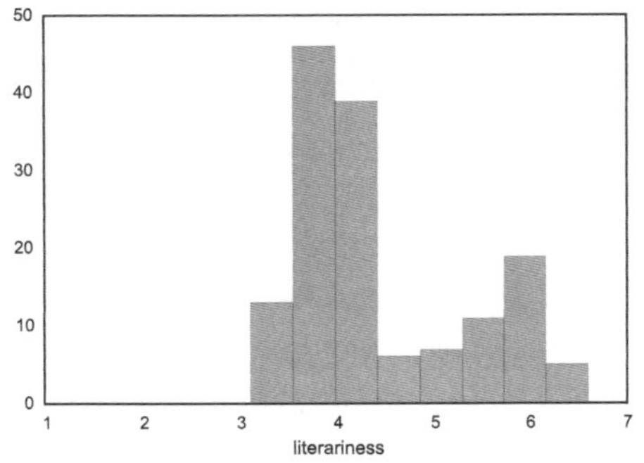

Figure 1: A histogram of the mean literary ratings.

3 Experimental setup

Three aspects of a machine learning model can be distinguished: the target of its predictions, the data which predictions are based on, and the kind of model and predictions it produces.

3.1 Machine Learning Tasks

We consider two tasks:

1. Literariness
2. Bad/good (general quality)

The target of the classification model is a binary classification whether a book is within the 25 % judged to be the most literary, or good. Figure 1 shows a histogram of the literary judgments. This cutoff divides the two peaks in the histogram, while ensuring that the number of literary novels is not too small.

A more difficult task is to try to predict the average rating for literariness of each book. This not only involves the large differences between thrillers and literary novels, but also smaller differences within these genres.

3.2 Textual Features

The features used to train the classifier are based on a bag-of-words model with relative frequencies. Instead of single words we use word bigrams. Bigrams are occurrences of two consecutive words observed in the texts. The bigrams are restricted to those that occur in between 60 % and 90 % of texts used in the model, to avoid the sparsity of rare bigrams on the one hand, and the most frequent function bigrams on

	Original	Translated
literature	Bernlef, Dis, Dorrestein, Durlacher, Enquist, Galen, Giphart, Hart, Heijden, Japin, Kluun, Koch, Kroonenberg, Launspach, Moor, Mortier, Rosenboom, Scholten, Siebelink, Verhulst, Winter.	Auel, Avallone, Baldacci, Binet, Blum, Cronin, Donoghue, Evans, Fragoso, George, Gilbert, Giordano, Harbach, Hill, Hodgkinson, Hosseini, Irving, James, Krauss, Lewinsky, Mastras, McCoy, Pick, Picoult, Rosnay, Ruiz Zafn, Sansom, Yalom.
literary thrillers	Appel, Dijkzeul, Janssen, Noort, Pauw, Terlouw, Verhoef, Vermeer, Visser, Vlugt	Coben, Forbes, French, Gudenkauf, Hannah, Haynes, Kepler, Koryta, Lackberg, Larsson, Lckberg, Nesbo, Patterson, Robotham, Rosenfeldt, Slaughter, Stevens, Trussoni, Watson.
thrillers		Baldacci, Clancy, Cussler, Forsyth, Gerritsen, Hannah, Hoag, Lapidus, McFadyen, McNab, Patterson, Roberts, Rose.

Table 2: Authors in the dataset

the other. No limit is placed on the total number of bigram features. We consider two feature sets:

content bigrams: Content words contribute meaning to a sentence and are thus topic related; they consist of nouns, verbs, adjectives, and adverbs. Content bigrams are extracted from the original tokenized text, without further preprocessing.

style bigrams: Style bigrams consist of function words, punctuation, and part-of-speech tags of content words (similar to Bergsma et al. 2012). In contrast with content words, function words determine the structure of sentences (determiners, conjunctions, prepositions) or express relationships (pronouns, demonstratives). Function words are identified by a selection of part-of-speech tags and a stop word list. Function words are represented with lemmas, e.g., auxiliary verbs appear in uninflected form. Lemmas and part-of-speech tags were automatically assigned by the Alpino parser.[2]

3.3 Models

All machine learning experiments are performed with `scikit-learn` (Pedregosa et al., 2011). The classifier is a linear Support Vector Machine (SVM) with regularization tuned on the training set. The cross-validation is 10-fold and stratified (each fold has a distribution of the target class that is similar to that of the whole data set).

For regression the same setup of texts and features is used as for the classification experiments, but the machine learning model is a linear Support Vector Regression model.

4 Results

Before we train machine learning models, we consider a dimensionality reduction of the data. Figure 2 shows a non-negative matrix factorization of the style bigrams. In other words, this is a visualization of a decomposition of the bigram counts, without taking into account whether novels are literary or not (i.e., an unsupervised model). Notice that most of the non-literary novels (red) cluster together in one corner, while the literary books (blue) show more variation. When content bigrams are used, a similar cluster of non-literary books emerges, but interestingly, this cluster only consists of translated works. With style bigrams this does not occur.

This result seems to suggest that non-literary books are easier to recognize than literary books, since the literary novels show more variation. However, note that this decomposition present just one way to summarize and visualize the data. The classification

[2]Cf. `http://www.let.rug.nl/vannoord/alp/Alpino/`

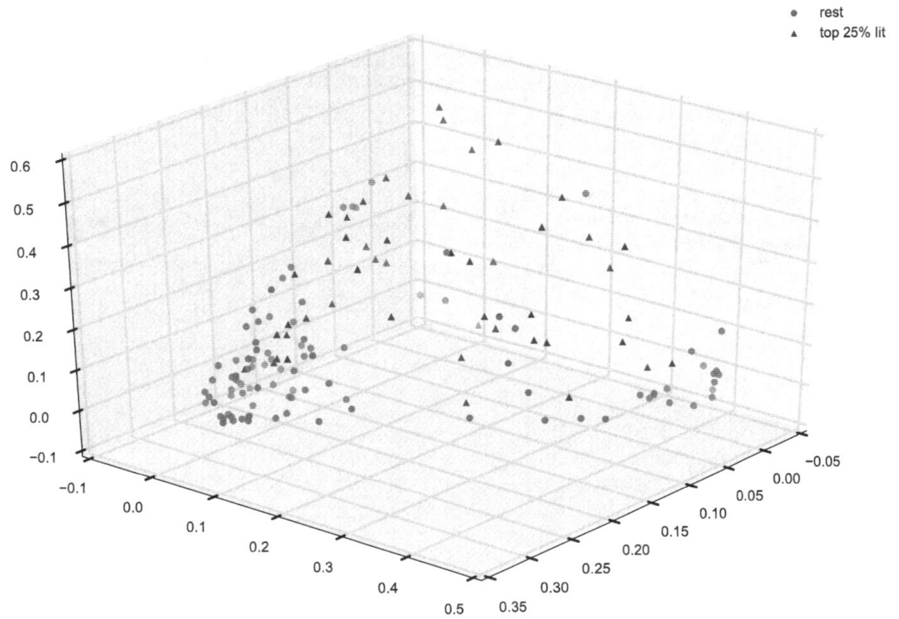

Figure 2: Non-negative matrix factorization based on style bigrams (literary novels are the blue triangles).

Features	Literary	Bad/good
Content bigrams	90.4	63.7
Style bigrams	89.0	63.0

Table 3: Classification accuracy (percentage correct).

Features	Literary	Bad/Good
Content bigrams	61.3 (0.65)	33.5 (0.49)
Style bigrams	57.0 (0.67)	22.2 (0.52)

Table 4: Evaluation of the regression models; R^2 scores (percentage of variation explained), root mean squared error in parentheses (1–7).

model, when trained specifically to recognize literary and non-literary texts, can still identify particular discriminating features.

4.1 Classification

Table 3 shows the evaluation of the classification models. The content bigrams perform better than the style bigrams. The top-ranked bigram features of the model for literary classification are shown in Table 5.

If we look only at the top 20 bigrams that are most predictive of literary texts according to our model and plot how often they occur in each genre as specified by the publishers, we see that these bigrams occur significantly more often in literary texts; cf. the plot in Figure 4. This indicates that there are features specific to literary texts, despite the variance among literary texts shown in Figure 2.

When trained on the bad/good dimension, the classification accuracy is around 60 %, compared to around 90 % for literariness, regardless of whether the features are about content or style bigrams. This means that the bad/good judgments are more difficult to predict from these textual features. This is not due to the variance in the survey responses themselves. If literariness were a more clearly defined concept for the survey participants than general quality, we would expect there to be less consensus and thus more variance on the latter dimension. But this is not what we find; in fact the mean of the standard deviations of the bad/good responses is lower than for the literariness responses (1.08 vs. 1.33). Rather, it is likely that the bad/good dimension depends on higher-level, plot-related characteristics, or text-extrinsic social factors.

4.2 Regression

The regression results cannot be evaluated with a simple 'percentage correct' accuracy metric, because

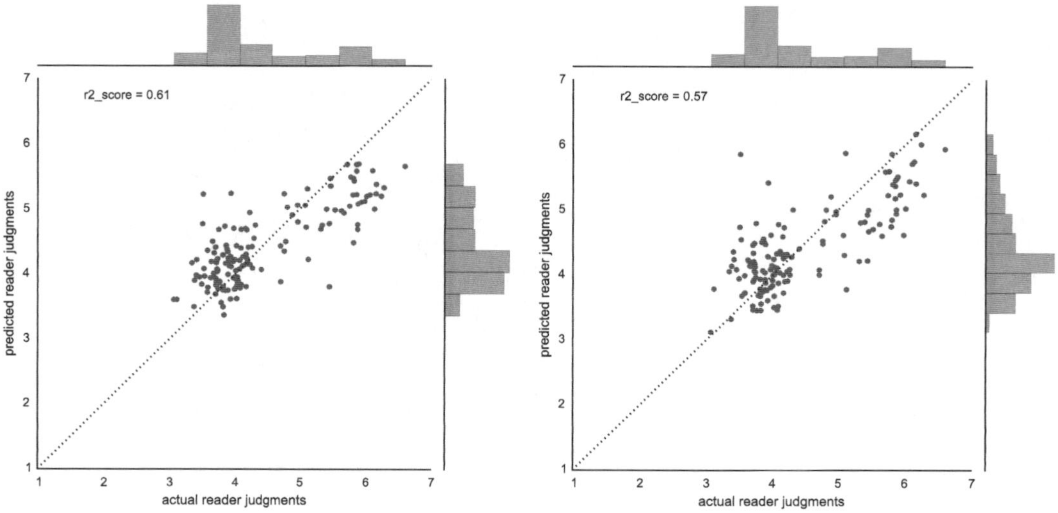

Figure 3: Regression results for predicting literary judgments with content bigrams (left) and style bigrams (right).

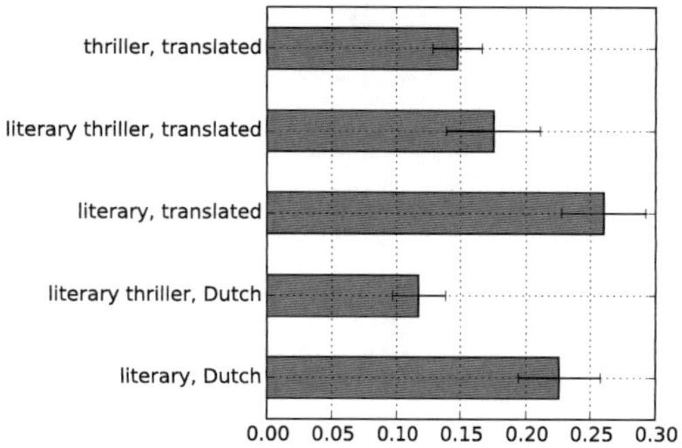

Figure 4: A barplot of the number of occurrences of the top 20 most important literary features (cf. Table 5) across the genres given by the publisher (error bars show 95 % confidence interval).

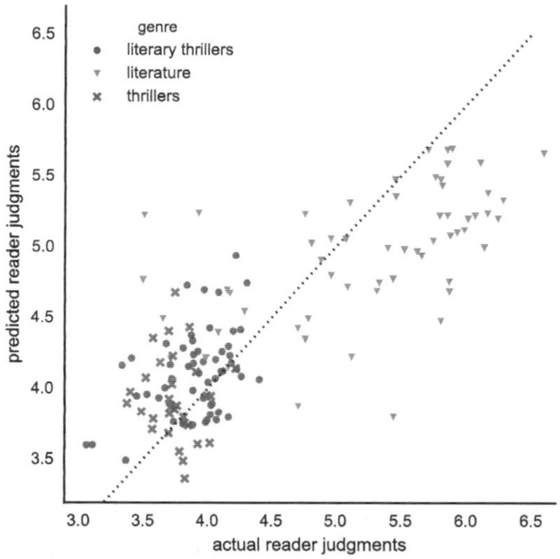

Figure 5: Regression results for predicting literary judgments with content bigrams, with data points distinguished by the publisher-assigned genre.

it is not feasible to predict a continuous variable exactly. Instead we report the coefficient of determination (R^2). This metric captures the percentage of variation in the data that the model explains by contrasting the errors of the model predictions with those of the null model which always predicts the mean of the data. R^2 can be contrasted with the root mean squared error, also known as the standard error of the estimate, or the norm of residuals, which measures how close the predictions are to the target on average. In contrast with R^2, this metric has the same scale as the original data, and lower values are better.

The regression scores are shown in Table 4. Predicting the bad/good scores is again more difficult. The regression results for literariness predictions are visualized in Figure 3. Each data point represents a single book. The x-axes show the literariness ratings from survey participants, while the y-axes show the predictions from the model. The diagonal line shows what the perfect prediction would be, and the further the data points (novels) are from this line, the greater the error. On the sides of the graphs the histograms show the distribution of the literariness scores. Notice that the model based on content bigrams mirrors the bimodal nature of the literariness ratings, while the histogram of predicted literariness scores based on style bigrams shows only a single peak.

Figure 5 shows the same regression results with the publisher-assigned genres highlighted. The graph shows that predicting the literariness of thrillers is more difficult than predicting the literariness of the more literary rated novels. Most thrillers have ratings between 3.4 and 4.3, while the model predicts a wider range of ratings between 3.3 and 5.0; i.e., the model predicts more variation than actually occurs. For the literary novels both the predicted and actual judgments show a wide range between 4.5 and 6.5. The actual judgments of the literary novels are about 0.5 points higher than the predictions. However, there are novels at both ends of this range for which the ratings are well predicted. Judging by the dispersion of actual and predicted ratings of the literary novels compared to the thrillers, the model accounts for more of the variance within the ratings of literary novels.

It should be noted that while in theory 100 % is the perfect score, the practical ceiling is much lower due to the fact that the model is trying to predict an average rating—and because part of the variation in literariness will only be explainable with richer features, text-extrinsic sociological influences, or random variation.

5 Interpretation

As the experiments show, there are textual elements that allow a machine learning model to distinguish between works that are perceived as highly literary as opposed to less literary ones—at least for this dataset and survey. We now take a closer look at the features and predictions of the literary classification task to interpret its success.

5.1 Content

When we look at the forty bigrams that perform best and worst for the literary novels (cf. Table 5), we can identify a few tendencies.

The book, *a book*, *a letter*, and *to write* are also part of the most important features, as well as *the bar*, *a cigarette*, and *the store*. This suggests a certain pre-digital situatedness, as well as a reflection on the writing process. Interestingly enough, in contrast to *the book* and *letter* that are most discriminating, negative indicators contain words related to modern technology: *mobile phone* and *the computer*. Inspection of the novels shows that the literary novels are not necessarily set in the pre-digital age, but that they have fewer markers of recent technology. This might be tied to the adage in literary writing that good writing should be 'timeless'—which in practice means that at the very least a novel should not be too obvious in relating its settings to the current day. It could also show a hint of nostalgia, perhaps connected to a romantic image of the writer.

In the negative features, we find another time-related tendency. The first is indications of time—*little after*, and in Dutch 'tot nu' and 'nu toe', which are part of the phrase 'tot nu toe' (*so far* or *up until now*), *minutes after* and *ten minutes*; another indicator that awareness of time, albeit in a different sense, is not part of the 'literary' discourse. Indicators of location are *the building*, *the garage/car park*, and *the location*, showing a different type of setting than the one described above. We also see indicators of homicide: *the murder*, and *the investigation*. Some markers of colloquial speech are also found in the negative markers: *for god's sake* and *thank you*, which aligns with a finding of Jautze et al (2013), where indicators of colloquial language were found in low-brow literature.

It is possible to argue, that genre is a more important factor in this classification than literary style. However, we state that this is not particular to this research, and in fact unavoidable. The discussion of how tight genre and literariness are connected, has been held for a long time in literary theory and will probably continue for years to come. Although it is not impossible for so called 'genre novels' to gain literary status (cf. Margaret Atwood's scifi(-like) work for instance—although she objects to such a classification; Hoby 2013), it is the case that certain topics and genres are considered to be less literary than others. The fact that the literary novels are apparently not recognised by proxy, but on an internal coherence (cf. section 4), does make an interesting

weight	literary features, content		weight	non-literary features, content	
12.1	*de oorlog*	the war	-6.1	*de moeder*	the mother
8.1	*het bos*	the forest	-5.1	*keek op*	looked up
8.1	*de winter*	the winter	-4.9	*mijn hoofd*	my head
6.6	*de dokter*	the doctor	-4.9	*haar moeder*	her mother
5.8	*zo veel*	so much	-4.7	*mijn ogen*	my eyes
4.8	*nog altijd*	yet still	-4.7	*ze keek*	she looked
4.5	*de meisjes*	the girls	-4.5	*mobiele telefoon*	mobile telephone
4.3	*zijn vader*	his father	-4.2	*de moord*	the murder
4.0	*mijn dochter*	my daughter	-4.0	*even later*	a while later
3.9	*het boek*	the book	-3.8	*nu toe*	(until) now
3.8	*de trein*	the train	-3.5	*zag ze*	she saw
3.7	*hij hem*	he him	-3.4	*ik voel*	I feel
3.7	*naar mij*	at me	-3.3	*mijn man*	my husband
3.5	*zegt dat*	says that	-3.2	*tot haar*	to her
3.5	*het land*	the land	-3.2	*het gebouw*	the building
3.5	*een sigaret*	a cigarette	-3.2	*liep naar*	walked to
3.4	*haar vader*	her father	-3.1	*we weten*	we know
3.4	*een boek*	a book	-3.1	*enige wat*	only thing
3.2	*de winkel*	the shop	-3.1	*en dus*	and so
3.1	*elke keer*	each time	-3.0	*in godsnaam*	in god's name
weight	**literary features, style**		**weight**	**non-literary features, style**	
21.8	*! WW*	! VERB ,	-13.8	*nu toe*	until now
20.5	*u ,*	you (FORMAL) ,	-13.4	*en dus*	and so
18.0	*haar haar*	her her	-13.4	*achter me*	behind me
16.5	*SPEC :*	NAME :	-13.2	*terwijl ik*	while I
15.4	*worden ik*	become I	-13.1	*tot nu*	until now

Table 5: The top 20 most important content features and top 5 most important style features of literary (left), and non-literary texts (right), respectively.

case for the literary novel to be a genre on its own. Computational research into genre differences has proven that there are certain markers that allow for a computer to make an automated distinction between them, but it also shows that interpretation is often complex (Moretti, 2005; Allison et al., 2011; Jautze et al., 2013). Topic modelling might give some more insight into our findings.

5.2 Style

A stronger case against genre determining the classification is the success of the function words in the task. Function words are not directly related to themes or topics, but reflect writing style in a more general sense. Still, the results do not rule out the existence of particular conventions of writing style in genres, but in this case the distinction between literariness and genre becomes more subtle. Function words are hard to interpret manually, but we do see in the top 20 (Table 5 shows the top 5) that the most discriminating features of less literary texts contain more question marks (and thus questions), and more numerals ('TW')—which can possibly be linked to the discriminative qualities of time-indications in the content words. Some features in the less-literary set appear to show more colloquial language again, such as *ik mezelf* ('I myself'), *door naar* ('through/on to'; an example can be found in the sentence *'Heleen liep door naar de keuken.'*, which translates to 'Heleen walked on to the kitchen', a sound grammatical construction in Dutch, but perhaps not a very aesthetically pleasing one). A future close reading of the original texts will give more information on this intuition.

In future work, more kinds of features should be applied to the classification of literature to get more insight. Many aspects could be studied, such as readability, syntax, semantics, discourse relations, and topic coherence. Given a larger data set, the factors genre and translation/original can be controlled for.

The general question which needs to be answered is whether a literary interpretation of a computational model is even possible. The material to work with (the features), consist of concise sets of words or even part-of-speech tags, which are not easy to interpret manually; and they paint only a small part of the picture. The workings of the machine learning model remain largely hidden to the interpreter. This is an instance of the more general problem of the interpretability of results in computational humanities (Bod, 2013). In the specific case of literature, we can observe that readers of literature follow a similar pattern: literature can be recognized and appreciated, but it is hard to explain what makes texts literary, let alone to compose a highly literary work.

5.3 Good and bad predictions

In Figure 5, we can see both outliers and novels that are well predicted by the regression model. Here we discuss a few and suggest why the model does or does not account for their perceived literariness.

Emma Donoghue - Room A literary novel that is rated as highly literary (5.5), but with a lower prediction (3.8). This may be because this novel is written from the perspective of a child, with a correspondingly limited vocabulary.

Elizabeth Gilbert - Eat, Pray Love A novel with a low literariness rating (3.5), but a high prediction (5.2) by the model. This novel may be rated lower due to the perception that it is a novel for women, dealing with new age themes, giving it a more specific audience than the other novels in the dataset.

Charles Lewinsky - Melnitz A novel that is both rated (5.7) and predicted (5.7) as highly literary. This novel chronicles the history of a Jewish family including the events of the second world war. This subject, and the plain writing style makes it stand out from the other novels.

Erwin Mortier - While the Gods Were Sleeping The most highly rated (6.6) literary novel in the dataset, with a high prediction (5.7). A striking feature of this novel is that it consists of short paragraphs and short, often single line sentences. It features a lot of metaphors, analogies, and generally a poetic writing style. This novel also deals with war, but the writing style contrasts with Lewinsky, which may explain why the model's prediction is not as close for this novel.

6 Related Work

Previous work on classification of literature has focused on authorship attribution (e.g., Hoover, 2003; van Cranenburgh, 2012) and popularity (Ashok et al., 2013). The model of Ashok et al. (2013) classifies novels from Project Gutenberg as being successful or not using stylometric features, where success is based on their download counts. Since many of the most downloaded novels are classics, their results indirectly relate to literariness. However, in our data set all texts are among the most popular books in a fixed time span (cf. section 2), whereas the less successful novels in their data set differ much more in popularity from the successful novels. To the best of our knowledge, our work is the first to directly predict the literariness of texts in a computational model.

There is also work on the classification of the quality of non-fiction texts. Bergsma et al. (2012) work on scientific articles with a similar approach to ours, but including syntactic features in addition to bag-of-words features. Louis and Nenkova (2013) present results on science journalism by modelling what makes articles interesting and well-written.

Salganik et al. (2006) present an experimental study on the popularity of music. They created an artificial "music market" to study the relationship between quality and success of music, with or without social influence as a factor. They found that social influence increases the unpredictability of popularity in relation to quality. A similar effect likely plays a role in the reader judgments of the survey.

7 Conclusion

Our experiments have shown that literary novels share significant commonalities, as evidenced by the performance of machine learning models. It is still a challenge to understand what these literary commonalities consist of, since a large number of word features interact in our models. General quality is harder to predict than literariness.

Features related to genre (e.g., *the war* in literary novels and *the homicide* in thrillers) indicate that genre is a possible confounding factor in the classification, but we find evidence against the notion that the results are solely due to genre. One aspect that stood out in our analysis of content features, which is not necessarily restricted to genre (or which might indicate that the literary novel is a genre in and of itself), is that setting of space and time rank high among the discriminating features. This might be indicative of a 'timeless quality' that is expected of highly literary works (where words as *book* and *letter* are discriminative)—as opposed to more contemporary settings in less literary novels (*computer* and *mobile phone*). Further study is needed to get more insight into these themes and to what extent these are related to genre differences or a literary writing style.

The good performance of style features shows the importance of writing style and indicates that the classification is not purely based on topics and themes. Although genres may also have particular writing styles and thus associated style features, the fact that good results are obtained with two complementary feature sets suggests that the relation between literariness and text features is robust.

Finally, the regression on content and function words shows that the model accounts for more than just genre distinctions. The predictions within genres are good enough to show that it is possible to distinguish highly literary works from less literary works. This is a result that merits further investigation.

Acknowledgments

We are grateful to Karina van Dalen-Oskam, Rens Bod, and Kim Jautze for commenting on drafts, and to the anonymous reviewers for useful feedback. This work is part of The Riddle of Literary Quality, a project supported by the Royal Netherlands Academy of Arts and Sciences through the Computational Humanities Program.

References

Sarah Danielle Allison, Ryan Heuser, Matthew Lee Jockers, Franco Moretti, and Michael Witmore. 2011. Quantitative formalism: an experiment. Stanford Literary Lab pamphlet. http://litlab.stanford.edu/LiteraryLabPamphlet1.pdf.

Vikas Ashok, Song Feng, and Yejin Choi. 2013. Success with style: Using writing style to predict the success of novels. In *Proceedings of EMNLP*, pages 1753–1764. http://aclweb.org/anthology/D13-1181.

Shane Bergsma, Matt Post, and David Yarowsky. 2012. Stylometric analysis of scientific articles. In *Proceedings of NAACL*, pages 327–337. http://aclweb.org/anthology/N12-1033.

Rens Bod. 2013. Who's afraid of patterns?: The particular versus the universal and the meaning of humanities 3.0. *BMGN – Low Countries Historical Review*, 128(4). http://www.bmgn-lchr.nl/index.php/bmgn/article/view/9351/9785.

Pierre Bourdieu. 1996. *The rules of art: Genesis and structure of the literary field.* Stanford University Press.

Hermione Hoby. 2013. Margaret Atwood: interview. The Telegraph, Aug 18. http://www.telegraph.co.uk/culture/books/10246937/Margaret-Atwood-interview.html.

David L. Hoover. 2003. Frequent collocations and authorial style. *Literary and Linguistic Computing*, 18(3):261–286. http://llc.oxfordjournals.org/content/18/3/261.abstract.

Kim Jautze, Corina Koolen, Andreas van Cranenburgh, and Hayco de Jong. 2013. From high heels to weed attics: a syntactic investigation of chick lit and literature. In *Proc. of workshop Computational Linguistics for Literature*, pages 72–81. http://aclweb.org/anthology/W13-1410.

Annie Louis and Ani Nenkova. 2013. What makes writing great? first experiments on article quality prediction in the science journalism domain. *Transactions of the Association for Computational Linguistics*, 1:341–352. http://aclweb.org/anthology/Q13-1028.

Franco Moretti. 2005. *Graphs, maps, trees: abstract models for a literary history*. Verso.

Fabian Pedregosa, G. Varoquaux, A. Gramfort, V. Michel, B. Thirion, O. Grisel, M. Blondel, P. Prettenhofer, R. Weiss, V. Dubourg, J. Vanderplas, A. Passos, D. Cournapeau, M. Brucher, M. Perrot, and E. Duchesnay. 2011. Scikit-learn: Machine learning in Python. *Journal of Machine Learning Research*, 12:2825–2830.

Matthew J. Salganik, Peter Sheridan Dodds, and Duncan J. Watts. 2006. Experimental study of inequality and unpredictability in an artificial cultural market. *Science*, 311(5762):854–856.

Andreas van Cranenburgh. 2012. Literary authorship attribution with phrase-structure fragments. In *Proceedings of CLFL*, pages 59–63. Revised version: `http://andreasvc.github.io/clfl2012.pdf`.

Visualizing Poetry with *SPARSAR* – Visual Maps from Poetic Content

Rodolfo Delmonte
Department of Language Studies & Department of Computer Science
Ca' Foscari University - 30123, Venezia, Italy
delmont@unive.it

Abstract

In this paper we present a specific application of SPARSAR, a system for poetry analysis and TextToSpeech "expressive reading". We will focus on the graphical output organized at three macro levels, a *Phonetic Relational View* where phonetic and phonological features are highlighted; a *Poetic Relational View* that accounts for a poem rhyming and metrical structure; and a *Semantic Relational View* that shows semantic and pragmatic relations in the poem. We will also discuss how colours may be used appropriately to account for the overall underlying attitude expressed in the poem, whether directed to sadness or to happiness. This is done following traditional approaches which assume that the underlying feeling of a poem is strictly related to the sounds conveyed by the words besides their meaning. This will be shown using part of Shakespeare's Sonnets.

1 Introduction

The contents of a poem cover many different fields from a sensorial point of view to a mental and a auditory linguistic one. A poem may please our hearing for its rhythm and rhyme structure, or simply for the network of alliterations it evokes be they consonances or assonances; it may attract our attention for its structure of meaning, organized on a coherent lattice of anaphoric and coreferential links or suggested and extracted from inferential and metaphorical links to symbolic meanings obtained by a variety of rhetorical devices. Most if not all of these facets of a poem are derived from the analysis of SPARSAR, the system for poetry analysis which has been presented to a number of international conferences (Delmonte 2013a; 2013b; 2014) - and to Demo sessions in its TextToSpeech "expressive reading" version (Delmonte & Bacalu, 2012; Delmonte & Prati, 2014; Delmonte, 2015).

Most of a poem's content can be captured considering three basic views on the poem itself: one that covers what can be called the overall sound pattern of the poem - and this is related to the phonetics and the phonology of the words contained in the poem - ***Phonetic Relational View***. Another view is the one that captures the main poetic devices related to rhythm, that is the rhyme structure and the metrical structure - this view will be called ***Poetic Relational View***. Finally, the semantic and pragmatic contents of the poem which are related to relations entertained by predicates and arguments expressed in the poem, relations at lexical semantic level, relations at metaphorical and anaphoric level - this view will be called ***Semantic Relational View***.

In this paper we will concentrate on the three views above, which are visualized by the graphical output of the system and has been implemented by extracting the various properties and features of the poem and are analyzed in ten separate poetic maps. These maps are organized as follows:

- *A General Description map* including seven Macro Indices with a statistical evaluation of such descriptors as: Semantic Density Evaluation; General Poetic Devices; General Rhetoric Devices etc., Prosodic Distribution; Rhyming Schemes; Metrical Structure. This map is discussed and presented in previous publications, so I will not show it here;
- *Phonetic Relational Views*: five maps,
    - Assonances, i.e. all vowels contained in stressed vowel nuclei which have been repeated in the poem within a certain interval – not just in adjacency;
    - Consonances, i.e. all consonant onsets of stressed syllables again repeated in the poem within a certain interval;
    - All word repetitions, be it stressed or unstressed;

Proceedings of NAACL-HLT Fourth Workshop on Computational Linguistics for Literature, pages 68–78,
Denver, Colorado, June 4, 2015. ©2015 Association for Computational Linguistics

- one for the Unvoiced/Voiced opposition as documented in syllable onset of stressed words (stress demotion counts as unstressed);
  - another for a subdivision of all consonant syllable onsets, including consonant cluster onsets, and organized in three main phonological classes:
  - Continuants (only fricatives);
  - Obstruents (Plosives and Affricates);
  - Sonorants (Liquids, Vibrants, Approximants; Glides; Nasals).
- *Poetic Relation Views*:
  - Metrical Structure, Rhyming Structure and Expected Acoustic Length all in one single map.
- *Semantic Relational View*: four maps,
  - A map including polarity marked words (Positive vs Negative) and words belonging to Abstract vs Concrete semantic class[1];
  - A map including polarity marked words (Positive vs Negative) and words belonging to Eventive vs State semantic class;
  - A map including Main Topic words; Anaphorically linked words; Inferentially linked words; Metaphorically linked words i.e. words linked explicitly by "like" or "as", words linked by recurring symbolic meanings (woman/serpent or woman/moon or woman/rose);
  - A map showing predicate argument relations intervening between words, marked at core argument words only, indicating predicate and semantic role; eventive anaphora between verbs.

Graphical maps highlight differences using colours. The use of colours associated to sound in poetry has a long tradition. Rimbaud composed a poem devoted to "Vowels" where colours where specifically associated to each of the main five vowels. Roman Jakobson wrote extensively about sound and colour in a number of papers (1976; Jakobson & Waugh, 1978:188; lately Mazzeo, 2004). As Tsur (1992) notes, Fónagy in 1961 wrote an article in which he connected explicitly the use of certain types of consonant sounds associated to certain moods: unvoiced and obstruent consonants are associated with aggressive mood; sonorants with tender moods. Fónagy mentioned the work of M.Macdermott (1940) who in her study identified a specific quality associated to "dark" vowels, i.e. back vowels, that of being linked with dark colours, mystic obscurity, hatred and struggle. For this reason, we then decided to evaluate all information made available by SPARSAR at the three macro levels in order to check these findings about the association of mood and sound. This will be discussed in a final section of the paper devoted to correlations in Shakespeare's sonnets.

As a result, we will also be using darker colours for highlighting back and front vowels as opposed to low and middle vowels, these latter with light colours. The same will apply to representing unvoiced and obstruent consonants as opposed to voiced and sonorants. But as Tsur (1992:15) notes, this sound-colour association with mood or attitude has no real significance without a link to semantics. In the Semantic Relational View, we will be using dark colours for Concrete referents vs Abstract ones with lighter colours; dark colours also for Negatively marked words as opposed to Positively marked ones with lighter colours. The same strategy will apply to other poetic maps: this technique has certainly the good quality of highlighting opposing differences at some level of abstraction[2].

The usefulness of this visualization is intuitively related to various potential users and for different purposes. First of all, translators of poetry would certainly benefit from the decomposition of the poem and the fine-grained analysis, in view of the need to preserve as much as possible of the original qualities of the source poem in the target language. Other possible users are literary critics and literature teachers at various levels. Graphical output is essentially produced to allow immediate and direct comparison between different poems

[1] see in particular Brysbaert et al. 2014 that has a database of 40K entries. We are also using a manually annotated lexicon of 10K entries and WordNet supersenses or broad semantic classes. We are not using MRCDatabase which only has some 8,000 concrete + some 9,000 imagery classified entries because it is difficult to adapt and integrated into our system.

[2] our approach is not comparable to work by Saif Mohammad (2011a;2011b), where colours are associated with words on the basis of what their mental image may suggest to the mind of annotators hired via Mechanical Turk. The resource only contains word-colour association for some 12,000 entries over the 27K items listed.

and different poets. In order to show the usefulness and power of these visualization, I have chosen two different English poets in different time periods: Shakespeare with Sonnet 1 and 60; and Sylvia Plath, with Edge.

The paper is organized as follows: a short state of the art in the following section; then the views of three poems accompanied by comments; some conclusion.

2. Related Work

Computational work on poetry addresses a number of subfields which are however strongly related. They include automated annotation, analysis, or translation of poetry, as well as poetry generation, that we comment here below. Other common subfields regard automatic grapheme-to-phoneme translation for out of vocabulary words as discussed in (Reddy & Goldsmith, 2010). Genzel et al. (2010) use CMU pronunciation dictionary to derive stress and rhyming information, and incorporate constraints on meter and rhyme into a machine translation system. There has also been some work on computational approaches to characterizing rhymes (Byrd and Chodorow, 1985) and global properties of the rhyme network (Sonderegger, 2011) in English.

Green et al. (2010) use a finite state transducer to infer the syllable-stress assignments in lines of poetry under metrical constraints. They contribute variations similar to the schemes below, by allowing an optional inversion of stress in the iambic foot. This variation is however only motivated by heuristics, noting that "poets often use the word 'mother' (S* S) at the beginnings and ends of lines, where it theoretically should not appear." So eventually, there is no control of the internal syntactic or semantic structure of the newly obtained sequence of feet: the optional change is only positionally motivated. They employ statistical methods to analyze, generate, and translate rhythmic poetry. They first apply unsupervised learning to reveal word-stress patterns in a corpus of raw poetry. They then use these word-stress patterns, in addition to rhyme and discourse models, to generate English love poetry. Finally, they translate Italian poetry into English, choosing target realizations that conform to desired rhythmic patterns. They, however, concentrate on only one type of poetic meter, the iambic pentameter. And they use the audio transcripts - made by just one person - to create the syllable-based word-stress gold standard corpus for testing, made of some 70 lines taken from Shakespeare's sonnets. Audio transcripts without supporting acoustic analysis[3] are not always the best manner to deal with stress assignment in syllable positions which might or might not conform to a strict sequence of iambs. There is no indication of what kind of criteria have been used, and it must be noted that the three acoustic cues may well not be congruent (see Tsur, 2014). So eventually results obtained are rather difficult to evaluate. As the authors note, spoken recordings may contain lexical stress reversals and archaic pronunciations[4]. Their conclusion is that "this useful information is not available in typical pronunciation dictionaries". Further on, (p. 531) they comment "the probability of stressing 'at' is 40% in general, but this increases to 91% when the next word is 'the'. " We assume that demoting or promoting word stress requires information which is context and syntactically dependent. Proper use of one-syllable words remains tricky. In our opinion, machine learning would need much bigger training data than the ones used by the authors for their experiment.

There's a large number of papers on poetry generation starting from work documented in a number of publications by P. Gérvas (2001;2010) who makes use of Case Based Reasoning to induce the best line structure. Other interesting attempts are by Toivonen et al.(2012) who use a corpus-based approach to generate poetry in Finnish. Their idea is to contribute the knowledge needed in content and form by two separate corpora, one providing semantic content, and another for grammatical and poetic structure. Morphological analysis and synthesis is used together with text-mining methods. Basque poetry generation is the

[3] One questions could be "Has the person transcribing stress pattern been using pitch as main acoustic correlate for stress position, or loudness (intensity or energy) or else durational patterns?". The choice of one or the other acoustic correlated might change significantly the final outcome.

[4] At p.528 they present a table where they list a number of words - partly function and partly content words - associated to probability values indicating their higher or lower propensity to receive word stress. They comment that "Function words and possessives tend to be unstressed, while content words tend to be stressed, though many words are used both ways".

topic of Agirrezabal et al. 2013 paper which uses POS-tags to induce the linear ordering and WordNet to select best semantic choice in context.

Manurung et al., 2000 have explored the problem of poetry generation under some constraints using machine learning techniques. With their work the authors intended to fill the gap in the generation paradigm, and "to shed some light on what often seems to be the most enigmatic and mysterious forms of artistic expression". The conclusion they reach is that "...despite our implementation being at a very early stage, the sample output succeeds in showing how the stochastic hillclimbing search model manages to produce text that satisfies these constraints." However, when we come to the evaluation of metre we discover that they base their approach on disputable premises. The authors quote the first line of what could be a normal limerick but totally misinterpret the metrical structure. In limericks, what we are dealing with are not dactyls - TAtata - but anapests, tataTA, that is a sequence of two unstressed plus a closing stressed syllable. This is a well known characteristic feature of limericks and the typical rhythm is usually preceded and introduced by a iamb "there ONCE", and followed by two anapests, "was a MAN", "from maDRAS". Here in particular it is the syntactic-semantic phrase that determines the choice of foot, and not the scansion provided by the authors[5].

Reddy & Knight (2011) produce an unsupervised machine learning algorithm for finding rhyme schemes which is intended to be language-independent. It works on the intuition that "a collection of rhyming poetry inevitably contains repetition of rhyming pairs. ... This is partly due to sparsity of rhymes – many words that have no rhymes at all, and many others have only a handful, forcing poets to reuse rhyming pairs." The authors harness this repetition to build an unsupervised algorithm to infer rhyme schemes, based on a model of stanza generation. "We test the algorithm on rhyming poetry in English and French." The definition of rhyme the authors used is the strict one of perfect rhyme: two words rhyme if their final stressed vowels and all following phonemes are identical. So no half rhymes are considered. Rhyming lines are checked from CELEX phonological database.

3. Three Views via Poetic Graphical Maps

The basic idea underlying poetic graphical maps is that of making available to the user an insight of the poem which is hardly realized even if the analysis is carried out manually by an expert literary critic. This is also due to the fact that the expertise required for the production of all the maps ranges from acoustic phonetics to semantics and pragmatics, a knowledge that is not usually possessed by a single person. All the graphical representations associated to the poems are produced by SWI Prolog, inside the system which is freely downloadable from its website, at sparsar.wordpress.com. For lack of space, we will show maps related to two of Shakespeare's Sonnets, Sonnet 1 and Sonnet 60 and compare them to Sylvia Plath's Edge, to highlight similarities and to show that the system can handle totally different poems still allowing comparisons to be made neatly. All Phonetic Views are shown in Arpabet, i.e. the computer based phonetic alphabet .

Poem and Poetic Devices :- Assonance Alliterations

sonnet_1

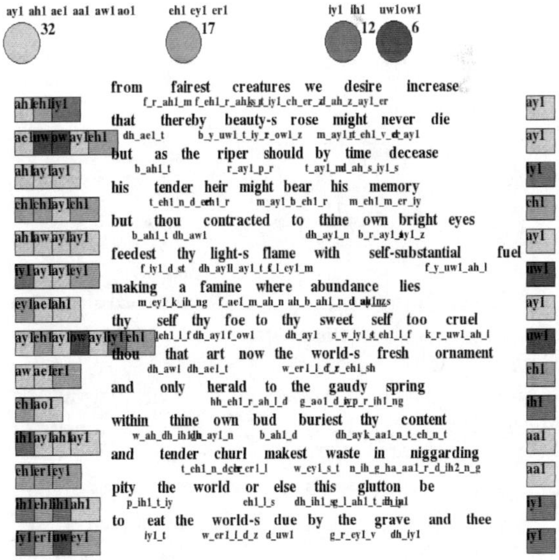

---

[5] "For instance, the line 'There /once was a /man from Ma/dras', has a stress pattern of (w,s,w,w,s,w,w,s). This can be divided into feet as (w),(s,w,w),(s,w,w),(s). In other words, this line consists of a single upbeat (the weak syllable before the first strong syllable), followed by 2 dactyls (a classical poetry unit consisting of a strong syllable followed by two weak ones), and ended with a strong beat."(ibid.7)

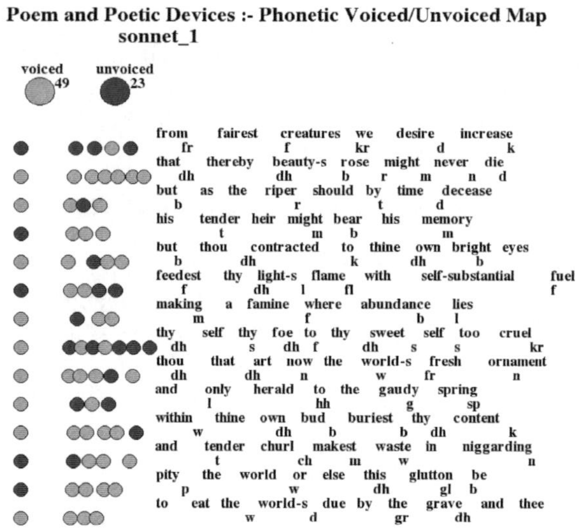

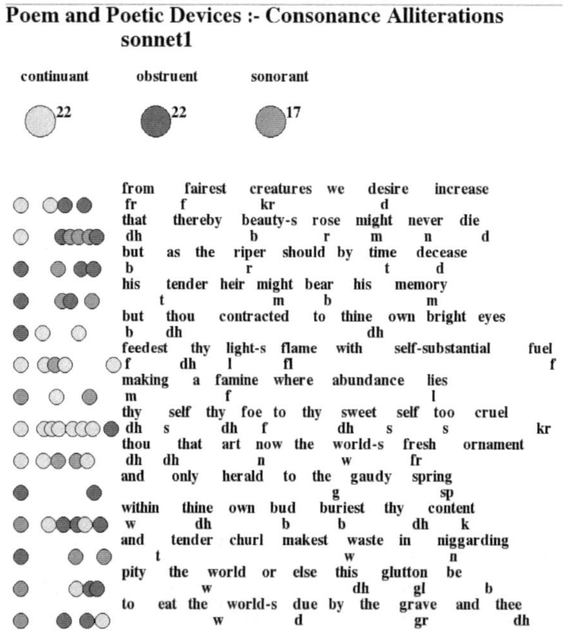

We will start commenting the Phonetic Relational View and its related maps. The first map is concerned with Assonances. Here sounds are grouped into Vowel Areas, as said above, which include also diphthongs: now, in area choice what we have considered is the onset vowel. We have disregarded the offset glide which is less persistent and might also not reach its target articulation. We will have also combined together front high vowels, which can express suffering and pain, with back dark vowels: both can be treated as marked vowels, compared to middle and low vowels[6].

Assonances and Consonances are derived from syllable structure in stressed position of repeated sounds within a certain line span: in particular, Consonances are derived from syllable onset while Assonances from syllable nuclei in stressed position. The Voiced/Unvoiced View is taken from all consonant onsets of stressed words. As can be noticed from the maps above, the choice of warm colours is selected for respectively, CONTINUANT (yellow), VOICED (orange), SONORANT (green), Centre/Low Vowel Area (gold), Middle Vowel Area (green); and cold colours respectively for UNVOICED (blue), Back Vowel Area (brown). We used then red for OBSTRUENT (red), Front High Vowel Area (red), to indicate suffering and surprise associated to speech signal interruption in obstruents.

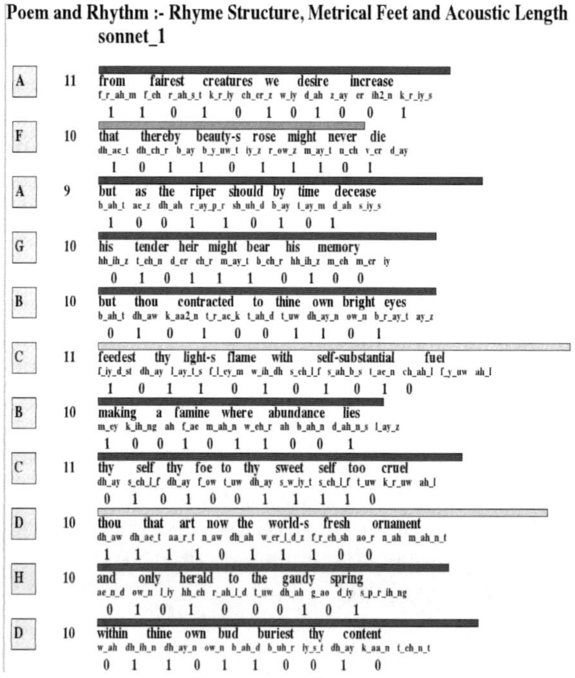

The second set of views is the Poetic Relations View. It is obtained by a single graphical map which however condenses five different levels of

[6] Area low: ae aa ah ao aw ay; area high front: iy ih ia y; area high back: uw uh ow ua w; area middle: er ea ax oh eh ey oy. Voiced consonants: l m n ng r z zh dh d b g v jh; unvoiced consonants: p s sh th h hh f ch t k. Obstruents: t d b p g k jh ch; continuants: f v z zh s sh th dh h hh; sonorants: l m n ng r.

analysis. The Rhyming Structure is obtained by matching line endings in its phonetic form. The result is an capital letter associated with each line on left. This is accompanied by a metrical measure indicating the number of syllables contained in the line. Then the text of the poem and underneath the phonetic translation at syllable level. Finally, another annotation is added mapping syllable type with sequences of 0/1. This should serve a metrical analysis which can be accomplished by the user – completed by comments on poetry type which will be presented at the conference. The additional important layer of analysis that this view makes available is an acoustic phonetic image of each line represented by a coloured streak computed on the basis of the average syllable length in msec derived from our database of syllables of British English.

Finally, the third set of views, the Semantic Relational View, produced by the modules of the system derived from VENSES (Delmonte et al., 2005). This view is organized around four separate graphical poetic maps: a map which highlights Event and State words in the poem; a map which highlights Concrete vs Abstract words. Both these two maps address nouns and adjectives. They also indicate Affective and Sentiment analysis (Delmonte & Pallotta, 2011; Delmonte 2014), an evaluation related to nouns and adjective – which however will be given a separate view when the Appraisal-based dictionary will be completed at the conference. A map which contains main Topics, Anaphoric and Metaphoric relations, and a final map with Predicate-arguments relations.

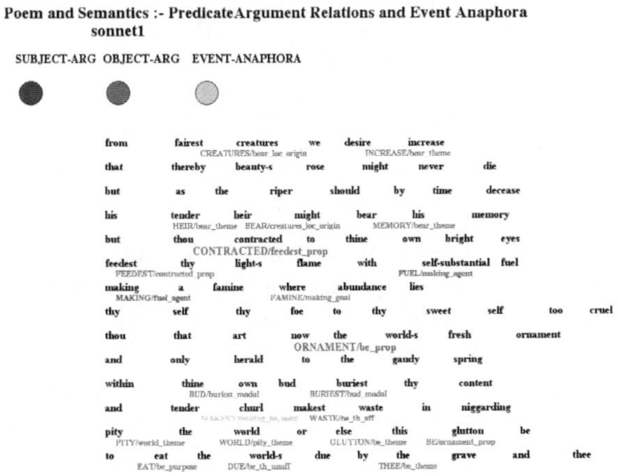

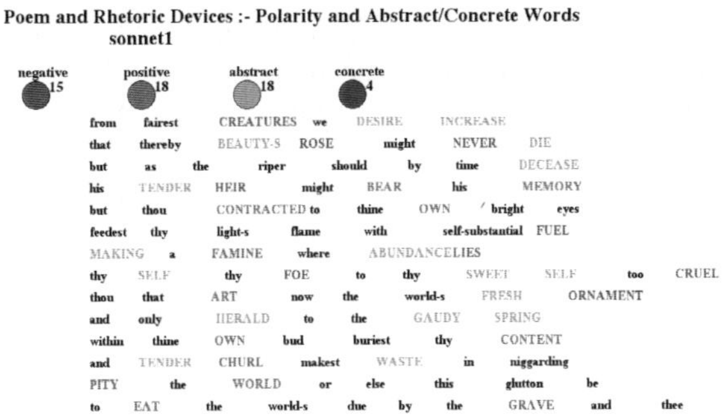

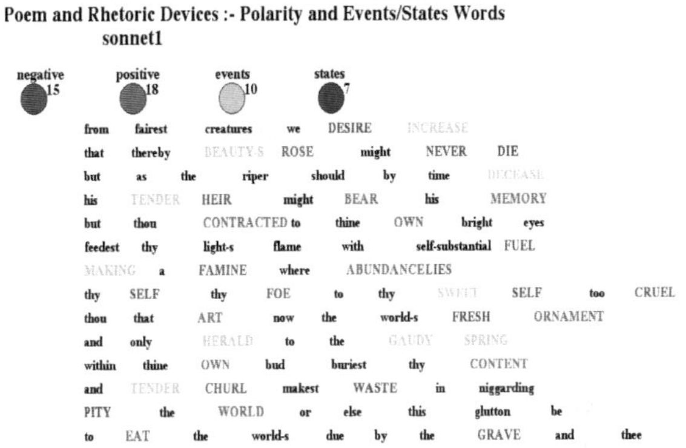

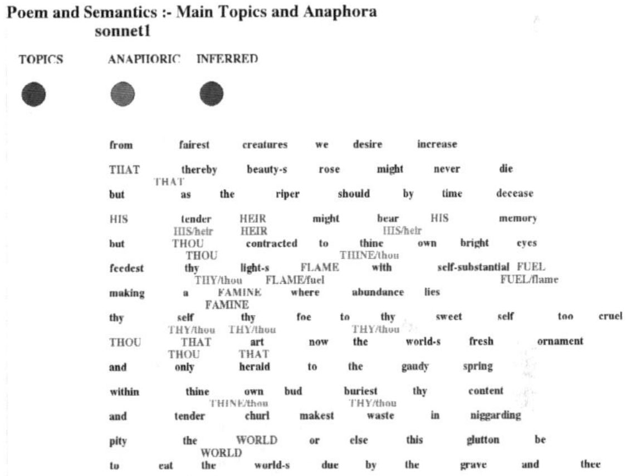

We will now compare a love sonnet like Sonnet 1 to Sonnet 60, which like many other similar sonnets depicts the condition of man condemned to succumb to the scythe of Time - the poet though, will survive through his verse. Here we will restrict ourselves to showing only part of the maps and omit less relevant ones.

In the Phonetic Relations Views the choice of words is strongly related to the main theme and the result is a gloomier, hasher overall sound quality of the poem: number of unvoiced is close to that of voiced consonants; in particular, number of obstruents is higher than the sum of sonorants and continuants. As to Assonances, we see that even though A and E sounds - that is open and middle vowels - constitute the majority of sounds, there is a remarkable presence of back and high front vowels. Proportions are very different from what we found in Sonnet 1: 18/49, i.e. dark are one third of light, compared to 21/46, almost half the amount. Also consider number of Obstruents which is higher than number of Sonorants and Continuants together: in Sonnet 1 it was identical to number of Continuants.

**Poem and Poetic Devices :- Assonance Alliterations
sonnet_60**

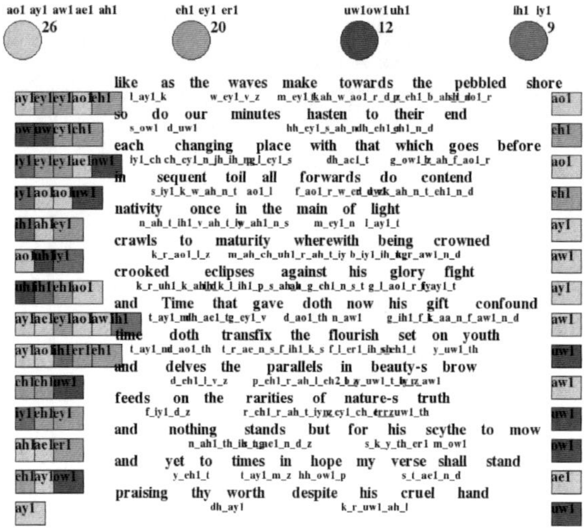

**Poem and Poetic Devices :- Phonetic Voiced/Unvoiced Map
sonnet_60**

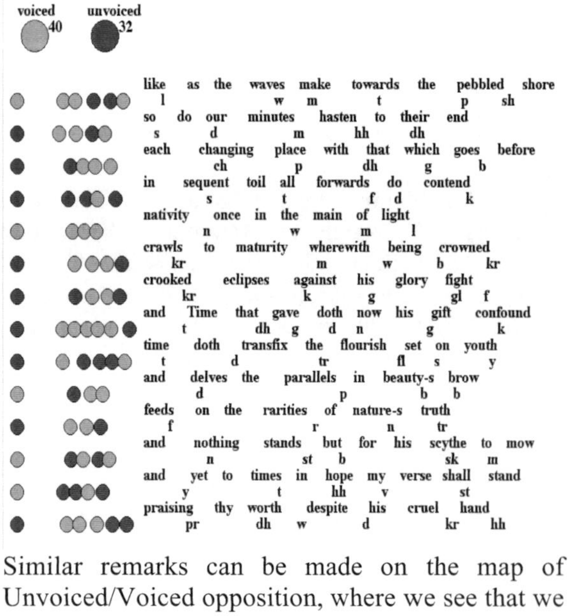

Similar remarks can be made on the map of Unvoiced/Voiced opposition, where we see that we go from 29/43 that is dark sounds are a little bit more than half light ones in Sonnet 1, to 32/40 in Sonnet 60, i.e. they are almost the same amount. Eventually, the information coming from affective analysis confirms our previous findings: in Sonnet 1 we see a majority of positive words/propositions, 18/15; the opposite applies to Sonnet 60, where the ratio is reversed 10/21.

**Poem and Poetic Devices :- Consonance Alliterations
sonnet_60**

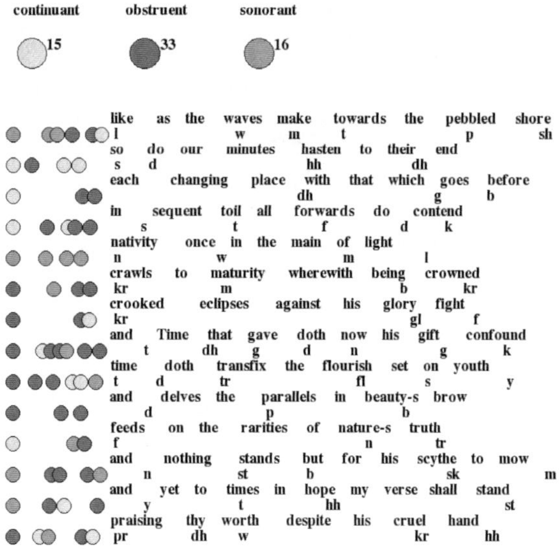

**Poem and Rhetoric Devices :- Polarity and Abstract/Concrete Words
sonnet_60**

This interpretation of the data is expected also for other poets and is proven by Sylvia Plath's Edge, a poem the author wrote some week before her suicidal death. It's a terrible and beautiful poem at the same time: images of death are evoked and explicitly mentioned in the poem, together with images of resurrection and nativity. The poem starts with an oxymoron: "perfected" is joined with "dead body" and both are predicated of the "woman". We won't be able to show all the maps for lack of space, but the overall sound pattern is strongly reminiscent of a death toll. In the Consonances map, there's a clear majority of obstruent sounds and the balance between voiced/unvoiced consonants is in favour of the latter. In the Assonances map we see that dark vowel sounds are almost in same amount of light sounds 28/30.

Poem and Semantics :- Main Topics and Anaphora
edge

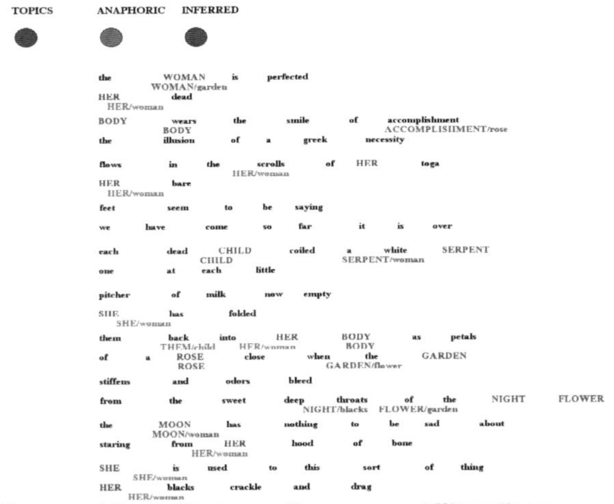

Poem and Poetic Devices :- Consonance Alliterations
edge

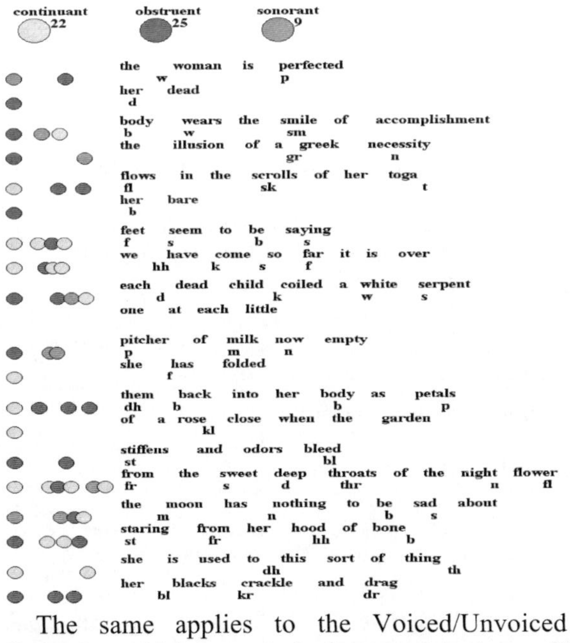

The same applies to the Voiced/Unvoiced distinction which is again in favour of the latter. If we look at the topics and the coherence through anaphora, we find that the main topic is constituted by concepts WOMAN, BODY and CHILD. There's also a wealth of anaphoric relations expressed by personal and possessive pronouns which depend on WOMAN. In addition, he system has found metaphoric referential links with such images as MOON GARDEN and SERPENT. In particular the Moon is represented as human - "has nothing to be sad about".

Poem and Poetic Devices :- Phonetic Voiced/Unvoiced Map
edge

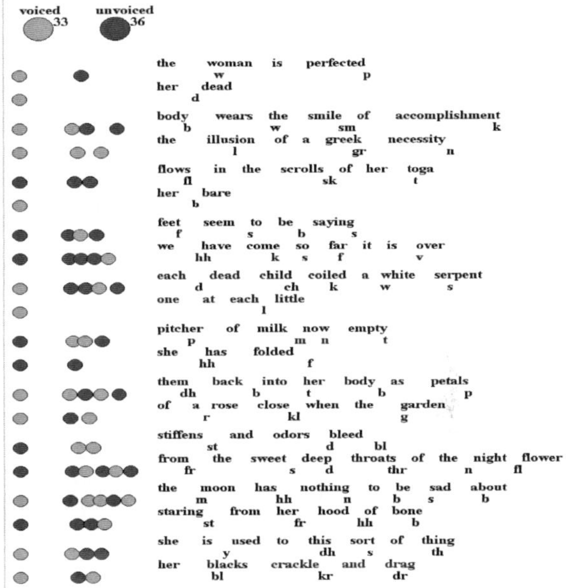

Poem and Rhetoric Devices :- Polarity and Abstract/Concrete Words
edge

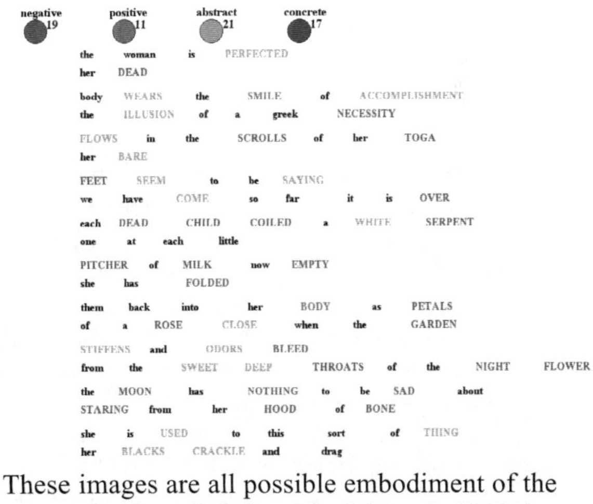

These images are all possible embodiment of the WOMAN, either directly - the Moon is feminine (she) - or indirectly, when the CHILD that the woman FOLDS the children in her BODY, and the children are in turn assimilated to WHITE SERPENTS.

4. Computing Mood from the Sonnets

In this final section we will show data produced by SPARSAR relatively to the relation holding between Mood, Sound and Meaning in half of William Shakespeare's Sonnets. This is done to confirm data presented in the sections above. As will be made clear from Table 1. below, choice of words by Shakespeare has been carefully done in relating the theme and mood of the sonnet to the sound intended to be produced while reading it. Shakespeare's search for the appropriate word is a well-known and established fact and a statistics of his corpus speak of some 29,000 types, a lot more than any English poet whose corpus has been quantitatively analyzed so far (see Delmonte, 2013a).

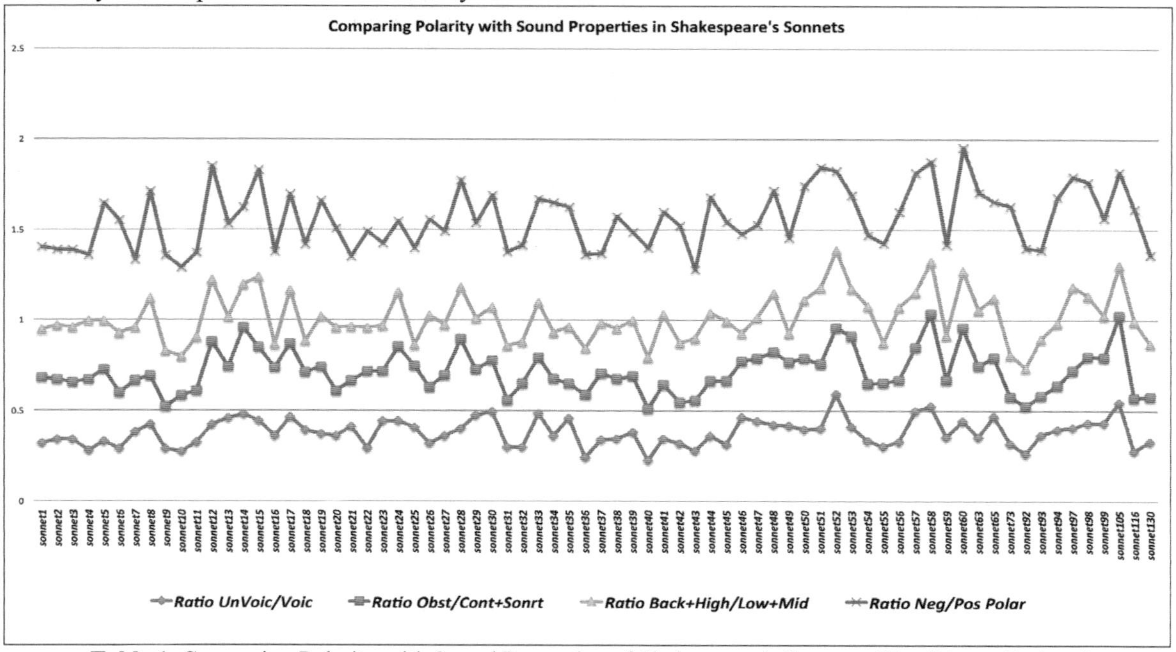

Table 1. Comparing Polarity with Sound Properties of Shakespeare's Sonnets: Blue Line = Ratio of Unvoiced/Voiced Consonants; Red Line = Ratio of Obstruents/Continuants+Sonorants; Green Line = Ratio of Marked Vowels/Unmarked Vowels; Violet Line = Ratio of Negative/Positive Polarity Words/Propositions.

1. sonnets with an overall happy mood; 2. sonnets about love with a contrasted mood – the lover have betrayed the poet but he still loves him/her, or the poet is doubtful about his friend's love; 3. sonnets about the ravages of time, the sadness of human condition (but the poet will survive through his verse); 4 sonnets with an overall negative mood. We will look at peaks and dips in the Table 1. and try to connect them to the four possible interpretations of the sonnets.

1. POSITIVE peaks (11): sonnet 6, sonnet 7, sonnet 10, sonnet 16, sonnet 18, sonnet 25, sonnet 26, sonnet 36, sonnet 43, sonnet 116, sonnet 130

4. NEGATIVE dips (15): sonnet 5, sonnet 8, sonnet 12, sonnet 14, sonnet 17, sonnet 19, sonnet 28, sonnet 33, sonnet 41, sonnet 48, sonnet 58, sonnet 60, sonnet 63, sonnet 65, sonnet 105

2. POSITIVE-CONTRAST (6): sonnet 22, sonnet 24, sonnet 31, sonnet 49, sonnet 55, sonnet 59

3. NEGATIVE-CONTRAST (1): sonnet 52

Overall, the system has addressed 33 sonnets out of 75 with the appropriate mood selection, 44%. The remaining 42 sonnets have been projected in the intermediate zone from high peaks to low dips.

Conclusion

We presented a visualization algorithm that works on two XML files, the output of SPARSAR system for poetry analysis. The algorithm decomposes the content of the two XML files into 10 graphical maps whose content can in turn be organized into three macro views that encompass most of a poem's poetic content. In a final section we also verified (successfully) the hypothesis regarding the existence of an implicit association between sound and meaning carried by the words making up a poem, by a study of 75 Shakespeare's sonnets. More work needs to be done to improve the Polarity analysis which we intend to project onto the "Appraisal Theory" of meaning. A complete analysis of Shakespeare's sonnets is also under way and will be presented at the conference, together with a comparison with the work of more recent poets.

References

Agirrezabal Manex, Bertol Arrieta, Aitzol Astigarraga, Mans Hulden, 2013. POS-tag based poetry generation with WordNet, Proceedings of the 14th European Workshop on Natural Language Generation, pages 162–166.

Baayen R. H., R. Piepenbrock, and L. Gulikers. 1995. *The CELEX Lexical Database (CD-ROM).* Linguistic Data Consortium.

Bacalu C., Delmonte R. 1999. Prosodic Modeling for Syllable Structures from the VESD - Venice English Syllable Database, in Atti 9° Convegno GFS-AIA, Venezia.

Bacalu C., Delmonte R. 1999. Prosodic Modeling for Speech Recognition, in Atti del Workshop AI*IA - "Elaborazione del Linguaggio e Riconoscimento del Parlato", IRST Trento, pp.45-55.

Brysbaert, M., Warriner, A.B., & Kuperman, V. 2014. Concreteness ratings for 40 thousand generally known English word lemmas. Behavior Research Methods, 46, 904-911.

Byrd Roy J. and M. S. Chodorow. 1985. Using an online dictionary to find rhyming words and pronunciations for unknown words. In Proceedings of the 23rd Annual Meeting of ACL, 277–283.

Delmonte R., 2013a. Transposing Meaning into Immanence: The Poetry of Francis Webb, in Rivista di Studi Italiani, Vol. XXX1, n° 1, 835-892.

Delmonte R., et al. 2005. VENSES – a Linguistically-Based System for Semantic Evaluation, in J. Quiñonero-Candela et al.(eds.), Machine Learning Challenges. LNCS, Springer, Berlin, 344-371.

Delmonte R. and V. Pallotta, 2011. Opinion Mining and Sentiment Analysis Need Text Understanding, in "Advances in Distributed Agent-based Retrieval Tools", Springer, 81-96.

Delmonte R. & C. Bacalu. 2013. SPARSAR: a System for Poetry Automatic Rhythm and Style AnalyzeR, SLATE 2013 - Demonstration Track, Grenoble.

Delmonte R. 2013b. Computing Poetry Style, in C. Battaglino, C. Bosco, E. Cambria, R. Damiano, V. Patti, P. Rosso (eds.), Proceeding ESSEM - Emotion and Sentiment in Social and Expressive Media: approaches and perspectives from AI (ESSEM 2013), CEUR Workshop Proceedings, Torino, 148-155, http://ceur-ws.org/Vol-1096/.

Delmonte R. & A.M. Prati. 2014. SPARSAR: An Expressive Poetry Reader, Proceedings of the Demonstrations at the 14th Conference of the EACL, Gotheborg, 73–76.

Delmonte R. 2014. A Computational Approach to Poetic Structure, Rhythm and Rhyme, in R. Basili, A. Lenci, B. Magnini (eds), Proceedings of CLiC-it - The First Italian Conference on Computational Linguistics, Pisa University Press, Vol.1, 144-150.

Delmonte R. 2014. ITGETARUNS A Linguistic Rule-Based System for Pragmatic Text Processing, in C. Bosco, P. Cosi, F. Dell'Orletta, M. Falcone, S. Montemagni, Maria Simi (eds.), Proceedings of Fourth International Workshop EVALITA, Pisa University Press, Vol. 2, 64-69.

Delmonte R., 2015. SPARSAR - Expressivity in TTS and its Relations to Semantics, Invited Talk at AISV 2015, Bologna.

Genzel Dmitriy, J. Uszkoreit, and F. Och. 2010. "Poetic" statistical machine translation: Rhyme and meter. In Proceedings of EMNLP.

Fónagy, Iván (1971) "The Functions of Vocal Style", in Seymour Chatman (ed.), *Literary Style*: A Symposium. London: Oxford UP, 159-174.

Gérvas, P. (2001). An expert system for the composition of formal Spanish poetry. Knowledge-Based Systems,14(3):181–188.

Gérvas, P. (2010). Engineering linguistic creativity: Bird flight and jet planes. In Proceedings of the NAACL HLT 2010 Second Workshop on Computational Approaches to Linguistic Creativity, pages 23–30.

Greene E., T. Bodrumlu, K. Knight. 2010. Automatic Analysis of Rhythmic Poetry with Applications to Generation and Translation, in Proceedings of the 2010 Conference on EMNLP, 524–533.

Jakobson, R. 1978. Six lectures on sound and meaning (Trans.: J. Mepham). Cambridge: MIT Press (Original work published in 1976).

Jakobson, R., & Waugh, L. 1978. The sound shape of language. Bloomington: Indiana University Press.

Kao Justine and Dan Jurafsky. 2012. "A Computational Analysis of Style, Affect, and Imagery in Contemporary Poetry". in *Proc. NAACL Workshop on Computational Linguistics for Literature*.

Keppel-Jones David. 2001. The Strict Metrical Tradition: Variations in the Literary Iambic Pentameter from Sidney and Spenser to Matthew Arnold, Mcgill Queens Univ. Pr., 280.

Manurung Hisar Maruli, G. Ritchie, and H. Thompson. 2000. Towards a computational model of poetry generation. In Proceedings of AISB Symposium on

Creative and Cultural Aspects and Applications of AI and Cognitive Science, 17-20.
Manurung M.H., G. Ritchie, H. Thompson. 2000. A Flexible Integrated Architecture For Generating Poetic Texts. in Proceedings of the Fourth Symposium on Natural Language Processing (SNLP 2000), Chiang Mai, Thailand, 7-22.
Macdermott M.M. 1940. Vowel Sounds in Poetry: Their Music and Tone Colour, Psyche Monographs, No.13, London: Kegan Paul, 148 pp.
Mazzeo, M. 2004. Les voyelles colorées: Saussure et la synesthésie. Cahiers Ferdinand de Saussure, 57,129–143.
Mohammad Saif, Colourful Language: Measuring Word-Colour Associations, 2011a. In Proceedings of the ACL 2011 Workshop on Cognitive Modeling and Computational Linguistics (CMCL), June 2011, Portland, OR.
Mohammad Saif, Even the Abstract have Colour: Consensus in Word Colour Associations, 2011b. In Proceedings of the 49th Annual Meeting of the Association for Computational Linguistics: Human Language Technologies, June 2011, Portland, OR.
Sonderegger Morgan. 2011. Applications of graph theory to an English rhyming corpus. Computer Speech and Language, 25:655–678.
Sravana Reddy & Kevin Knight. 2011. Unsupervised Discovery of Rhyme Schemes, in Proceedings of the 49th Annual Meeting of ACL: shortpapers, 77-82.
Toivanen Jukka, Hannu Toivonen, Alessandro Valitutti, & Oskar Gross, 2012. Corpus-based generation of content and form in poetry. In Proceedings of the Third International Conference on Computational Creativity.
Tsur, Reuven. 1992. What Makes Sound Patterns Expressive: The Poetic Mode of Speech-Perception. Durham N. C.: Duke UP.
Tsur Reuven. 1997a. "Poetic Rhythm: Performance Patterns and their Acoustic Correlates". Versification: An Electronic Journal Devoted to Literary Prosody. (http://sizcol1.u-shizuoka-ken.ac.jp/versif/Versification.html)
Tsur Reuven. 2012. Poetic Rhythm: Structure and Performance: An Empirical Study in Cognitive Poetics, Sussex Academic Press, 472.

Towards a better understanding of Burrows's Delta in literary authorship attribution

Stefan Evert and **Thomas Proisl**
FAU Erlangen-Nürnberg
Bismarckstr. 6
91054 Erlangen, Germany
stefan.evert@fau.de
thomas.proisl@fau.de

Fotis Jannidis, Steffen Pielström, Christof Schöch and **Thorsten Vitt**
Universität Würzburg
Am Hubland
97074 Würzburg, Germany
fotis.jannidis@uni-wuerzburg.de

Abstract

Burrows's Delta is the most established measure for stylometric difference in literary authorship attribution. Several improvements on the original Delta have been proposed. However, a recent empirical study showed that none of the proposed variants constitute a major improvement in terms of authorship attribution performance. With this paper, we try to improve our understanding of how and why these text distance measures work for authorship attribution. We evaluate the effects of standardization and vector normalization on the statistical distributions of features and the resulting text clustering quality. Furthermore, we explore supervised selection of discriminant words as a procedure for further improving authorship attribution.

1 Introduction

Authorship Attribution is a research area in quantitative text analysis concerned with attributing texts of unknown or disputed authorship to their actual author based on quantitatively measured linguistic evidence (Juola, 2006; Stamatatos, 2009; Koppel et al., 2008). Authorship attribution has applications e.g. in literary studies, history, and forensics, and uses methods from Natural Language Processing, Text Mining, and Corpus Stylistics. The fundamental assumption in authorship attribution is that individuals have idiosyncratic habits of language use, leading to a stylistic similarity of texts written by the same person. Many of these stylistic habits can be measured by assessing the relative frequencies of function words or parts of speech, vocabulary richness, and other linguistic features. This, in turn, allows using the relative similarity of the texts to each other in clustering or classification tasks and to attribute a text of unknown authorship to the most similar of a (usually closed) set of candidate authors.

One of the most crucial elements in quantitative authorship attribution methods is the distance measure used to quantify the degree of similarity between texts. A major advance in this area has been Delta, as proposed by Burrows (2002), which has proven to be a very robust measure in different genres and languages (Hoover, 2004b; Eder and Rybicki, 2013). Since 2002, a number of variants of Burrows's Delta have been proposed (Hoover, 2004a; Argamon, 2008; Smith and Aldridge, 2011; Eder et al., 2013). In a recent publication, empirical tests of authorship attribution performance for Delta as well as 13 precursors and/or variants of it have been reported (Jannidis et al., 2015). That study, using three test corpora in English, German and French, has shown that Burrows's Delta remains a strong contender, but is outperformed quite clearly by Cosine Delta as proposed by Smith and Aldridge (2011). The study has also shown that some of the theoretical arguments by Argamon (2008) do not find empirical confirmation. This means that, intriguingly, there is still no clear theoretical model which is able to explain why these various distance measures yield varying performance; we don't have a clear understanding why Burrows's Delta and Cosine Delta are so robust and reliable.

In the absence of compelling theoretical arguments, systematic empirical testing becomes paramount, and this paper proposes to continue such

Proceedings of NAACL-HLT Fourth Workshop on Computational Linguistics for Literature, pages 79–88,
Denver, Colorado, June 4, 2015.

investigations. Previous work has focused on feature selection either in the sense of deciding what type of feature (e.g. character, word or part-of-speech n-grams) has the best discriminatory power for authorship attribution (Forsyth and Holmes, 1996; Rogati and Yang, 2002), or in the sense of deciding which part of the list of most frequent words yields the best results (Rybicki and Eder, 2011). Other publications explored strategies of deliberately picking a very small numbers of particularly disciminative features (Cartright and Bendersky, 2008; Marsden et al., 2013). Our strategy builds on such approaches but differs from them in that we focus on word unigrams only and examine how the treatment of the input feature vector (i.e., the list of word tokens used and their frequencies) interacts with the performance of distance measures. Each distance measure implements a specific combination of standardization and/or normalization of the feature vector. In addition, the feature vector can be preprocessed in several ways before submitting it to the distance measure.

In the following, we report on a series of experiments which assess the effects of standardization and normalization, as well as of feature vector manipulation, on the performance of distance measures for authorship attribution.

Although we use attribution success as our performance indicator, our ultimate goal is not so much to optimize the results, but rather to gain a deeper understanding of the mechanisms behind distance measures. We hope that a deeper theoretical understanding will help choose the right parameters in authorship attribution cases.

2 Notation

All measures in the Delta family share the same basic procedure for measuring dissimilarities between the text documents D in a collection $\mathcal{D}$ of size $n_{\mathcal{D}}$.[1]

- Each text $D \in \mathcal{D}$ is represented by a profile of the relative frequencies $f_i(D)$ of the n_w most frequent words (mfw) $w_1, w_2, \ldots w_{n_w}$.
- The complete profile of D is given by the feature vector $\mathbf{f}(D) = (f_1(D), \ldots, f_{n_w}(D))$.
- Features are re-scaled, usually with a linear transformation, in order to adapt the weight given to each of the mfw. The most common choice is to standardize features using a z-transformation

$$z_i(D) = \frac{f_i(D) - \mu_i}{\sigma_i}$$

where μ_i is the mean of the distribution of f_i across the collection $\mathcal{D}$ and σ_i its standard deviation (s.d.). After the transformation, each feature z_i has mean $\mu = 0$ and s.d. $\sigma = 1$.
- Dissimilarities between the scaled feature vectors are computed according to some distance metric. Optionally, feature vectors may first be normalized to have length 1 under the same metric.

Different choices of a distance metric lead to various well-known variants of Delta. The original Burrows's Delta Δ_B (Burrows, 2002) corresponds to the Manhattan distance between feature vectors:

$$\Delta_B(D, D') = \|\mathbf{z}(D) - \mathbf{z}(D')\|_1 = \sum_{i=1}^{n_w} |z_i(D) - z_i(D')|$$

Quadratic Delta Δ_Q (Argamon, 2008) corresponds to the squared Euclidean distance:

$$\Delta_Q(D, D') = \|\mathbf{z}(D) - \mathbf{z}(D')\|_2^2 = \sum_{i=1}^{n_w} (z_i(D) - z_i(D'))^2$$

and is fully equivalent to Euclidean distance $\sqrt{\Delta_Q}$.

Cosine Delta $\Delta_\angle$ (Smith and Aldridge, 2011) measures the angle α between two profile vectors

$$\Delta_\angle(D, D') = \alpha$$

which can be computed from the cosine similarity of $\mathbf{x} = \mathbf{z}(D)$ and $\mathbf{y} = \mathbf{z}(D')$:

$$\cos \alpha = \frac{\mathbf{x}^T \mathbf{y}}{\|\mathbf{x}\|_2 \cdot \|\mathbf{y}\|_2}$$

where $\mathbf{x}^T\mathbf{y} = \sum_{i=1}^{n_w} x_i y_i$ is the dot product and $\|\mathbf{x}\|_2 = \sqrt{\sum_{i=1}^{n_w} x_i^2}$ denotes the length of the vector $\mathbf{x}$ according to the Euclidean norm. All three variants of Delta agree in using standardized frequencies of the most frequent words as their underlying features.

[1] The notation introduced here follows Argamon (2008) and Jannidis et al. (2015).

3 Understanding the parameters of Delta

Different versions of Delta can be obtained by setting the parameters of the general procedure outlined in Sec. 2, in particular:

- n_w, i.e. the number of words used as features in the frequency profiles;
- how these words are selected (e.g. taking the most frequent words, choosing words based on the number df of texts they occur in, etc.);
- how frequency profiles $\mathbf{f}(D)$ are scaled to feature vectors $\mathbf{z}(D)$
- whether feature vectors are normalized to unit length $\|\mathbf{z}(D)\| = 1$ (and according to which norm); and
- which distance metric is used to measure dissimilarities between feature vectors.

We focus here on three key variants of the Delta measure:

(i) the original Burrows's Delta Δ_B because it is consistently one of the best-performing Delta variants despite its simplicity and lack of a convincing mathematical motivation (Argamon, 2008);

(ii) Quadratic Delta Δ_Q because it can be derived from a probabilistic interpretation of the standardized frequency profiles (Argamon, 2008); and

(iii) Cosine Delta $\Delta_\angle$ because it achieved the best results in the evaluation study of Jannidis et al. (2015).

All three variants use some number n_w of mfw as features and scale them by standardization (z-transformation). At first sight, they appear to differ only with respect to the distance metric used: Manhattan distance (Δ_B), Euclidean distance (Δ_Q), or angular distance ($\Delta_\angle$).

There is a close connection between angular distance and Euclidean distance because the (squared) Euclidean norm can be expressed as a dot product $\|\mathbf{x}\|_2^2 = \mathbf{x}^T\mathbf{x}$. Therefore,

$$\begin{aligned}\|\mathbf{x}-\mathbf{y}\|_2^2 &= (\mathbf{x}-\mathbf{y})^T(\mathbf{x}-\mathbf{y}) \\ &= \mathbf{x}^T\mathbf{x} + \mathbf{y}^T\mathbf{y} - 2\mathbf{x}^T\mathbf{y} \\ &= \|\mathbf{x}\|_2^2 + \|\mathbf{y}\|_2^2 - 2\|\mathbf{x}\|_2\|\mathbf{y}\|_2 \cos\alpha\end{aligned}$$

If the profile vectors are normalized wrt. the Euclidean norm, i.e. $\|\mathbf{x}\|_2 = \|\mathbf{y}\|_2 = 1$, Euclidean distance is a monotonic function of the angle α:

$$\|\mathbf{x}-\mathbf{y}\|_2^2 = 2 - 2\cos\alpha$$

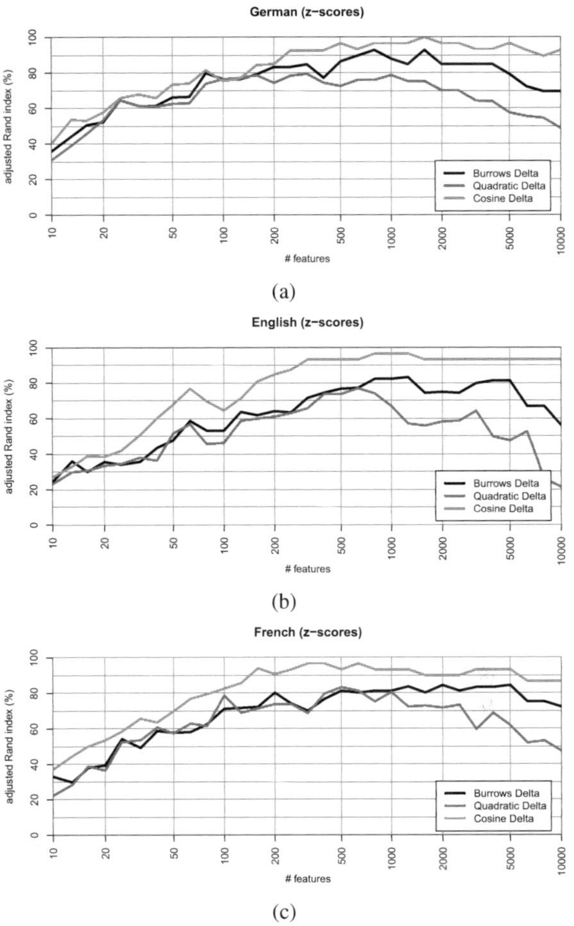

Figure 1: Clustering quality for German, English and French texts in our replication of Jannidis et al. (2015)

As a result, Δ_Q and $\Delta_\angle$ are equivalent for normalized feature vectors. The difference between Quadratic and Cosine Delta is a matter of the normalization parameter at heart; they are not based on genuinely different distance metrics.

3.1 The number of features

As a first step, we replicate the findings of Jannidis et al. (2015). Their data set is composed of three collections of novels written in English, French and German. Each collection contains 3 novels each from 25 different authors, i.e. a total of 75 texts. The collection of British novels contains texts published between 1838 and 1921 coming from Project Gutenberg.[2] The collection of French novels con-

[2] www.gutenberg.org

tains texts published between 1827 and 1934 originating mainly from Ebooks libres et gratuits.[3] The collection of German novels consists of texts from the 19th and the first half of the 20th Century which come from the TextGrid collection.[4]

Our experiments extend the previous study in three respects:

1. We use a different clustering algorithm, partitioning around medoids (Kaufman and Rousseeuw, 1990), which has proven to be very robust especially on linguistic data (Lapesa and Evert, 2014). The number of clusters is set to 25, corresponding to the number of different authors in each of the collections.
2. We evaluate clustering quality using a well-established criterion, the chance-adjusted Rand index (Hubert and Arabie, 1985), rather than cluster purity. This improves comparability with other evaluation studies.
3. Jannidis et al. (2015) consider only three arbitrarily chosen values $n_w = 100, 1000, 5\,000$. Since clustering quality does not always improve if a larger number of mfw is used, this approach draws an incomplete picture and does not show whether there is a clearly defined optimal value n_w or whether the Delta measures are robust wrt. the choice of n_w. Our evaluation systematically varies n_w from 10 to 10 000.

Fig. 1(a) shows evaluation results for the German texts; Fig. 1(b) and 1(c) show the corresponding results on English and French data. Our experiments confirm the observations of Jannidis et al. (2015):

- For a small number of mfw as features (roughly $n_w \leq 500$), Δ_B and Δ_Q achieve the same clustering quality. However, Δ_Q proves less robust if the number of features is further increased ($n_w > 500$), despite the convincing probabilistic motivation given by Argamon (2008).
- $\Delta_\angle$ consistently outperforms the other Delta measures, regardless of the choice of n_w. It is robust for values up to $n_w = 10\,000$, degrading much more slowly than Δ_B and Δ_Q.
- The clustering quality achieved by $\Delta_\angle$ is very impressive. With an adjusted Rand index above 90% for a wide range of n_w, most of the texts in the collections are correctly grouped by author.

[3] www.ebooksgratuits.com

[4] www.textgrid.de/Digitale-Bibliothek

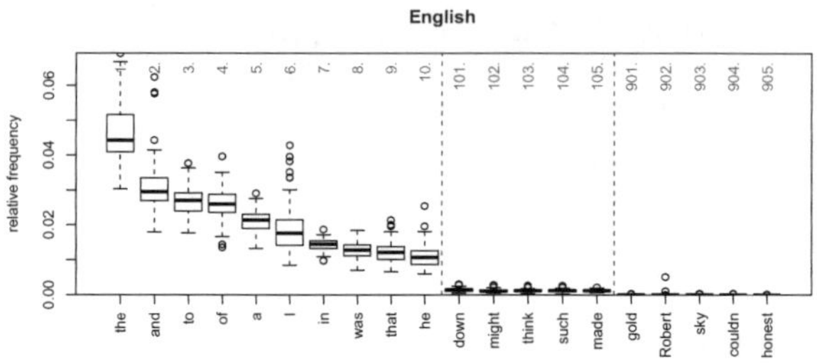

Figure 2: Distribution of relative frequencies for selected English words (numbers at the top show mfw rank)

It is obvious from these evaluation graphs that an appropriate choice of n_w plays a crucial role for Δ_Q, and to a somewhat lesser extent also for Δ_B. In all three languages, clustering quality is substantially diminished for $n_w > 5\,000$. Since there are already noticeable differences between the three collections, it has to be assumed that the optimal n_w depends on many factors – language, text type, length of the texts, quality and preprocessing of the text files (e.g. spelling normalization), etc. – and cannot be known *a priori*. It would be desirable either to re-scale the relative frequencies in a way that gives less weight to "noisy" features, or to re-rank the most frequent words by a different criterion for which a clear cut-off point can be determined.

Alternatively, more robust variants of Delta such as $\Delta_\angle$ might be used, although there is still a gradual decline, especially for the French data in Fig. 1(c). Since $\Delta_\angle$ differs from the least robust measure Δ_Q only in its implicit normalization of the feature vectors, vector normalization appears to be the key to robust authorship attribution.

3.2 Feature scaling

Burrows applied a z-transformation to the frequency profiles with the explicit intention to "treat all of these words as markers of potentially equal power" (Burrows, 2002, p. 271). Fig. 2 and 3 illustrate this intuition for some of the most frequent words in the English collection.

Without standardization, words with mfw ranks above 100 make a negligible contribution to the frequency profiles (Fig. 2). The evaluation graph in Fig. 4 confirms that Delta measures are hardly affected at all by words above mfw rank 100 if no z-

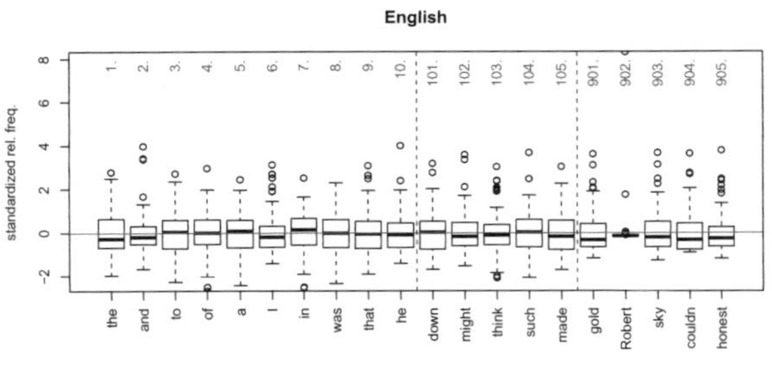

Figure 3: Distribution of standardized z-scores

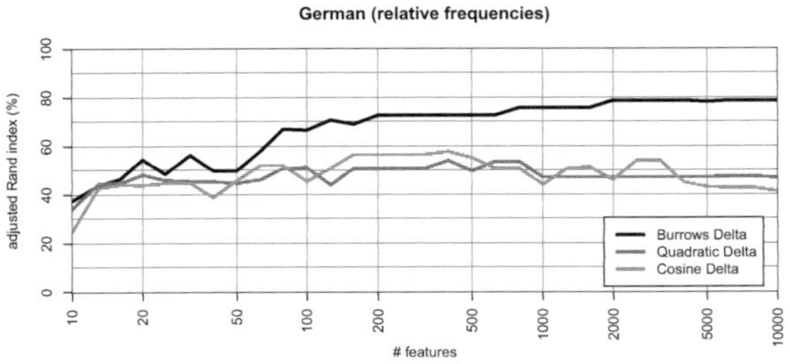

Figure 4: Clustering quality of German texts based on unscaled relative frequencies (without standardization)

transformation is applied. While results are robust with respect to n_w, the few mfw that make a noticeable contribution are not sufficient to achieve a reasonable clustering quality. After standardization, the z-scores show a similar distribution for all features (Fig. 3).

Argamon (2008) argued that standardization is only meaningful if the relative frequencies roughly follow a Gaussian distribution across the texts in a collection $\mathcal{D}$, which is indeed the case for high-frequency words (Jannidis et al., 2015). With some further assumptions, Argamon showed that $\Delta_Q(D, D')$ can be used as a test statistic for authorship attribution, with an asymptotic $\chi^2_{n_w}$ distribution under the null hypothesis that both texts are from the same author. It can also be shown that standardization gives all features equal weight in Δ_Q in a strict sense, i.e. each feature makes exactly the same average contribution to the pairwise squared Euclidean distances (and analogously for $\Delta_\angle$).

This strict interpretation of equal weight does not hold for Δ_B, so Burrows's original intention has not been fully realized. Fig. 5 displays the actual contribution made to each feature to $\Delta_B(D, D')$, i.e. to the pairwise Manhattan distances between

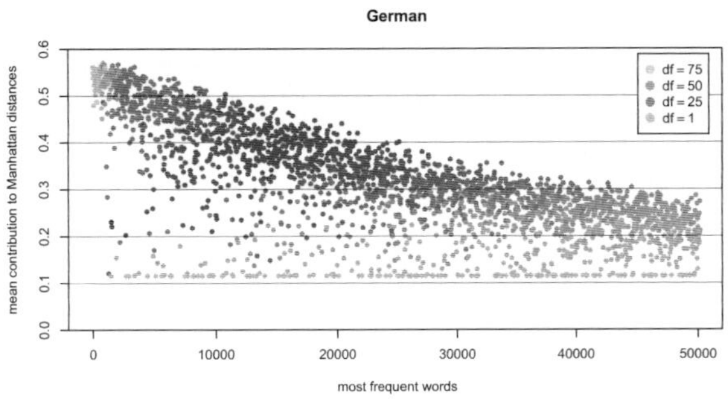

Figure 5: Average contribution of features to pairwise Δ_B distances; colour indicates document frequency (*df*)

z-transformed feature vectors $\mathbf{z}(D)$ and $\mathbf{z}(D')$. It shows that less frequent words have a moderately smaller weight than the mfw up to rank 5 000. Words that occur just in a small number of texts (their document frequency *df*, indicated by point colour in Fig. 5) carry a low weight regardless of their overall frequency.

Our conclusion is that Δ_B appears to be more robust than Δ_Q precisely because it gives less weight to the standardized frequencies of "noisy" words above mfw rank 5 000 in contrast to the claim made by Burrows. Moreover, it strongly demotes words that concentrate in a small number of texts, which are likely idiosyncratic expressions from a particular novel (e.g. character names) or a narrow sub-genre. It is plausible that such words are of little use for the purpose of authorship attribution.

Surprisingly, ranking the mfw by their contribution to Δ_B (so that e.g. words with $df < 10$ are never included as features) is less effective than ranking by overall frequency (not shown for space reasons). We also experimented with a number of alternative scaling methods – including the scaling suggested by Argamon (2008) for a probabilistic interpretation of Δ_B – obtaining consistently worse clustering quality than with standardization.

3.3 Vector normalization

As shown at the beginning of Sec. 3, the main difference between $\Delta_\angle$ (the best and most robust measure in our evaluation) and Δ_Q (the worst and least robust measure) lies in the normalization of feature vectors. This observation suggests that other Delta measures such as Δ_B might also benefit from vector normalization. We test this hypothesis with the evaluation

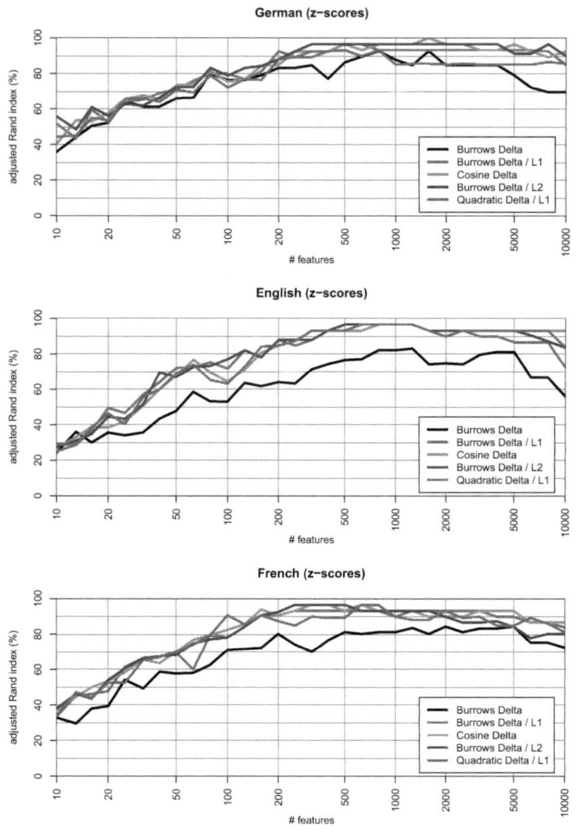

Figure 6: The effect of vector normalization on clustering quality (L2 = Euclidean norm, L1 = Manhattan norm)

shown in Fig. 6.

The quality curves for Δ_Q with Euclidean normalization are in fact identical to the curves for Cosine Delta ($\Delta_\angle$) and are not shown separately here. Δ_B is also improved substantially by vector normalization (contrast the black curve with the red and blue ones), resulting in clustering quality equal to $\Delta_\angle$, although Δ_B might be slightly less robust for $n_w > 5\,000$. Interestingly, it seems to make little difference whether an appropriate normalization is used (L1 for Δ_B and L2 for Δ_Q) or not (vice versa).

Our tentative explanation for these findings is as follows. We conjecture that authorial style is primarily reflected by the pattern of positive and negative deviations z_i of word frequencies from the "norm", i.e. the average frequency across the text collection. This characteristic pattern is not expressed to the same degree in all texts by a given author, leading to differences in the average magnitude of the values z_i and hence the length $\|\mathbf{z}(D)\|$ of the feature vectors. If this is indeed the case, vector normalization makes the stylistic pattern of each author stand out more clearly because it equalizes the average magnitude of the z_i.

Fig. 7 visualizes the Euclidean length of feature vectors for texts written by different German authors. In the situation depicted by the left panel ($n_w = 150$) normalization has no substantial effect, whereas in the situation depicted by the right panel ($n_w = 5\,000$) unnormalized Δ_Q performs much worse than normalized $\Delta_\angle$ (cf. Fig. 1(a)).

Each point in the plots represents the feature vector $\mathbf{z}(D)$ of one text. The distance from the origin indicates its Euclidean (L2) norm $\|\mathbf{z}(D)\|_2$, relative to the average vector length $\sqrt{n_w}$. All points on a circle thus correspond to feature vectors of the same Euclidean length. The angular position of a text shows the relative contribution of positive features ($z_i > 0$, i.e. words used with above-average frequency) and negative features ($z_i < 0$, words used with below-average frequency) as a rough indicator of its stylistic pattern. Texts below the dashed diagonal thus have more (or larger) positive deviations z_i, texts above the diagonal have more (or larger) negative deviations. In both panels, some authors are characterized quite well by vector length and the balance of positive vs. negative deviations. For other authors, however, one of the texts shows a much larger deviation from the norm than the other two, i.e. larger Euclidean length (Freytag and Spielhagen in the right panel). Similar patterns can be observed for the Manhattan (L1) norm as well as among the English and French novels. In such cases, normalization reduces the distances between texts from the same author and thus improves clustering quality.

Fig. 7 also reveals a plausible explanation for the poor evaluation results of Δ_Q as n_w is increased. Because of the skewed distribution of z_i for lower-frequency words (see Fig. 3), the contribution of positive values to the Euclidean norm outweighs the negative values (but this is not the case for the Manhattan norm and Δ_B). Therefore, all points in the right panel are below the diagonal and their stylistic profiles become increasingly similar. Differences in vector length between texts from the same author have a stronger influence on Δ_Q distances in this situation, resulting in many clustering errors.

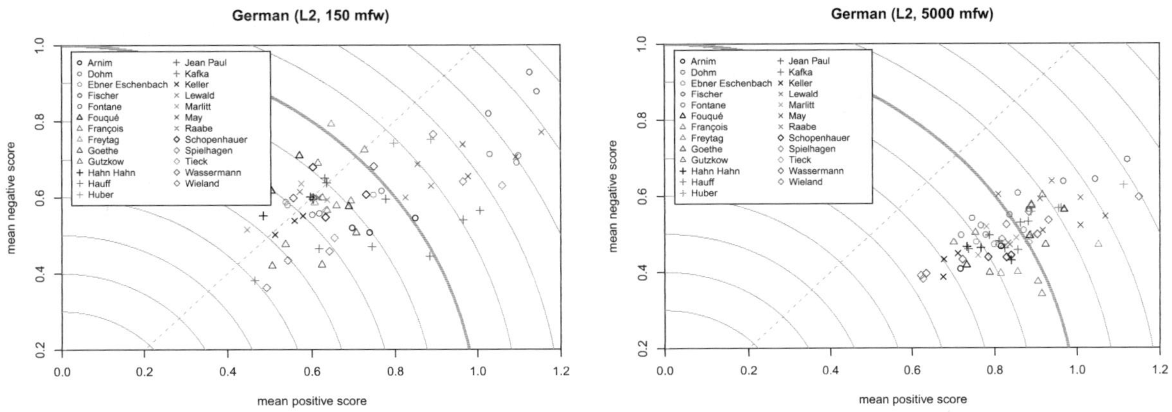

Figure 7: Euclidean length of unnormalized vectors for texts in the German corpus. Coordinates of the points indicate the average contribution of positive and negative features to the total length of the vector.

	English	French	German
nr. of features	246	381	234
SVC accuracy	0.99 ($\pm$0.04)	1.00 ($\pm$0.00)	1.00 ($\pm$0.00)
MaxEnt accuracy	1.00 ($\pm$0.00)	1.00 ($\pm$0.00)	1.00 ($\pm$0.00)
Cosine Delta ARI	0.966	1.000	1.000

Table 1: Results for cross-validation and clustering experiments

4 Feature selection as a contribution to explanation

In this section, we explore another strategy for obtaining an optimal set of features. Instead of using a threshold on (document) frequencies of words for feature selection, we systematically identify a set of discriminant words by using the method of recursive feature elimination. The resulting feature set is much smaller and not only works well in a machine learning setting, but also outperforms the most-frequent-words approach when clustering a test corpus of mainly unseen authors.

4.1 Recursive feature elimination

Recursive feature elimination is a greedy algorithm that relies on a ranking of features and on each step selects only the top ranked features, pruning the remaining features. For our feature elimination experiments we rely on a Support Vector Classifier (SVC) with linear kernel for feature ranking.[5] During training, an SVC assigns weights to the individual features, with greater absolute weights indicating more important features. We can use the weight magnitude as ranking criterion and perform recursive feature elimination by repeating the following three steps:

1. Train the classifier, i. e. assign weights to the features.
2. Rank the features according to the absolute value of their weights.
3. Prune the n lowest ranking features.

Since it is more efficient to remove several features at a time (with the possible disadvantage of introducing a slight degradation in classification performance) and we are starting with a few hundreds of thousands of features and are aiming for a much smaller set, we first reduce the number of features to 500 in three stages. First we reduce the number of features to 50 000 by recursively pruning the 10 000 lowest ranking features, then we reduce those 50 000 features to 5 000 features by pruning 1 000 features at a time and finally we reduce the number of fea-

[5]The scikit-learn implementation of Support Vector Machines we used is based on libsvm and supports multiclass classification via a one-vs.-one scheme. We used it with default parameter settings.

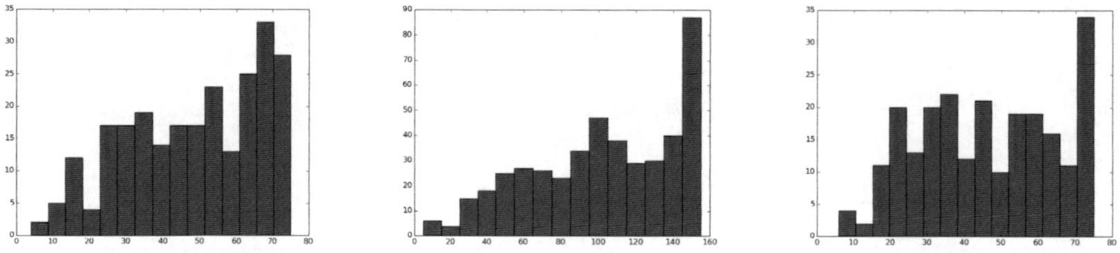

(a) English (b) French (c) German

Figure 8: Distributions of document frequencies for selected features

	unscaled full fs	rescaled full fs	selected fs
SVC accuracy	0.91 (± 0.03)	0.57 (± 0.13)	0.84 (± 0.14)
MaxEnt accuracy	0.95 (± 0.03)	0.95 (± 0.03)	0.90 (± 0.08)
Cosine Delta ARI	0.835	0.835	0.871

Table 2: Evaluation results for the selected features on the second additional test set compared to all features (for Cosine Delta clustering, 2 000 mfw are used in this case)

tures to 500 by pruning the 100 lowest ranking features at a time.

Once we have reduced the number of features to 500, we try to find an optimal number of features by pruning only one feature at a time, doing a stratified threefold cross-validation on the data after each pruning step to test classification accuracy.

Since Support Vector Machines are not scale-invariant, we rescaled each feature to [0, 1] during preprocessing. Simply rescaling the data should work better than standardization because it preserves sparsity (the standardized feature matrix is dense, replacing every zero by a small negative value). As an additional preprocessing step we removed all words with a document frequency of 1.

4.2 Examination and validation

The recursive feature elimination process can choose from an abundance of features, and therefore it is no surprise that it is able to find a subset of features that yields perfect results for both classification (accuracy was determined using stratified threefold cross-validation and is given as the mean plus/minus two standard deviations) and clustering using $\Delta_\angle$.[6] Cf. Table 1 for an overview of the results.

Figures 8(a)-8(c) show the distribution of the document frequencies of those features. For all corpora there are some highly specific features that occur only in a fraction of the texts, but most selected features have a rather high document frequency.

The features which turn out to be maximally distinctive of authors show a number of interesting patterns. For example, they are not limited to function words. This is a relevant finding, because it is often assumed that function words are the best indicators of authorship. However, content words may be more prone to overfitting than function words. Also, in the English and French collections, a small number of roman numerals are included (such as "XL" or "XXXVVII"), which may be characteristic of novels with an unusually high number of chapters. This, in turn, may in fact be characteristic of certain authors. Finally, in the German collection, a certain number of words show historical orthographic variants (such as "Heimath" or "giebt"). These are most likely artifacts of the corpus rather than actual stylistic characteristics of certain authors.

Perfect cross-validation and clustering results suggest that there may be severe overfitting. In order to verify how well the set of selected features performs on unseen data, we used two additional evaluation data sets:

1. An unbalanced set of 71 additional unseen nov-

[6] We used agglomerative clustering with complete linkage.

els by 19 authors from the German collection;

2. An unbalanced set of 155 unseen novels by 34 authors, with at least 3 novels per author (6 authors are also in the original collection).

For the first test set, we trained an SVC and a Maximum Entropy classifier (MaxEnt) on the original German corpus using the set of 234 selected features and evaluated classifier accuracy on the test set. Both SVC and MaxEnt achieved 0.97 accuracy on that test set, indicating that the selected features are not overfit to the specific novels in the training corpus but generalize very well to other works from the same authors. Since this test set includes singletons (a single novel by an author), cross-validation and clustering experiments cannot sensibly be conducted here.

For the second test set, we evaluated classification accuracy with stratified threefold cross-validation using only the set of 234 selected features. We also clustered the texts using $\Delta_{\angle}$ based on the same features. To have a point of reference, we furthermore evaluated classification and clustering using the full feature set, once using relative frequencies and once using rescaled relative frequencies. For the clustering we used the 2 000 mfw as features, which our experiments in Section 3.1 showed to be a robust and nearly optimal number. The results are summarized in Table 2.[7]

Comparing evaluation results for the 234 selected features from the original corpus with the full rescaled feature set, we see a considerable increase in SVC accuracy (due to the smaller number of features),[8] a small decrease in MaxEnt accuracy and an increase in clustering quality, indicating that the selected features are not overfitted to the training data and generalize fairly well to texts from other authors. Nevertheless, the difference in clustering accuracy between the first and the second test set indicates that these features are author-dependent to some extent.

5 Conclusion

The results presented here shed some light on the properties of Burrows's Delta and related text distance measures, as well as the contributions of the underlying features and their statistical distribution. Using the most frequent words as features and standardizing them with a z-transformation (Burrows, 2002) proves to be better than many alternative strategies (Sec. 3.2). However, the number n_w of features remains a critical factor (Sec. 3.1) for which no good strategy is available. Vector normalization is revealed as the key factor behind the success of Cosine Delta. It also improves Burrows's Delta and makes all measures robust wrt. the choice of n_w (Sec. 3.3). In Sec. 4 we showed that supervised feature selection may be a viable approach to further improve authorship attribution and determine a suitable value for n_w in a principled manner.

Although we are still not able to explain in full how Burrows's Delta and its variants are able to distinguish so well between texts of different authorship, why the choices made by Burrows (use of mfw, z-scores, and Manhattan distance) are better than many alternatives with better mathematical justification, and why vector normalization yields excellent and robust authorship attribution regardless of the distance metric used, the present results constitute an important step towards answering these questions.

[7]Clustering results on the unscaled and rescaled full feature sets are identical because of the z-transformation involved in cosine delta.

[8]While Support Vector Machines are supposed to be effective for data sets with more features than training samples, they don't deal very well with huge feature sets that exceed the training samples by several orders of magnitude. For this reason, the poor performance of SVC on the full features set was to be expected. It is surprising, however, that SVC performs much better on unscaled features. We believe this to be a lucky coincidence: The SVC optimization criterion prefers high-frequency words that require smaller feature weights; they also happen to be the most informative and robust features in this case.

References

Shlomo Argamon. 2008. Interpreting Burrows's Delta: Geometric and Probabilistic Foundations. *Literary and Linguistic Computing*, 23(2):131 –147, June.

John Burrows. 2002. Delta: a Measure of Stylistic Difference and a Guide to Likely Authorship. *Literary and Linguistic Computing*, 17(3):267 –287.

Marc-Allen Cartright and Michael Bendersky. 2008. Towards scalable data-driven authorship attribution. *Center for Intelligent Information Retrieval.*

Maciej Eder and Jan Rybicki. 2013. Do birds of a feather really flock together, or how to choose training samples for authorship attribution. *Literary and Linguistic Computing*, 28(2):229–236, June.

Maciej Eder, Mike Kestemont, and Jan Rybicki. 2013. Stylometry with R: a suite of tools. In *Digital Humanities 2013: Conference Abstracts*, pages 487–489, Lincoln. University of Nebraska.

R. S. Forsyth and D. I. Holmes. 1996. Feature-finding for text classification. *Literary and Linguistic Computing*, 11(4):163–174, December.

David L. Hoover. 2004a. Delta Prime? *Literary and Linguistic Computing*, 19(4):477 –495, November.

David L. Hoover. 2004b. Testing Burrows's Delta. *Literary and Linguistic Computing*, 19(4):453 –475, November.

Lawrence Hubert and Phipps Arabie. 1985. Comparing partitions. *Journal of Classification*, 2:193–218.

Fotis Jannidis, Steffen Pielström, Christof Schöch, and Thorsten Vitt. 2015. Improving Burrows' Delta - An empirical evaluation of text distance measures. In *Digital Humanities Conference 2015*, Sydney.

Patrick Juola. 2006. Authorship attribution. *Foundations and Trends in Information Retrieval*, 1(3):233–334.

Leonard Kaufman and Peter J. Rousseeuw. 1990. *Finding Groups in Data: An Introduction to Cluster Analysis*. John Wiley and Sons, New York.

M. Koppel, J. Schler, and S. Argamon. 2008. Computational methods in authorship attribution. *Journal of the American Society for information Science and Technology*, 60(1):9–26.

Gabriella Lapesa and Stefan Evert. 2014. A large scale evaluation of distributional semantic models: Parameters, interactions and model selection. *Transactions of the Association for Computational Linguistics*, 2:531–545.

John Marsden, David Budden, Hugh Craig, and Pablo Moscato. 2013. Language individuation and marker words: Shakespeare and his maxwell's demon. *PloS one*, 8(6):e66813.

Monica Rogati and Yiming Yang. 2002. High-performing feature selection for text classification. In *Proceedings of the eleventh international conference on Information and knowledge management*, CIKM '02, pages 659–661, New York, NY, USA. ACM.

Jan Rybicki and Maciej Eder. 2011. Deeper delta across genres and languages: do we really need the most frequent words? *Literary and Linguistic Computing*, 26(3):315–321, July.

Peter W. H. Smith and W. Aldridge. 2011. Improving Authorship Attribution: Optimizing Burrows' Delta Method*. *Journal of Quantitative Linguistics*, 18(1):63–88, February.

Efstathios Stamatatos. 2009. A survey of modern authorship attribution methods. *J. Am. Soc. Inf. Sci. Technol.*, 60(3):538–556, March.

Gender-Based Vocation Identification in Swedish 19th Century Prose Fiction using Linguistic Patterns, NER and CRF Learning

Dimitrios Kokkinakis
Department of Swedish, Språkbanken
University of Gothenburg
Sweden
dimitrios.kokkinakis@gu.se

Ann Ighe
Economic History, School of Business Economics and Law
University of Gothenburg
Sweden
ann.ighe@gu.se

Mats Malm
Department of Literature, History of Ideas and Religion
University of Gothenburg
Sweden
mats.malm@lir.gu.se

Abstract

This paper investigates how literature could be used as a means to expand our understanding of history. By applying macroanalytic techniques we are aiming to investigate how women enter literature and particularly which functions do they assume, their working patterns and if we can spot differences in how often male and female characters are mentioned with various types of occupational titles (vocation) in Swedish literary texts. Modern historiography, and especially feminist and women's history has emphasized a relative invisibility of women's work and women workers. The reasons to this are manifold, and the extent, the margin of error in terms of women's work activities is of course hard to assess. Therefore, vocation identification can be used as an indicator for such exploration and we present a hybrid system for automatic annotation of vocational signals in 19th century Swedish prose fiction. Beside vocations, the system also assigns gender (male, female or unknown) to the vocation words, a prerequisite for the goals of the study and future in-depth explorations of the corpora.

1 Introduction

Can we use literary text as a (valid) source for historical research? Evidence shows that the answer is probably yes and in this paper we investigate how literature can be used as a means to expand our understanding of history; (Rutner & Schonfeld, 2012). This paper presents a system for the automatic annotation of vocational signals in Swedish text, namely 19th century prose fiction. *Vocation* in this context is defined as a single word or a multi word expression intended to capture the (professional) activities with which one occupies oneself, such as employment or other, wider, forms of productive occupations not necessarily paid. Therefore *vocation* is used here in a rather broad sense since we do not want to disallow word candidates that might not fit in a strict definition of the term. Apart from vocation identification, the described system recognizes and assigns gender, i.e. male, female or unknown, to the vocations by using various Natural Language Processing (NLP) technologies.

The purpose of this work is to use literature as means to expand our understanding of history (Pasco, 2014) by applying macroanalytic techniques (Moretti, 2013; Jockers, 2013) in order to start exploring how women enter literature as characters, which functions do they assume and their working patterns. The research questions themselves are not new, but in fact central to the field of gender studies and to a certain extent, economic history. From a historical point of view, the 19th century in Sweden, and several other western countries, is a period with a dramatic restructuring of gender relations in formal institutions such as the civil law, and also a period where the separation of home and workplace came to redefine the spatial arenas for human interaction. Singular works of fiction can be analyzed and interpreted in historical research and current development in digital humanities certainly opens new possibilities in this direction. Therefore, vocation identification can be used as one such indicator for achieving some of the above stated goals. The starting point of this study has been to create an infrastructure of suitable lexical resources and computational tools for empirical NLP in the cultural heritage domain and digital humanities area. Supporting future users of digitized literature collections

Proceedings of NAACL-HLT Fourth Workshop on Computational Linguistics for Literature, pages 89–97,
Denver, Colorado, June 4, 2015.

with tools that enable the discovery and exploration of text patterns and relationships, or even allow them to semantically search and browse (Don et al., 2007; Vuillemot et al., 2009; Oelke et al., 2013), using computer-assisted literary analysis with more semantically oriented techniques, can lay the foundations to more distant reading or macroanalysis of large corpora in novel ways, impossible to investigate using traditional qualitative methods or close reading.

2 Background

Digital humanities is an umbrella term used for any humanities research with potential for real interdisciplinary exchange between various fields and can be seen as an amalgamation of methodologies from traditional humanities disciplines (such as literature and art, corpus linguistics), and social sciences, with computational approaches and tools provided by computer science (such as text and data mining) and digital publishing. During the last couple of decades there has been a lot of research on applying automatic text analytic tools to annotate, enrich, explore and mine historical or other digital collections in various languages and for several reasons (Pennacchiotti & Zanzotto, 2008; Mueller, 2009; Manning, 2011; Piotrowski, 2012; Jockers, 2013; McEnery & Baker, 2014). The focus of such research is to reduce the time consuming, manual work that is often carried out e.g. by historians or other literature scholars, in order to identify valid, useful and meaningful results such as semantic associations, gender patterns and features of human networks (Agarwal et al., 2012). Also, recently, a small number of studies have been published where gender and other biographical characteristics are explored (Hota et al., 2006; Argamon et al., 2007; Garera & Yarowsky, 2009; Bullard & Oveesdotter Alm, 2014). These methods apply various types of classifiers with good performance results.

Boes (2014) discusses the content of the "Vocations of the Novel Project" which consists of a database of roughly 13,000 German-language prose works, published between 1750-1950, and in which each entry in this database is tagged with vocational metadata identifying occupations that receive extended narrative treatment. Fifteen occupational clusters, such as *agricultural professions*, *health* and *nautical professions*, are used for estimating the proportional distribution of those with the database content, showing for instance that members of the *clergy* diminished after about 1885 or that agricultural professions first declined in importance but then become to rise around the turn of the century, after which they rapidly sank again. However, even closer to our goals is the research by Pettersson & Nivre (2011); Fiebranz et al. (2011) and Pettersson et al. (2012; 2014), who in cooperation with historians, study what men and women did for a living in the early modern Swedish society ("The Gender and Work project", GaW) between 1550-1800. In the context of GaW's verb-orientated studies, historians are building a database with relevant information, by identifying working activities often described in the form of verb phrases, such as *chop wood* or *sell fish*. Automatically extracted verb phrases from historical texts are presented to historians as a list of candidate phrases for revision and database inclusion. Since Swedish NLP tools for that period are very scarce, the historical texts are first normalized to a more modern spelling, before tagging and parsing is applied – the techniques applied in GaW are different and thus complementary to the ones we apply in the research described in this paper.

3 Material

The textual data we use in this work is the content of an 18-19th century Swedish Prose Fiction database – Spf[1]. Spf is comprised by ca 300 prose works that were originally published as books during the years 1800, 1820, 1840, 1860, 1880 and 1900. The material is representational of its times in ways that the canonized literatures are not, in the sense that it contains not only canonized literature but mainstream as well as marginalized treatments of 19th century society. The database makes it possible to examine a particular year span and compare it to the material of other years in order to obtain a comprehensive view of societal development across an entire century. However, the main part of this work deals with the construction and adaptation of several lexical and semantic resources developed for modern Swedish to the language of Spf and algorithmic resources that use those for automatic labeling, and we have left as future work the fine-grained comparison between different time spans.

Furthermore, there are several classificatory systems available where occupations are organized into clearly defined sets of groups according to the tasks and duties undertaken in the job;

[1] <http://spf1800-1900.se/#!/om/inenglish>.

such as the *International Standard Classification of Occupations*[2] or the *National Occupational Classification*[3] which is the nationally accepted reference on occupations in Canada. Such classifications are basically structured by skill type, e.g. *Agricultural, Animal Husbandry and Forestry Workers*, *Fishermen and Hunters* which can further increase the usability of such resources. However, in this study we did not have the human resources to structure the collected occupations in a finer-grained manner, apart from some very basic and coarse encoding (see further Section 3.1); therefore this task is left as a future work. A large number of vocation and other related terms from three lexically-oriented resources were collected and structured. As our starting point we used ca 3,500 lexical units found in relevant frames, such as *Medical_professionals* and *People_by_origin*, from the Swedish *FrameNet*[4]. Moreover, several other lexical units in related frames, that are slightly more general but still relevant, were used, i.e. entries that belong to other types of both generic and more specific frames that indicate person activities, relationships or qualities of various kinds, such as *Kinship* or *Performer*. Secondly, we used several hundred of vocation names from the Swedish dictionary *Svensk Ordbok*[5] 'Swedish Dictionary' (SO) and finally, several thousand vocation names from the *Alfabetiskt yrkesregister* 'Alphabetically list of professional designators' published by the Statistics Sweden[6].

3.1 Vocation Lexicon Structure

Semi-automatically, all lexicon entries were assigned two features. The first one was *gender* (i.e. Male, Female or Unknown) and the second one *Vocation*. Depending on the content and structure of the three resources we used to extract occupations and similar entries from, we tried to keep and encode any kind of relevant to our goals descriptive information for these entries in tab-separated fields. For our study we only use *Vocation* and combinations with *Vocation* and other labels. For instance, in FrameNet, vocation related frames such as *Medical_professionals* (a label that was transformed to a more generic and shorter one, *Health*, and which consists of single and compound lexical units for health-related occupations) was encoded using both *Vocation* and *Health*, e.g. *patolog* 'pathologist' or *sjuksköterska* 'nurse'. Similarly other combinations of FrameNet-originating labels were extracted and encoded in a similar manner. Since we adopted a broad definition of the term *Vocation* we allow such words to be included in the knowledge base, but not all were used for the study described here if there were not directly vocation-related. For instance, *tjuvpojke* 'thief boy' is coded as *Morality-negative*; here *Morality-negative* is of course not a vocation but rather a general human quality and not used in the study. Also words with the label *Person,* which is the most generic category, including mentions such as *baldrottning* 'prom queen'; *äventyrerska* 'adventuress' or *söndagsskoleelev* 'Sunday school student', are not used in the study presented in this paper.

Gender assignment is based on reliable orthographic features of the lexicon entry in question (if available), these include:

- typical gender bearing morphological suffixes, such as –inna [female] *värdinna* 'hostess', *prestinna* 'priestess'or –rska [female] *ångfartygskokerska* 'steamboat's cook', *städerska* 'cleaning woman'.
- gender bearing head noun words that unambiguously can assign gender in compound word forms; for instance *hustru* 'wife' [female]: *soldathustru* 'soldier's wife', *bagarehustru* 'baker's wife'; or *dräng* [male] 'farmhand': *stalledräng* 'stable farmhand', *fiskardräng* 'fisherman farmhand'.

After consulting international efforts in the area, we automatically normalized and attempted to group together and harmonize the labels of all available lexical units (these labels are primarily encoded in the Swedish FrameNet) to the following 14 single types and 4 complex ones, without putting too much effort to introduce finer-grained types for practical reasons (see the previous section for discussion on this issue). Thus, the final set of categories we applied are: *Age* (*yngling* 'youth'), *Expertise-Neg* (*okunnige* 'ignorant'), *Expertise-Pos* (*specialist*), *Jurisdiction* (*invånare* 'resident'), *Kinship* (*dotterdotter* 'granddaughter'), *Morality-Neg* (*tjuv* 'thief'), *Morality-Pos* (*nationalhjälte* 'national hero'), *Origin* (*jugoslav* 'yugoslavian'), *Person* (*vän* 'friend'), *Politics* (*socialdemokrat* 'social-democrat'), *Religion*

[2] <http://www.ilo.org/ public/english/bureau/stat/isco/>.

[3] <http://www5.hrsdc.gc.ca/NOC/Eng lish/NOC/ 2011/OccupationIndex.aspx>.

[4] <http://spraakbanken.gu.se/eng/swefn>.

[5] <http://www.svenskaakademien.se/publikationer/bocker_ om_svenska_spraket>.

[6] <http://www.scb.se/>.

(*metodistpredikant* 'methodist preacher'), *Residence* (*granne* 'neighbour'), *Vocation* (*bussförare* 'bus driver'), *Vocation+Health, Vocation+Military* (*kavallerilöjtnant* 'cavalry lieutenant'), *Vocation+Performer* (*dragspelare* 'accordionist') and *Person+Disease* (*autistiker* 'autistic person'). The resulting lexicon consists of 19,500 terms, of which over 77% (15,000) are distinct occupational titles (vocations), and used in various ways by the system, mainly as the core lexicon for rule based pattern matching and as a feature for supervised machine learning (see Section 4.4). Moreover, 75% (or 11,000) of all these vocations in the lexical resources have been assigned *Unknown* gender as a default since no classificatory orthographic features, as previously described, could be applied for that purpose.

4 Methods

Figure 1 provides a general outline of the methods applied in the study.

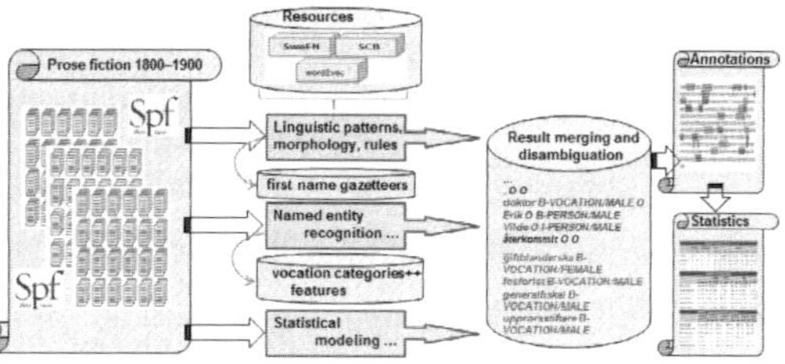

Figure 1. The major steps used to extract gender-bearing vocations from raw text.

4.1 Linguistic Patterns: Morphology, Compounding and Continuous Space Word Representations

The previously outlined lexicon[7] is used for pattern matching based on a number of manually coded rules that explore regularities in the surrounding context of potential vocation words. Inflectional morphology is determined programmatically, while the lexicon's content is also used for discovering "new" terms (not in the static lexicon) using compound segmentation and matching of the head of a candidate vocation to the content of the knowledge base.

For instance, a potential new term candidate, that is a word over 6 characters long not in the lexicon, is de-compounded and its head is matched against the lexicon's content. If a match is found, the new term gets the vocation annotation of the matched head. The length of six characters is determined after testing with other lower values and six is the lowest number that can be safely used and which minimizes the number of false positives returned to a minimum. Suppose *prestinna* 'priestess' is in the lexicon with features *Vocation* and *Female* and a new word, over six characters long, e.g. *öfverprestinna* 'head priestess', is found in a text, *öfverprestinna* will be then decomposed to *öfver+prestinna* and the head *prestinna* will match an existing lexicon entry with the same form; consequently *öfverprestinna* will inherit the annotation *Vocation* and *Female*. Alternative surface text forms, e.g. with hyphenation (*solo-sångare* 'solo singer' versus *solosångare*) are treated in a similar manner, breaking the compound at the hyphen. This processing allows a set of potential new terms to be efficiently recognized, while the results using the lexicon based pattern matching approach show nearly perfect precision scores. The recognition step is made using case insensitive matching against the lexicon's content.

Furthermore, we also experimented with continuous space word representations (Mikolov et al., 2013) in order to extract, manually review and incorporate lists of near synonyms to vocation-specified words. For instance, the top-10 closest words for the word *soldat* 'soldier' were: *bonde* 'farmer', *officer*, *simple** 'simple', knekt 'foot soldier', *tapper** 'brave', *sjöman* 'seaman', *adelsman* 'nobleman', *munk* 'monk', *duktig** 'capable' and *matros* 'sailor'; only three of these words, marked with '*', are not directly associated with vocations. This experiment resulted into roughly a hundred of new vocation words integrated in the knowledge base.

4.2 Person Entity Recognition

During processing we also use named entity recognition (NER) (Borin et al., 2007), but only a component that deals with person entity identification. Since gender is a prominent attribute for a very large number of *first names,* we apply a NER component that uses a first name gazetteer with 21,000 first names, in which each name has been pre-assigned gender and thus used to assign gender to recognized person first names. For instance the NER processing of the sentence: *Jan och Johan skulle just gå in i stugan, då Maja ropade dem tillbaka* 'Jan and John were about to go into the cottage, when Maja called them back' will recognize three first names (*Jan*, *Johan* and *Maja*) and assign male gender to the first two,

[7] All lexicon entries annotated with the Vocation label are available from: <http://spraakbanken.gu.se/swe/personal/dimitrios#research>.

Jan and *Johan* and female to the last one, *Maja*. Thereafter, the results obtained during the application of the method described in Section 4.1 and the results from the NER will be merged, and a post-NER pattern matching script will try to assign gender to vocation words for which gender is marked as *Unknown* by the process described in 4.1 and there is a first name annotation close by. This is accomplished under the condition that the NER has assigned a gender to a first name in the near context of a "genderless" vocation. For instance, a vocation word, for which its surface characteristics does not reveal any gender affiliation according to the vocation lexicon, can be assigned appropriate gender if a recognized first name appears in its near context; e.g. *bonden Petter* '(the) farmer Petter' or *Gusten är en fiskare* 'Gusten is a fisherman'. In these examples *bonden* and *fiskare* are coded in the knowledge base as vocation words with unknown gender and the process outlined in 4.1 recognizes it as such. *Petter* and *Gusten*, on the other hand, are recognized by the NER as human with *male* gender. The gender attribute will be then propagated to the vocation words *bonden* and *fiskare* which will get the same gender as its appositive *Petter* in the first case and the person entity's gender close by in the second case.

4.3 Local Context Regularities

Since not all vocation annotations get gender assignment during recognition, we use hand-coded rules based on various lexical patterns for that purpose. The heuristics applied to these rules include four major types of reliable information: personal pronouns, gender-bearing adjectives, gender-bearing suffixes and certain forms of local context:

- personal pronouns, e.g. the Swedish *hans* 'his' and *hennes* 'her', are used for gender assignment if they appear in a context very close to a vocation (1 to 5 tokens); e.g. in the text fragment *...fiskaren och hans barn* '... the fisherman and his children', *fiskaren* is identified as a vocation but with unknown gender which at this stage will be assigned male since the pronoun *hans* is male and refers to the *fiskaren* 'fisherman'; while in the text fragment *...hon var en agitator* '... she was an agitator', *agitator* is identified as a vocation but with unknown gender which at this stage will be assigned female since the pronoun *hon* is female referring to *agitator*
- historical forms of Swedish adjectives used to be gender bearing; e.g. the majority of adjectives ending in *-e* designate male gender. For example, *fattige bonden* 'the poor farmer', here *bonden* is identified as a vocation with unknown gender which will be assigned male since the adjective *fattige* is indicating a *male* noun
- similarly to the process described in Section 4.1, we also here take advantage of the fact that many noun suffixes or head words of compounds are also gender bearing; e.g. suffixes *-erska* or *-inna* designate female gender; e.g. *tvätterska* 'laundress' or *värdinna* 'hostess' are assigned female gender because of their gender bearing suffixes. Gender bearing head words are also used for gender assignment; e.g. compounds ending in *-fru* 'wife' such as *bondefru* [bonde+fru] 'peasant wife' will be assigned female gender; while compounds ending in e.g. *karl* 'man' such as *besättningskarl* [besättning+s+karl] 'crew man' will be assigned male gender
- local context is also used to merge two or more consecutive vocation and related annotations into one; typically when a genitive form of a noun precedes another noun. For instance, the text snippet: *ryttmästarns betjent* '[the] rittmeister's servant' will initially receive two vocation annotations (with unknown gender) that will be merged into one *[ryttmästarns+betjent]* which unknown gender; while the snippet *drottningens hofmästarinna* '(the) queen's hofmeisteress' will initially receive two vocation annotations (with female gender) that will be merged into one *[drottningens+hofmästarinna]* with female gender.

4.4 Statistical Modeling

Finally, we also use a complementary statistical modelling method, conditional random fields (CRF) for learning gender-assigned vocations in combination with the results of the rule-based system and the NER (the vocation words together with basic features such as n-grams and word shape were used as features for training the learner). For that purpose we use the Stanford CRF off-the-shelf software (Finkel et al., 2005). The purpose of the CRF is to identify vocations and (possibly) correct gender not captured by the previous techniques, in order to increase recall. Training and testing is based on a pre-annotated and manually inspected sample (by the first author). This sample was randomly selected from Spf and it was first automatically annotated by the rule based and NER components, and then sentences with at least one annotation were selected, manually inspected, corrected and used for training (390,000) and testing (50,000).

5 Results, Evaluation and Analysis

The fact that a large number of vocations in the lexical resources have been assigned *Unknown* gender implies that the computational processing requires to heavily relying on a (wider) context to assign proper gender to these words. This is a serious drawback since there is not always reliable near context, e.g. at the sentence level, that can be used. This fact is mirrored on the results of e.g. the CRF classifier. Different complementary techniques have been tested, but still, a large number of vocations remains with unknown gender. More elaborated ways are probably required to identify gender, perhaps using discourse information, e.g. CRF is used with default features, new features might be necessary to test.

Female	Male	Unknown
hustru [wife] (2016)	kung [king] (976)	präst [priest] (1341)
majorska [majoress] (1054)	prost [provost] (614)	kapten [captain] (532)
grefvinna [countess] (805)	brukspatron [ironmaster] (582)	löjtnant [lieutenant] (487)
jungfru [maid] (698)	patron [land tenure] (430)	major (382)
grevinna [countess] (593)	kyrkoherde [vicar] (325)	bonde [farmer] (343)
överstinna [colonel's wife] (308)	konung [king] (258)	*don (322)
prostinna [minister's wife] (304)	biskop [bishop] (242)	tjänare [servant] (283)
drottning [queen] (274)	grefve [count] (227)	överste [colonel] (241)
hushållerska [housekeeper] (260)	baron (215)	tiggare [beggar] (236)
prästfru [minister's wife] (218)	kejsare [emperor] (208)	husbonde [master] (217)

Table 1. The top-10 most frequent lemmatized vocations (and their occurrences) in the *Selma Lagerlof Archive* ('*': error).

Table 1 above shows the top-20 occurrences of three automatically extracted lists of male, female and unknown gender vocations from the *Selma Lagerlof Archive* (a collection of the author's works of fiction published as books during her lifetime), a completely new corpus, not used for the development of the resources in the study with 3.341.714 tokens.

5.1 Evaluation of the CRF

The results of the classifier's evaluation[8] are given in tables 2 and 3. Low recall scores can be possibly attributed to two facts; one is the amount of test and training texts used for training the classifier and second the use of default features for training. Addition of new features, such as part-of-speech, syntactic and/or co-reference links could have possibly being beneficial, including larger training corpora. Moreover, various types of errors could be identified during all stages of processing. With respect to the CRF component evaluation, most of the errors had to do with the occurrences of e.g. male designated adjectives, such as *svenske* 'Swedish' or *danske* 'Danish'. A number of last names and also common words that were homographic to vocations were also annotated erroneously as such; for instance the last names *Skytte* 'Shooter' (e.g. in the context *Malin Skytte*) and *Snickare* 'carpenter' (e.g. in the context *Gorius Snickare*); and common nouns such as *simmaren* '(the) swimmer' or *vakt* 'guard' in idiomatic contexts such as *hålla vakt* 'be on one's guard'.

	Precision	Recall	f-score
B[9]	96.33%	58.22%	72.57%
I	89.09%	72.06%	79.67%

Table 2. Precision, recall and f-scores for the CRF learner.

	Precision	Recall	f-score
F	97.03%	43.75%	60.31%
M	94.52%	55.44%	69.89%
U	53.25%	45.00%	48.78%

Table 3. Precision, recall and f-scores for the CRF learner on gender (M=male; F=female; U=unknown).

Another type of important omission has been the fact that a large number of vocations are assigned

[8] For the evaluation we used the *conlleval* script, vers. 2004-01-26 by Erik Tjong Kim Sang.

[9] We use the IOB tags for file representation: I (inside), O (outside), or B (begin). A token is tagged as B if it marks the beginning of a chunk. Subsequent tokens within the chunk are tagged I. All other tokens are tagged O. E.g. the context *Fru majorskan skrek till majorn...* 'Mrs. major's wife shouted to the major ...' is represented as:

Fru B-Female
majorskan I-Female
skrek O
till O
majorn B-Male ...

unknown gender since there is no reliable context (at the sentence level) that could be used. Moreover, we have been restrictive to the gender assignment of certain vocations in the resources, although, in principle, and considering the nature and publication time of the texts, we could by default assign gender to a large number of these vocations. For instance, a large number of military-related vocations, such as *löjtnant* 'lieutenant' or *generalmajor* 'major general' are assigned unknown gender, although these, predominantly, refer to males in the novels. Moreover, identical singular and plural forms of vocation terms are yet another difficult problem, e.g. *politiker* 'politician' or 'politicians' or *spritfabrikarbetare* 'distillery worker' or 'distillery workers'. Some sort of linguistic pre-processing, such as idiom identification and part of speech annotation, could probably exclude word tokens in plural form (or verbs in that matter, but such cases were extremely rare in our data), nevertheless part of speech tagging is not used at the moment. Also, more elaborative models could be used to first determine who the personal pronouns refer to before an attempt could be made to assign the pronoun's gender to a vocation word with unknown one.

5.2 Evaluation of the Knowledge-based Components

Besides the evaluation of the CRF learner, we also conducted an analysis on a small random sample of similar text from different, but comparable, corpora, in order to investigate the contribution of the different components for the vocation identification. A selection of a randomized subset of 1000 sentences from two sources was conducted from the *August Strindberg's Collected Works* ("August Strindbergs Samlade Verk") and the *Selma Lagerlof Archive* ("Selma Lagerlöf-arkivet"), both parts of the Swedish Literature Bank[10]. These 1000 sentences were automatically annotated by: i) the rule-based system without any sort of disambiguation or other processing only lexicon look-up; this can be considered as a baseline system where only inflectional morphology is considered; and ii) all the rest without the CRF. That included the rule-based system *with* the use of lexical patterns for disambiguation, compound segmentation and the named entity recognition.

A total of 341 of vocation identifiers could be manually recognised and confirmed the assumption that best results are produced by using all available resources at hand. Moreover, the precision of the rule-based system (i.e. the lexicon lookup) is very high. Out of the 341 possible vocations, the baseline, i.e. the rule-based system without any sort of disambiguation, compound analysis etc., identified 329 vocations (46% with the correct gender and the rest with unknown gender); 12 (most of them compounds such as *klädessömmerska* 'clothing dressmaker') and a few others such as *penitentiarius* 'confessor', could not be found and 15 tokens were annotated as vocations but were wrong. These 15 wrong ones originate from (possibly) inappropriate lexicon vocation entries, entries that shouldn't have entered the lexicon as *vocations*, such *Sachsare* 'a person from Saxony' *befrämjare* 'promoter' (a borderline case) and homographs with proper names, such as *Jarl* (which is a title given to members of medieval royal families before their accession to the throne, but also used as a last name).

The combination of all available tools and resources improved these figures; marginally on the gender but substantially on the recognition of the compounds. All vocation compounds were recognized (10) and also four more that were wrong, such as *Nekropolis* 'Nekro+polis' (since *polis* 'police' is in the lexicon) and Notre-Dame 'Notre-+Dame' (since *dame* 'female equivalent of the honour of knighthood' is in the lexicon as well). These compounds could be identified because of the compound decomposition step and matching of the compounds' heads to the lexicon content. Compared to the baseline results the percentage of vocations with correct gender raised to 49.6%.

6 Conclusions

Women's history has emphasized a relative invisibility of women's work and women workers. The reasons to this are manifold, and the extent, the margin of error in terms of women's work activities is of course hard to assess, e.g. work wasn't a tax base also work wasn't the point of departure for a collective political interest (i.e. labour) as it later developed into; while the political organisation also excluded women from some certain areas and particularly from formal authority. This means that women were to a lesser extent mentioned, authorised, appointed or nominated in formal sources. This is obviously

[10] Information about the Literature Bank is here: <http://litteraturbanken.se/#!/om/inenglish>.

the case for many but not all traditional sources, population registers, cameral, and fiscal sources. However, we still don't have good reasons to believe that this means *either* that women didn't work *or* that other types of material couldn't be more rewarding. And the suggestion of this paper is that prose fiction is still possible to utilise further and that the methodological developments in digital humanities should be tried in this endeavour, e.g. by investigating women's work and economic activities represented longitudinally in prose fiction and the differences between the texts of female, male (and unknown) authors, in all those aspects. In this work we have applied automatic text analytic techniques in order to identify vocation signals in 19th century Swedish prose fiction. Our goal has been to reduce the time consuming, manual work that is usually carried out by historians, literature scholars etc., in order to e.g. identify and extract semantically meaningful information such as gender patterns and semantic associations. Literature is a comprehensive source for data on employment and occupation, economy and society, and to e.g. an economic historian or gender researcher such data can be of immense value, particularly for the period between 1800-1900 since gender relations in and through work is a long-standing problem due to repeated underestimation of women's work attributed to among other compelling reasons, the systematic under-reporting of women's work in the used sources (Humphries & Sarasua, 2012; Ighe & Wiechel, 2012). Prose fiction does not necessarily have the same limitations and can be utilized as a fruitful point of departure.

For future work we would like to explore even in more detail the variation of both the performance of the processing steps and also compare the results across time periods and authors' gender. Deeper analysis could provide interesting insights on the nature of which types of person activities are used by different authors or compare and explore other types of collections[11] from the same period, and thus confirm or reject established hypotheses about the kind of vocabulary used; e.g. do male authors use more vocation or kinship labels?

[11] Such collections could be the *Dramawebben* (<http://www.dramawebben.se/>), i.e. digital versions of over 500 plays of Swedish drama from the 1600s to modern times; or the *Digidaily*, i.e. digitized Swedish newspapers from the 18-19th century (<https://riksarkivet.se/digidaily>).

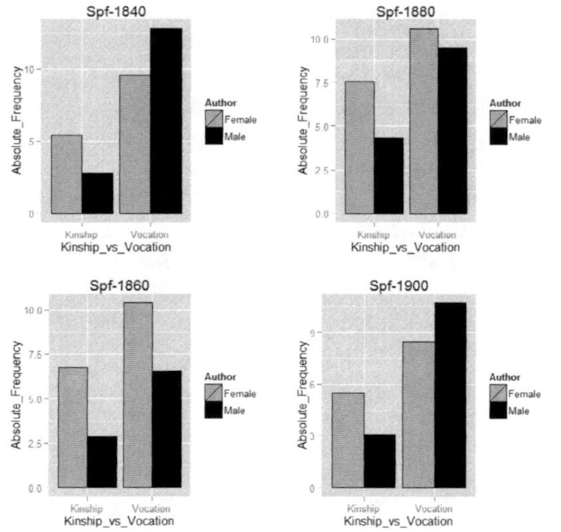

Figure 2. Comparison male and female authors (based on absolute frequencies) of the *Vocation* and *Kinship* categories during the period 1840-1860-1880-1900.

As Fig. 2 shows, other types of investigations are possible and the analysis can provide information about the kind of vocabulary used by various authors during different periods; e.g. do male authors use more vocation than kinship labels and of which type? Kinship (section 3.1) is one of the categories already encoded in the knowledge base and can be easily used to compare the style of authors diachronically.

Acknowledgements

This work is partially supported by the Swedish Research Council's framework grant "Towards a knowledge-based culturomics" dnr 2012-5738.

References

Apoorv Agarwal, Augusto Corvalan, Jacob Jensen and Owen Rambow. 2012. Social Network Analysis of Alice in Wonderland. *Workshop on Computational Linguistics for Literature*. Pp 88–96, Montréal, Canada.

Shlomo Argamon, Russell Horton, Mark Olsen and Sterling Stuart Stein. 2007. Gender, Race, and Nationality in Black Drama, 1850-2000: Mining Differences in Language Use in Authors and their Characters. *Digital Hum*. Pp. 8-10. U. of Illinois.

Tobias Boes. 2014. The Vocations of the Novel: Distant Reading Occupational Change in 19th Century German Literature. *Distant Readings – Topolo-*

gies of German Culture in the Long 19th Century. Erlin&Tatlock (eds). Pp. 259-283. Camden House.

Lars Borin, Dimitrios Kokkinakis and Leif-Jöran Olsson. 2007. Naming the past: Named entity and animacy recognition in 19th century Swedish literature. *1st LaTeCh.* Pp. 1-8. Prague.

Joseph Bullard and Cecilia Oveesdotter Alm. 2014. Computational analysis to explore authors' depiction of characters. *Proc. of the 3rd Workshop on Computational Linguistics for Literature.* Pp. 11–16. Gothenburg, Sweden.

Anthony Don et al. 2007. Discovering interesting usage patterns in text collections: Integrating text mining with visualization. *16th ACM Conf. on info & knowledge management (CIKM).* Pp. 213-222.

Rosemarie Fiebranz, Erik Lindberg, Jonas Lindström and Maria Ågren. 2011. Making verbs count: the research project 'Gender and Work' and its methodology. *Scan Econ Hist Rev.* 59:3, pp. 273-293.

Jenny Rose Finkel, Trond Grenager and Christopher Manning. 2005. Incorporating Non-local Information into Information Extraction Systems by Gibbs Sampling. *43rd ACL.* Pp. 363-370.

Nikesh Garera and David Yarowsky. 2009. Modeling latent biographic attributes in conversational genres. *47th Annual Meeting of the ACL and 4th IJCNLP.* Pp. 719–718. Singapore.

Sobhan Raj Hota, Shlomo Argamon and Rebecca Chung. 2006. Gender in Shakespeare: Automatic stylistics gender character classification using syntactic, lexical and lemma features. *Chicago Colloq. on Digital Humanities and Computer Science* (DHCS). Pp. 100-106. U. of Chicago, USA.

Jane Humphries and Carmen Sarasua. 2012. Off the Record: Reconstructing Women's Labor Force Participation in the European Past. *Feminist Economics.* Vol. 18:4. Taylor and Francis.

Ann Ighe and Anna-Helena Wiechel. 2012. Without title. The dynamics of status, gender and occupation in Gothenburg, Sweden, 1815-45. *Eur. Social Science History Conf.*. Glasgow, Scotland.

Matthew L. Jockers. 2013. *Macroanalysis - Digital Methods and Literary History. Topics in the Digital Humanities.* University of Illinois Press.

Christopher Manning. 2011. Natural Language Processing Tools for the Digital Humanities. Available at <http://nlp.stanford.edu/~manning/courses/DigitalHumanities/> (Visited 20150105).

Tony McEnery and Helen Baker. 2014. The Corpus as Social History - Prostitution in the 17th Century. *Exploring Historical Sources with LT: Results / Perspectives CLARIN Workshop.* Den Haag, The Netherlands. <https://www.clarin.eu/sites/default/files/Mcenery_DenHaag.pdf> (Visited 20150222)

Tomas Mikolov, Wen-tau Yih and Geoffrey Zweig. 2013. Linguistic Regularities in Continuous Space Word Representations. *Proc. of NAACL HLT.* Pp. 746–751. Atlanta, USA.

Franco Moretti. 2013. *Distant Reading.* Verso.

Martin Mueller. 2009. Digital Shakespeare, or towards a literary informatics. *Shakespeare.* 4:3, 284-301, Routledge.

Daniela Oelke, Dimitrios Kokkinakis and Daniel Keim. 2013. Visual Literature Analysis: Uncovering the dynamics of social networks in prose literature. *15th Eurographics Conf. on Visualization (EuroVis).* Pp. 371-380. Leipzig, Germany.

Allan H. Pasco. 2004. Literature as Historical Archive. *New Literary History.* Vol. 35:3, pp 373-394. John Hopkins University Press.

Marco Pennacchiotti and Fabio M. Zanzotto. 2008. Natural Language Processing across time: an empirical investigation on Italian. *Proc. of GoTAL.* LNAI. Vol. 5221. Pp 371-382. Springer.

Eva Pettersson and Joakim Nivre. 2011. Automatic Verb Extraction from Historical Swedish Texts. *5th LaTeCH.* Pp 87-95. Oregon, USA.

Eva Pettersson, Beáta Megyesi and Joakim Nivre. 2012. Parsing the Past – Identification of Verb Constructions in Historical Text. *6th LaTeCH.* Pp 65-74. Avignon, France.

Eva Pettersson, Beáta Megyesi and Joakim Nivre. 2014. Verb Phrase Extraction in a Historical Context. *Proc. of the first Swedish national SWE-CLARIN workshop.* Uppsala, Sweden.

Michael Piotrowski. 2012. *Natural Language Processing for Historical Texts.* Synthesis Lectures on HLT. 5(2):1. Morgan & Claypool Publ.

Jennifer Rutner and Roger C. Schonfeld. 2012. *Supporting the Changing Research Practices of Historians.* National Endowment for the Humanities. Ithaca S+R. New York.

Romain Vuillemot, Tanya Clement, Catherine Plaisant and Amit Kumar. 2009. What's being said near "Martha"? Exploring NEs in Literary Text Collections. *VAST.* Pp. 107-114. NJ, USA.

Rule-based Coreference Resolution in German Historic Novels

Markus Krug, Frank Puppe

Wuerzburg university,
Institute for Computer Science
Am Hubland
D-97074 Würzburg, Germany
markus.krug|frank.puppe@uni-wuerzburg.de

Fotis Jannidis, Luisa Macharowsky, Isabella Reger, Lukas Weimer

Wuerzburg university,
Institute for German Studies
Am Hubland
D-97074 Würzburg, Germany
fotis.jannidis@uni-wuerzburg.de

Abstract

Coreference resolution (CR) is a key task in the automated analysis of characters in stories. Standard CR systems usually trained on newspaper texts have difficulties with literary texts, even with novels; a comparison with newspaper texts showed that average sentence length is greater in novels and the number of pronouns, as well as the percentage of direct speech is higher. We report promising evaluation results for a rule-based system similar to [Lee et al. 2011], but tailored to the domain which recognizes coreference chains in novels much better than CR systems like CorZu. Rule-based systems performed best on the CoNLL 2011 challenge [Pradhan et al. 2011]. Recent work in machine learning showed similar results as rule-based systems [Durett et al. 2013]. The latter has the advantage that its explanation component facilitates a fine grained error analysis for incremental refinement of the rules.

1 Introduction

The overall goal of our research is the identification of characters in German novels from the 19th century and an analysis of their attributes. The main steps are named entity recognition (NER) of the persons, coreference resolution (CR), attribution of persons and character description with focus on sentiment analysis. While NER in novels is discussed in [Jannidis et al. 2015], we report on work in progress on rule-based coreference resolution in novels. Tests with existing rule-based or machine learning NLP tools on our novels had unsatisfying results. In contrast to newspaper texts novels not only exhibit different topics and wording, but also show a heavy use of pronouns (in our corpus 70% of all NEs) and relative few large clusters with long coreference chains opposed to many small clusters (see baseline analysis in table 1). Another important difference is the number and lengths of passages containing direct speech [Iosif, Mishra 2014].

We decided on a rule-based approach because:

- A key aspect in coreference resolution is feature and constraint detection. Features and constraints for ruling in or out candidates for coreference with a high precision can be combined to achieve a high recall. If such features and constraints are represented by rules, the explanation component of rule-based systems is very valuable in understanding the errors and thus enabling rapid rule refinement.
- We do not have a large corpus with annotated German novels to learn from. As mentioned above, there are substantial differences between e.g. newspapers and novels, so that machine learning approaches with domain adaptation (e.g. [Yang et al. 2012]) are difficult.
- We intend to use rule-based CR to semi-automatically create a large corpus of annotated novels for experimenting with machine learning CR approaches.

We present a state-of-the-art rule-based system tailored for CR in novels. In comparison to CorZu (see section 4) which recognizes CR well in newspapers, we achieve better results in novels (MUC

Proceedings of NAACL-HLT Fourth Workshop on Computational Linguistics for Literature, pages 98–104,
Denver, Colorado, June 4, 2015. ©2015 Association for Computational Linguistics

F1: 85.5% vs. 65.9%, B^3 F1: 56.0% vs. 33.6%). Our explanation component facilitates a fine grained error analysis for incremental rule refinement.

2 Related Work

Coreference Resolution itself is an old, but unsolved task on which a huge amount of effort was spent during the last 40 years. Large conferences like ConLL 2011 [Pradhan et al. 2011], CoNLL 2012 [Pradhan et al. 2012] and SemEval 2010 [Recasens et al. 2010]) have offered challenges for the topic not only with English text (ConLL 2011), but also for Chinese and Arabic (CoNLL 2012) and German, Dutch, Italian, Catalan and Spanish (SemEval 2010). Most approaches are based on machine learning algorithms. A large part of machine learning approaches use two phases: first classification of pairs of NEs (nouns, persons, etc.) followed by a clustering or ranking of the results (so called mention-pair model [Aone 1995, Soon et al. 2001]). Since the mention-pair model suffers from serious problems [Ng 2010], newer approaches try to match named entities directly to clusters of mentions (entity-mention model). A multitude of approaches was developed under the focus to model the affiliation of a mention to a specific entity. One goal of such an approach is to avoid problems of the mention-pair approach like (A = B, B = C, A ≠ C, e.g. A = "Mr. Clinton", B = "Clinton", C = "she"). Aside of mention-ranking approaches [Denis, Baldridge 2008], [Rahman 2009] the system developed by Durett, Hall and Klein [Durett et al. 2013] shows that task-specific graphical models perform well following the entity-mention approach. Since rules can model hard and soft constraints directly, e.g. for pronoun resolution, rule-based approaches like the multi pass sieve for CR [Lee et al. 2011] deliver promising results, e.g. the best result in the challenge of CoNLL 2011 for English documents. Although the problem of CR has been a topic for forty years [Hobbs 1976], even good results are between 60% and 70%: [Durett et al. 2013] report a MUC-Score of 63.7% and a B^3 Score of 67.8% for the CoNLL blind test set, with the system of Stanford performing comparably with 61.5% and 69.2% respectively – much worse than e.g. for NER. In [Lee et al. 2011] the Stanford system got better results with 78.6% and 80.5% showing the great influence of the data for the final results. In section 4 we therefore perform two separate experiments on two different datasets to manifest the reliability of our approach for the domain of literary novels.

3 Methods and data

Coreference resolution is based on a NLP-pipeline including tokenization, sentence splitting, part of speech tagging, lemmatization, named entity recognition and dependency parsing. In our pipeline we use the TreeTagger of Stuttgart university [Schmitt 1995] for tokenization and POS-tagging, OpenNLP[1] with the according German model for sentence splitting and the MATE-Toolkit [Bohnet 2010] for dependency parsing. Due to our overall goal, the identification and attribution of characters in German novels, we restrict coreference resolution to the resolution of persons, excluding e.g. geographic locations.

The data used for this development consists of roughly 80 segments, each sampled from a different novel. The sampling process determined a random (syntactic) sentence in the text and used all following 129 sentences, therefore forming a connected chunk of 130 sentences. This sampling process ignored the beginning of a chapter, which bears an even greater challenge for the human annotators and the algorithms, because now some segments can even start with uninformative mentions such as pronouns. With the long-term goal to get a detailed attribution of entities in the novels we developed our own annotation tool based on eclipse-rcp[2]. Since former studies showed that the coreference task does not exhibit many ambiguities for humans our data is only annotated by one annotator.

Our corpus used in the first evaluation comprises 48 different novels. Thus, the first test corpus contains 143 000 tokens with ca. 19 000 references including proper names, personal pronouns etc., while for our second experiment we used 30 additional fragments with about 11 600 NEs and 104 000 tokens. In comparison to the German TIGER corpus [Brants et al. 2004] which consists of newspaper articles, we have on average longer sentences with 24.2 tokens compared to 16.3 to-

[1] https://opennlp.apache.org/

[2] https://wiki.eclipse.org/index.php/Rich_Client_Platform

kens. On average, one sentence contains three references to the same character or other characters. Each character appeared 10 times on average within the small novel fragments of 130 sentences, compared to ca. 4 times in the ACE2004-nwire corpus used in [Lee et al. 2011]. The majority of references are pronouns (~ 70%). In German, pronoun resolution is more ambiguous than in English, e.g. the German "sie" has three possible meanings: "she", "they", and "you" in direct speech. Only for unambiguous pronouns like "er" [he] and "ihm" [him] we can use static features like in [Lee et al. 2011]. For pronoun resolution, our rules use features of NEs like gender (male, female, neuter, unknown), number (singular, plural, unknown), person (for pronouns: first, second, third person) and whether the NE is the subject of the sentence. In general, a substantial part of a novel is direct speech, so we segment the novels in narrative and direct speech parts in a preprocessing step. In order to detect the speaker of a given direct speech annotation we use the following rules:

- Explicit speaker detection.
- Speaker propagation for longer dialogues.
- Pseudo speaker propagation for situations where in longer dialogues two persons talking in turn can be recognized, but speaker detection failed.

In order to be able to determine features like gender from non-pronoun references we use various resources like lists of male and female first names from CorZu [Klenner 2011], the morphological analysis tool of Stuttgart University SMOR [Fitschen et al. 2004], the morphological tagger from the above mentioned Mate-toolkit [Bohnet 2010] and a self-trained classifier, a maximum entropy model trained on the TIGER corpus. After applying these tools in a precision based manner (lists, own system, mate, SMOR), where the subsequent system is only used if the previous system detects "unknown", we apply a set of correction rules in order to guarantee consistency among the NEs. The heuristic rules try to infer the gender of a NE by using context clues, e.g. a subsequent reference within the same "subsentence" (that is a sentence up to the next comma) of "his" or "her" and the propagation of a recognized gender of a NE along a local chain of unambiguous NEs (e.g. for old fashioned first names like "Günderode"). Other rules exist for determination of the number of an NE and dependency parsing is used for determining the subject of a sentence. An evaluation of the number attribute which we had annotated aside of the coreferences and NEs resulted in an accuracy of approximately 93% in the used test data. We split our documents into a small training set with just 5 documents, a first test set of 48 documents that we used to compare our performance with the system CorZu, and into another test set consisting of 30 completely unseen documents where we evaluated the robustness of our system.

Our system has a similar rule organization as [Lee et al. 2011] with passes, i.e. rule sets, which build on the results of former passes. While [Lee et al. 2011] uses 7 passes, we extend this by using 11 passes:

1. Pass: exact match: All identical non-pronouns are marked as coreferent. They are also considered as coreferent if their cases differ ("Annette" vs "ANNETTE").

2. Pass: Nameflexion: We designed a distance metric that allows us to detect derivations (or nicknames) from names and mark them as coreferent. ("Lydia", "Lyden","Lydchen").

3. Pass: Attributes: We use all modifiers (derived from the output of the parser) and match them against the strings of the NEs of the other cluster. Coreference occurs if there is an "equals-ignore-case"-match. ("Die alte Getrud" ,…"die Alte") ["the elderly Gertrud", "the elderly"]

4. Pass: precise constructs: Appositions, relative and reflexive pronouns are assigned to the preceding NE. In addition, these pronouns get the gender and number of the NE in order to support subsequent resolution of other pronouns.

5-7. Pass: 5. strict head match, 6. relaxed head match and 7. title match: These 3 passes recognize coreferent NEs, where an NE consists of several words. The first rule, named strict head match, removes all titles from the given mentions and then compares the remaining words. Two NEs are said to be coreferent if there is at least one word that appears in both mentions and they agree in number and gender ("Baron Landsfeld" , "Herr Landsfeld") ["Baron Landsfeld", "Mister Landsfeld"]. The relaxed head match only requires that one word of one NE is contained in a word of the other NE. Since titles were removed in the previous two rules we added another rule specifically for titles and match those to the most recent NE which contains the given title.

8. **Semantic pass:** For this semantic pass we use the synonyms in the German resource GermaNet[3], again, an agreement in gender is required. This matches for example "Gatte" and "Gemahl" ["spouse", "consort"].
9. **Pass: pronoun resolution:** pronouns are resolved to the most recent, suitable precedent NE. To respect salience we sorted our previous NEs in a manner that preferred the last subject of earlier sentences over the closest NEs in those sentences. A suitable precedent is a one that doesn't conflict with a given constraint. In the current implementation we respect the following constraints:
    - Compliance in gender/number and person.
    - Compliance in its context (are they both part of a direct speech or both part of a narrative segment).
    - The candidate and the actual pronoun do not harm a given constraint of binding theory.

. **10. Pass: Detection of the addressed person in direct speech:** For each direct speech annotation we try to find the addressed NE. We do this by using several handcrafted lexico-syntactic patterns (matching against expressions such as "*Alexander*, *you* are great"). Based on the results of speaker detection we use a propagation of the addressed persons in dialogues.

11. Pass: pronouns in direct speech: We then resolve all instances of <I> to the speaker and all instances of <you> to the person the speaker talks to (if known). If the speaker of two subsequent direct speech annotations doesn't change, but the addressed person differs, we assume that the speaker only uses a different naming for the person he is talking to and therefore set these NEs as coreferent.

Fig. 1 shows the explanation, annotation and error analysis component of our rule-based tool.

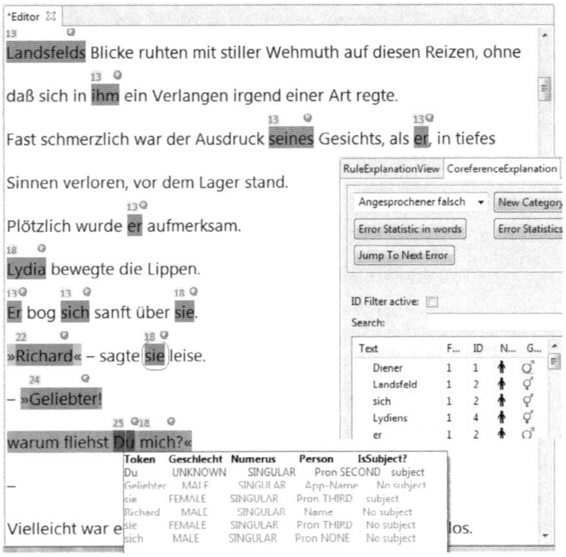

Fig. 1: Explanation and annotation editor for rule-based coreference resolution. All named entities (NE) are already marked. Identical numbers above the NE denote that they are coreferent to the same entity. For explanation, the user clicks on one NE (here: "Du" [you]) and the system shows in a pop up menu the last five NE tokens with some key attributes: Geschlecht ([gender]: male, female, neuter, unknown), number (singular, plural, unknown), Person (for pronouns: first, second third persons and for nouns the type of NE like real name, appellative name or pseudo-person) and whether the NE is the subject of the sentence. The annotator can classify errors like the missing coreference of "DU" to "Geliebter" [lover] with categories (here: "angesprochener falsch" [wrong reference]) with a drop down menu in the right frame. If there is direct speech, it is highlighted with a background color and the speaker (here "sie" [she]) is marked with a red circle.

4 Evaluation and error analysis

We evaluated the coreference resolution algorithm in two experiments. The first one uses the test corpus of 48 novel fragments with about 19.000 manually annotated character references in total. The following common evaluation metrics are used (see [Luo 2005]):

- The MUC-Score. It is based on the idea to count the minimum amount of links which need to be added to derive the true set of entities from the predicted set of entities or vice versa, divided by the amount of links in the spanning tree of the true partition. The MUC-Score itself is the harmonic mean out of both numbers that you get

[3] http://www.sfs.uni-tuebingen.de/GermaNet/

when you switch the true partition with the gold partition.

- The B^3-Score. The MUC Score cannot measure the influence of singleton clusters, that's why an additional evaluation metric is needed. The B^3-Score scales the overlap of predicted clusters and true clusters, based on how many markables were correctly assigned to a given cluster.

The effect of the different evaluation measures on a newspaper corpus with rather short coreference chains and on a novel corpus with long chains is shown in the baseline analysis in table 1. While for newspapers the baseline with n clusters for n NEs is very good, for novels the baseline with just one cluster for all NEs performs well. This can be explained using the structure of the underlying entities. While in newspaper texts many different entities with only a few mentions appear, our domain shows relatively few entities that tend to show up frequently.

Baseline	corpus	MUC			B^3		
		prec.	recall	F1	prec.	recall	F1
1 coreference cluster for all n named entities	newspaper	24%	100%	39%	100%	2%	5%
	novels	89%	100%	94%	100%	21%	34%
n coreference clusters for n named entities	newspaper	0%	0%	0%	76%	100%	86%
	novels	0%	0%	0%	11%	100%	19%

Table 1: Baseline analysis for a typical newspaper and novel corpus with assigning all n NEs to either just one cluster or to n different clusters.

We compared our system with the free coreference resolution software CorZu, using ParZu[4] [Sennrich 2009] as its parser from the university of Zurich, which was developed using a newspaper corpus. CorZu was given the same annotated named entities in the same novel fragments, so that the detected chains were comparable. Table 2 shows the results. Our system is about 20 percent points better than CorZu for both evaluation scores MUC F1 and B^3 F1.

Scores in %	MUC precision	MUC recall	MUC F1	B^3 prec.	B^3 recall	B^3 F1
our system	**89.1**	**83.2**	**85.5**	**70.5**	**83.2**	**56.0**
CorZu	77.0	57.7	65.9	69.5	22.7	33.6

Table 2: evaluation results of our system and CorZu on 48 novel fragments with about 19 000 named entities.

The effect of the passes (see section 3) in our system evaluated on the novel corpus is given in table 3. For reference, we added the results from Lee et al. [Lee et al. 2011], the results of the system of Stanford, evaluated on an ACE newspaper corpus. It shows that pronoun resolution is much more important in novels than in newspapers, while exact string matches and head matches already result in rather high scores on the ACE newspaper corpus.

Scores in %	our system evaluated with the novel corpus		Stanfords Sieve evaluated with ACE newspaper corpus	
Passes	MUC F1	B^3 F1	MUC F1	B^3 F1
1	27.5	24.6	47.8	69.4
1-4	37.7	28.1	59.9	73.3
1-8	38.9	28.9	67.1	76.9
1-9	83.3	52.6	78.6	80.5
1-11	85.5	56.0		

Table 3: Evaluation and comparison of the effects of the different passes of the rule-based algorithm.

We finally evaluated our system on our second test set, comprising 30 completely unseen fragments and achieved an F1-score of 86% MUC-F1 and a B^3-F1 of 55.5%. It is almost identical to the result of the first test set. Rule-based systems with an explanation component allow a fine-grained error analysis. Table 4 shows an error analysis for 5 randomly selected novel fragments from the 30 novels, drawn from the second test set that we used for evaluation:

Document (novel fragment)	# NEs	# Cluster (Gold)	# Cluster found	MUC F1	B^3 F1	# Errors	# Wrong g|n|p	# Ds related	# Heurisitics	# Semantic
1	332	16	64	86%	46%	58	3	22	21	12
2	185	8	22	94%	80%	16	1	4	3	8
3	261	31	44	90%	80%	22	6	0	6	10
4	283	28	47	77%	38%	48	5	2	20	21
5	469	39	39	90%	66%	61	13	1	22	25
Sum						205	28	29	72	76
Average	306	24	43	87%	62%	100%	14%	14%	35%	37%

Table 4: Number of named entities, clusters, evaluation metrics and error types for a sample of 5 novel fragments, drawn randomly from our second test set comprising 30 fragments. The category "Wrong g|n|p" refers to the sum of mistakes the algorithm made that were caused by a wrong assignment of gender, number or person. The category "Ds related", contains all errors related to direct speech, e.g. by assigning a wrong speaker or the wrong detection of the addressed person to a given direct speech annotation.

Table 4 shows that even though we combined 4 different morphological resources the recognition

[4] http://www.cl.uzh.ch/research/coreferenceresolution_en.html

of wrong number, gender and person still makes up a fraction of about 14% of the total amount of errors in the analyzed documents. Another part with 14% of the mistakes is the category that describes all errors related to direct speech, e.g. wrong speaker detection, missed detection of “Sie” [you] in the role of “du” or wrong detection of an addressed person. We intend to find some additional constraints to further reduce the errors made in these categories. The next category with 35% error contribution, labeled as heuristics, sums up all the errors which happened due to a wrong assumption of salience, parser errors or errors that were induced by former misclassified NEs. Still the biggest share of mistakes (37%) and probably also the ones that are most difficult to fix is the class of semantic errors. Most of these misclassifications can only be resolved with additional knowledge about the world or the entities in the novel itself (“a widow is a woman who lost her husband; “his profession is forester”; …). Apart from these, there are other mistakes related to an unmodeled context, such as thoughts, songs or letters that appear throughout the text. We plan to integrate the work of Brunner [Brunner 2015] to detect those instances and thereby improve the quality of our system.

5 Conclusion

CR for NE can be viewed as a task in which candidates for coreference are filtered out by constraints until only one candidate remains. Rule-based knowledge representation is well suited for this task. The more constraints can be modeled, the better the performance of the system. Our error analysis shows that we can cut our current error rate by roughly 28% with more precise grammatical constraints (14% for errors related to direct speech and 14% for gender, number and person related errors). However, we also plan the integration of semantic constraints and information, similar to Haghighi and Klein [Haghighi, Klein 2009]. A promising way is to collect information about the persons in the text, which is also the next step in our overall goal, the automated character analysis: determining all attributes assigned in a novel to a character.

References

Aone, C. and Bennett, S. 1995. *Evaluating Automated and Manual Acquisition of Anaphora Resolution Strategies.* Proceedings of the 33rd annual meeting on Association for Computational Linguistics (ACL '95). Association for Computational Linguistics, 122-129.

Bohnet, B. 2010. *Very High Accuracy and Fast Dependency Parsing is not a Contradiction*. The 23rd Int. Conf. on Computational Linguistics (COLING 2010), Beijing, China.

Brants, S., Dipper, S., Eisenberg, P., Hansen, S., König, E., Lezius, W., Rohrer, C., Smith, G. and Uszkoreit, H. 2004. *TIGER: Linguistic Interpretation of a German Corpus*. Journal of Language and Computation 2 (4), 597-620.

Brunner, A. 2015. *Automatische Erkennung von Redewiedergabe: Ein Beitrag zur Quantitativen Narratologie (Narratologia)*. [Automatic Recognition of Recorded Speech: a Contribution to Quantitative Narratologogia] Walter De Gruyter Inc.

Durrett G., Hall D., and Klein D. 2013. *Decentralized Entity-Level Modeling for Coreference Resolution.* In Proceedings of the 51st Annual Meeting of the Association for Computational Linguistics (Volume 1), 114-124.

Ferrucci, D. and Lally, A. 2004. *UIMA: An Architectural Approach to Unstructured Information Processing in the Corporate Research Environment.* Nat. Lang. Eng. 10, 327-348. http://dx.doi.org/10.1017/S1351324904003523

Fitschen, A., Schmid, H. and Heid, U. 2004. SMOR: *A German computational morphology covering derivation, composition, and inflection.* Proceedings of the IVth International Conference on Language Resources and Evaluation (LREC 2004), 1263-1266.

Haghighi, A. and Klein, D. 2009. *Simple Coreference Resolution with Rich Syntactic and Semantic Features*. In Proceedings of the 2009 Conference on Empirical Methods in Natural Language Processing. Association for Computational Linguistics, Singapore, 1152-1161.

Hinrichs, E., Kübler, S. and Naumann, K. 2005. *A unified representation for morphological, syntactic, semantic, and referential annotations*. Proceedings of the ACL Workshop on Frontiers in Corpus Anotation II: Pie in the Sky, pages 13–20, Ann Arbor, MI.

Hobbs, J.1976. *Pronoun Resolution*. Technical report, Dept. of Computer Science, CUNY, Technical Report TR761.

Iosif, E. and Mishra, T. 2014. *From Speaker Identification to Affective Analysis: A Multi-Step System for Analyzing Children`s Stories*. Proceedings of the 3rd Workshop on Computational Linguistics for Literature. Gothenburg, Sweden, 40-49.

Jannidis, F., Krug, M., Reger, I. Toepfer, M. Weimer, L, Puppe, F. 2015. *Automatische Erkennung von Figuren in deutschsprachigen Romanen*. [Automatic recognition of Characters in German novels] Digital Humanities im deutschsprachigen Raum (Dhd 2015), Graz, Austria, 2015.

Klenner, M; Tuggener, D. 2011. *An Incremental Entity-mention Model for Coreference Resolution with Restrictive Antecedent Accessibility.* Recent Advances in Natural Language Processing (RANLP 2011), Hissar, Bulgaria, 178-185.

Lee, H., Peirsman, Y., Chang, A., Chambers, N., Surdeanu, M. and Jurafsky, D. 2011. *Stanford's Multi-pass Sieve Coreference Resolution System at the CoNLL-2011 Shared Task*. Proc. of the 15th Conference on Computational Natural Language Learning: Shared Task (CONLL Shared Task '11). Association for Computational Linguistics, 28-34.

Luo, X. 2005. *On Coreference Resolution Performance Metrics*. Proc. of the conference on Human Language Technology and Empirical Methods in Natural Language Processing (HLT '05). Association for Computational Linguistics, 25-32.

Ng, V. 2010. *Supervised Noun Phrase Coreference Research: The First Fifteen Years.* Proceedings of the 48th Annual Meeting of the Association for Computational Linguistics (ACL '10). Association for Computational Linguistics, 1396-1411.

Pascal, D. and Baldridge, J. 2008. *Specialized models and ranking for coreference resolution*. In Proceedings of the Conference on Empirical Methods in Natural Language Processing (EMNLP '08). Association for Computational Linguistics, Stroudsburg, PA, USA, 660-669.

Pradhan, S., Moschitti, A., Xue, N., Uryupina, O. and Zhang, Y. 2012. *CoNLL-2012 Shared Task: Modeling Multilingual Unrestricted Coreference in OntoNotes*. In Proceedings of EMNLP and CoNLL-2012: Shared Task, 1-40.

Pradhan, S., Ramshaw, L., Marcus, M., Palmer, M., Weischedel, R., and Xue, N. 2011. *CoNLL-2011 Shared Task: Modeling Unrestricted Coreference in OntoNotes.* Proceedings of the Fifteenth Conference on Computational Natural Language Learning: Shared Task (CONLL Shared Task '11). Association for Computational Linguistics, 1-27.

Rahman, A and Ng, V. 2009. *Supervised Models for Coreference Resolution.* Proceedings of the 2009 Conference on Empirical Methods in Natural Language Processing, 968-977.

Recasens, M., Martí, T., Taulé, M., Màrquez, L., and Sapena, E. 2009. *Coreference Resolution in Multiple Languages.* Proceedings of the Workshop on Semantic Evaluations: Recent Achievements and Future Directions (SEW-2009), 70–75.

Schmid, H. 1995. *Improvements in Part-of-Speech Tagging with an Application to German*. Proceedings of the ACL SIGDAT-Workshop. Dublin, Ireland.

Sennrich, R., Schneider, G., Volk, M., Warin, M. 2009. *A New Hybrid Dependency Parser for German.* Proceedings of GSCL Conference, Potsdam.

Soon, W, Ng, H. and Lim, D. 2001. *A Machine Learning Approach to Coreference Resolution of Noun Phrases*. Comput. Linguist. 27 (4), 521-544.

Yang, J., Mao, Q., Xiang, Q., Tsang, I., Chai, K., Chieu, H. 2012. *Domain Adaptation for Coreference Resolution: An Adaptive Ensemble Approach.* Proceedings of the 2012 Joint Conference on Empirical Methods in NLP and CNLL, 744-753.

A computational linguistic approach to Spanish Golden Age Sonnets: metrical and semantic aspects

Borja Navarro-Colorado
Natural Language Processing Group
University of Alicante
Alicante, Spain
borja@dlsi.ua.es

Abstract

Several computational linguistics techniques are applied to analyze a large corpus of Spanish sonnets from the 16th and 17th centuries. The analysis is focused on metrical and semantic aspects. First, we are developing a hybrid scansion system in order to extract and analyze rhythmical or metrical patterns. The possible metrical patterns of each verse are extracted with language-based rules. Then statistical rules are used to resolve ambiguities. Second, we are applying distributional semantic models in order to, on one hand, extract semantic regularities from sonnets, and on the other hand to group together sonnets and poets according to these semantic regularities. Besides these techniques, in this position paper we will show the objectives of the project and partial results.

1 Introduction

16th- and 17th-Centuries Spanish poetry is judge as one of the best period of the History of Spanish Literature (Rico, 1980 2000; Terry, 1993; Mainer, 2010). It was the time of great, famous and "canonical" Spanish poets such as Miguel de Cervantes, Lope de Vega, Garcilaso de la Vega or Calderón de la Barca, among others. Due to the importance given to this period, it has been deeply studied by scholars from the 19th century to the present. We are persuaded that new approaches based on a "distant reading" (Moretti, 2007; Moretti, 2013) or "macroanalysis" (Jockers, 2013) framework could shed new light on this period.

We have two general objectives: first, we will try to extract regular patterns from the overall period; and second, in order to analyze each author inside the broad literary context in which they wrote (García Berrio, 2000), we will look for chains of relationships between them.

Nowadays both objectives are focused on metrical and semantic aspects of Spanish Golden Age Sonnets. In this position paper we will present the computational linguistic techniques used to achieve these objectives.

Next section shows how a large corpus of Spanish Golden-Age sonnets has been compiled and annotated; Section 3 describes a hybrid scansion system developed to extract metrical patterns; Section 4 presents how we use distributional semantic models to extract semantic patterns from the corpus; finally, Section 5 shows some preliminar conclusions.

2 Corpus compilation and XML annotation

A corpus of 5078 sonnets has been compiled. It includes all the main poets of the Spanish Golden Age: Juan Boscán, Garcilaso de la Vega, Fray Luis de León, Lope de Vega, Francisco de Quevedo, Calderón de la Barca, Sor Juana Inés de la Cruz, etc. Our objetive is to include all the authors of this period who wrote a significant amount of sonnets. Authors who wrote but few sonnets (less than ten) have been rejected. Most sonnets have been obtained from the Miguel de Cervantes Virtual Library[1].

[1] http://www.cervantesvirtual.com/

Proceedings of NAACL-HLT Fourth Workshop on Computational Linguistics for Literature, pages 105–113,
Denver, Colorado, June 4, 2015. ©2015 Association for Computational Linguistics

I must point out that sonnet quality is not taken into account. Following Moretti's Distant Reading framework (Moretti, 2007), we want a representative corpus of the kind of sonnets written in that period, not only the canonical sonnets. In other words, the corpus must represent the literary context of any Golden Age poet.

Each sonnet has been marked with the standard TEI-XML[2]. We have followed the standard TEI in order to ensure the re-usability of the corpus in further research. The main metadata annotated at the TEI-Header are:

- Project title and project manager (Title and Publication Statement),
- Title and author of each sonnet,
- Source publication and editor (Source Description).

Regarding the sonnet structure, we have annotated:

- Quatrains,
- Tercets,
- Verse line and number of line,
- Some extra lines included in the poem (called "estrambote")

The markup includes a representation of the metrical structure of each verse line. It will be explained in the next section.

Nowadays we have a first version of the corpus. We plan to publish it on the internet during 2016.

3 Metrical annotation and analysis

In order to extract the metrical pattern of each verse line, we have created a scansion system for Spanish based on Computational Linguistics techniques. In this section we will show how the metrical information is represented and what the main aspects of the scansion system are.

[2] www.tei-c.org/

3.1 Metrical representation

Spanish poetry measures poetic lines by syllables. The Spanish sonnet is an adaptation of the Italian sonnet, where each line has eleven syllables (hendecasyllable). The metrical pattern of each verse line is formed by a combination of stressed and unstressed syllables. There must be a stressed syllable in the tenth position. The rest of the stressed syllables can be combined in different ways, generating different rhythms or metrical patterns: Heroic (stressed syllables at position 2, 6 and 10), Melodic (at 3, 6, 10), sapphic (at 4, 8, 10), etc. (Quilis, 1984; Varelo-Merino et al., 2005)

For each verse line, we represent its metrical pattern by a combination of symbols "+" (stressed syllable) and "-" (unstressed syllable). For example:

```
<lg type="cuarteto">
<l n="1" met="---+---+-+-">
Cuando me paro a contemplar mi estado
</l>
```

"*lg*" tag represents the stanza (quatrain in this case), and "*l*" tag the line. Each line has the "*met* =" tag with the metrical pattern of the verse.

This verse from Garcilaso de la Vega has thirteen linguistic syllables, but it has only eleven metrical syllables. As we will show in the next section, "-ro a" (in "paro a") and "mi es-" (in "mi estado") conform a single syllable each due to the synaloepha phenomenon. Therefore this line is an hendecasyllable with stressed syllables in position 4, 8 and 10 (sapphic).

3.2 Scansion system

Metrical patterns extraction does not consist of a simple detection of syllables and accents. Due to the fact that there is not a direct relationship between linguistic syllables and metrical syllables, some ambiguity problems appear that must be solved by computational linguistics techniques. The main scansion problems are the following:

- The total amount of syllables could change according to the position of the last stressed syllable. If the last stressed syllable is the last one (oxytone), the line should have ten syllables and an extra syllable must be added. On contrary, if the last stressed syllable is the antepenultimate (proparoxytone), the line should have twelve syllables and the last syllable must be removed. This is a fixed phenomenon and can be solved with rules.

- Not every word with linguistic accent has a metrical accent. It depends on the Part of Speech. Words like nouns, verbs, adjectives or adverbs have always a metrical accent; but prepositions, conjunctions and some pronouns have no metrical accent.

- A vocalic sound at the end of a syllable and at the beginning of the next one tends to be blended in one single syllable (syneresis if the syllables belong to the same word and synaloepha if they belong to different words). This phenomenon is not always carried out: it depends on several factors, mainly the intention during declamation.

- The opposite is possible too: a one single syllable with two vowels (normally semivowel like an "i" or "u") that can be pronounced as two separated syllables (dieresis).

These phenomena could change the metrical pattern extracted in two different ways: the amount of syllables and the type of each one of them (stressed or unstressed). The main problem are those verses in which it is possible to extract two or more different patterns, all of them correct.

For example, for a verse with twelve syllables and paroxitonal final stress it is necessary to blend at least two syllables in one through a phenomenon of synaloepha or syneresis. The problem appears when there are two possible synaloephas or syneresis: which of them must be carried out? The final metrical pattern will be completely different.

For example, the next verse line:

cuando el padre Hebrero nos enseña

It has 12 syllables. It is necessary to blend two syllables in one through synaloepha. However, there are two possibles synaloephas: "cuando+el" and "padre+Hebrero". Different metrical patterns are generated for each synaleopha:

- - + - - + - - - + -
- - - + - + - - - + -

A ranking of natural and artificial synaloephas has been defined by traditional metrical studies. For example, it is more natural to join two unstressed vowels than two stressed vowels (Quilis, 1984). From our point of view, this is a "deliberate" ambiguity (Hammond et al., 2013): both metrical patterns are correct, choosing one depends on how the verse line is pronounced.

An automatic metrical scansion system must resolve this ambiguity[3]. There are several computational approaches to metrical scansion for different languages (Greene et al., 2010; Agirrezabal et al., 2013; Hammond, 2014). For Spanish, P. Gervás (2000) proposes a rule-based approach. It applies Logic-programming to detect stressed and unstressed syllables. It has a specific module to detect and resolve synaloephas that is applied recursively up to the end of the verse. However, I think that this system is not able to detect ambiguities: if there are two possible synalephas, this system always chooses the first one. Therefore, it does not detect other possible metrical patterns.

We follow a hybrid approach to metrical scansion. First, rules are applied in order to separate words in syllables (hyphenation module), detect metrical syllables with a Part of Speech tagger[4], and finally blend or segment syllables according to synaloephas, dieresis or syneresis.

Before the application of synaloephas or syneresis rules, the system counts the number of syllables. If the line has eleven syllables, then these rules are not applied. If there are more than eleven syllables, then the system counts how many synaloephas or syneresis must be resolved. If resolving all synaloephas or syneresis the syllables amount to eleven, then the system applies them all. If resolving all synaloephas or syneresis the syllables amount to a number lower than eleven, the verse is ambiguous: the system must select which rules must be applied and which must not.

[3]Or al least the system must select the most appropriate one, even if it could detect and represent alternative patterns.

[4]We use Freeling as PoS tagger (`http://nlp.lsi.upc.edu/freeling/`) (Padró and Stanilovsky, 2012). For each word, the scansion system selects the most general PoS tag (noun, verb, etc.) Only for a few cases it is necessary a deeper analysis. For example, the system must distinguish between personal pronouns (stressed) and clitic pronouns (unstressed)

For these ambiguous verses (with two or more possible metrical patterns) we follow a statistical approach. First, the system calculates metrical patterns frequencies from non-ambiguous patterns. These patterns are extracted from lines in which it has not been necessary to apply the rules for synaloephas, or lines in which applying all possible rules for synalopehas, a unique patter of eleven syllables is obtained. Each time the system analyzes one of these lines, the frequency of its pattern is increased one.

From a total amount of 82593 verses[5], 6338 are ambiguous and 76255 non-ambiguos. Therefore, only 7,67% of lines are ambiguous. In these cases, from the possible pattern that can be applied to a specific line, the system selects the most frequent one: the pattern that has been used more frequently in non-ambiguous verses.

Our approach tends to select common pattern and reject unusual ones. It must be noted that we do not claim that the metrical pattern selected in ambiguous lines is the correct one. We claim that it is the most frequent one. As we said before, this is a "deliberate" ambiguity (Hammond et al., 2013) in which there are not correct or incorrect solutions.

Table 1 shows the most frequent patterns extracted from the corpus and its frequency.

Metrical Pattern	Name	Frequency
- + - - - + - - - + -	Heroic	6457
- + - + - - - + - + -	Sapphic	6161
- - + - - + - - - + -	Melodic	5982
- + - + - + - - - + -	Heroic	5015
- - - + - + - - - + -	Sapphic	3947
- + - - - + - + - + -	Heroic	3549
- + - + - + - + - + -	Heroic	3310
+ - - + - - - + - + -	Sapphic	3164
+ - - + - + - - - + -	Sapphic	3150
- - - + - - - + - + -	Sapphic	3105
- - + - - + - + - + -	Melodic	2940

Table 1: Most frequent metrical patterns.

Therefore, the previous example is annotated with the first metrical pattern (Melodic):

[5]This is the total amount of verses, including authors with less than ten sonnets that were rejected for the final version of the corpus.

cuando el padre Hebrero nos enseña

```
<l n="1" met="--+--+---+-">
```

Nowadays we are manually reviewing the automatic annotation in order to correct errors, set up a Gold Standard and evaluate the system.

4 Semantic analysis

In order to develop a broad semantic analysis of Spanish Golden Age sonnets, we are applying Distributional Semantic Models (Turney and Pantel, 2010; Mitchell and Lapata, 2010). These models are based on the distributional hypothesis (Harris, 1951): words that occur in similar contexts have similar meanings. These models use vector space models to represent the context in which a word appears and, then, represent the meaning of the word.

Computational distributional models are able to establish the similarities between words according to the similarity of their contexts. Therefore, the application of these distributional models to corpora of sonnets can extract semantic similarities between words, texts and authors. A standard approach is based on a word-text matrix. Applying well-known distance metrics as Cosine Similarity or Euclidean Distance it is possible to find out the similarities between words or poems. In light of these similarities we can then establish the (distributional) semantic relations between authors.

We are applying two specific distributional semantic models: Latent Dirichlet Allocation (LDA) Topic Modeling (Blei et al., 2003) on one hand, and Distributional-Compositional Semantic Models (Mitchell and Lapata, 2010) on the other hand.

4.1 LDA Topic Modeling

During the last years several papers have proposed applying LDA Topic Modeling to literary corpora (Tangherlini and Leonard, 2013; Jockers and Mimno, 2013; Jockers, 2013; Kokkinakis and Malm, 2013) -among others-. Jokers and Mimno (2013), for example, use Topic Modeling to extract relevant themes from a corpus of 19th-Century novels. They present a classification of topics according to genre, showing that, in 19th-Century English novels, males and females tended to write about the same things but to very different degrees. For example, males preferred to write about guns and battles, while females preferred to write about education and children. From a computational point of view, this paper concludes that Topic Modeling must be applied with care to literary texts and it proves the needs for statistical tests that can measure confidence in results.

Rhody (2012) analyzes the application of Topic Modeling to poetry. The result will be different from the application of Topic Modeling to non-figurative texts. When it is applied to figurative texts, some "opaque" topics (topics formed by words with apparently no semantic relation between them) really shows symbolic and metaphoric relations. More than "topics", these topics represent symbolic meanings. She concludes that, in order to understand them, a closed reading of the poems is necessary.

We have run LDA Topic Modeling over our corpus of sonnets[6]. Using different configurations (10, 20, 50, 100 and 1000 topics), we are developing several analysis. In the next sections I will present these analysis together with some preliminary results and comments.

4.1.1 Common and regular topics

First, we have extracted the most common and regular topics from the overall corpus. We are analyzing them using as reference framework themes and topics established manually by scholars following a close reading approach (García Berrio, 1978; Rivers, 1993).

At this moment we have found four types of topics:

- Topics clearly related with classical themes. Table 2 shows some examples.
- Topics showing rhime relations: words that used to appear at the same sonnet because they rhyme between them. For example, "boca loca toca poca provoca" (Topic 14 of 100).
- Topics showing figurative and symbolic relations: words semantically related only in a symbolic framework. For example, topic 70 relates the words "río fuente agua" (river, fountain, water) with "cristal" (glass). This topic is showing the presence of Petrarchan tradition "rivers of glass"[7] in the Spanish poetry.
- Noise topics.

Topic Model	Traditional Theme
amor fuerza desdén arco niño cruel ciego flecha fuego ingrato sospecha	Unrequited Love
hoy yace sepulcro fénix mármol polvo ceniza ayer guarda muerta piedad cadáver	Funeral
españa rey sangre roma imperio grande baña valor extraña reino carlos hazaña engaña saña bárbaro	Decline of Spanish Empire

Table 2: Topic Models related to classical themes.

Once we detect an interesting topic, we analyze the sonnets in which this topic is relevant. For example, Topic 2 in table 2 represents clearly the funeral theme, sonnets composed upon the gravestone of a dead person. According to LDA, this topic is relevant in Francisco de Quevedo (10 poems), Góngora (6 poems), Lope de Vega (6 poems), Juan de Tassis y Peralta (6 poems), Trillo y Figueroa (3 poems), López de Zárate (3 poems), Bocángel y Unzueta (3 poems), Polo de Medina (2 poems), Pantaleón de Ribera (2 poems), etc. We can reach interesting conclusions from a close reading of these poems. For example,

- All these authors belong to 17th-century, the Baroque Period. This topic is related to the "brevity of life" theme, a typical Baroque topic. Topic Modeling is, then, confirming traditional studies.
- Most of these sonnets are really funeral sonnets, but not all of them. There are some love and satyrical sonnets too. However, these off-topic sonnets use words related to sepulcher, tomb, graves and death. In these cases, Topic Modeling is not showing topics but stylistic and figurative aspects of the poem. Francisco de Quevedo is an example of this aspect: he wrote quite a lot of funeral sonnets and, and the same

[6]We have used MALLET `http://mallet.cs.umass.edu/` (McCallum, 2002)

[7]"et giá son quasi di cristallo i fiumi" Petrarca *Canzoniere* LXVI.

time, he used words related to death in satyrical and mainly love sonnets. It is what Terry (1993) calls "ceniza amante" (loving ash), as a specific characteristic of Quevedos's sonnets.

Therefore, we benefit of the relations between sonnets and authors stablished by LDA Topic Modeling. Then we follow a close reading approach in order to (i) reject noise and random relations, (ii) confirm relations detected by manual analysis, and (iii) detect non-evident relations. This last situation is our main objective.

4.1.2 Cluster of sonnets and poets

Second, we are automatically clustering sonnets and authors that share the same topics. At this moment we have run a k-means cluster over an author-topic matrix [8]. Each author is represented by all the sonnets that they wrote. The matrix is formed by the weight that each topic has in the overall sonnets of each author[9]. Then a k-means cluster has been run using Euclidean distance and different amounts of clusters.

Some preliminary analysis shows that with 20 topics and clustering authors in only two groups, 16th-Century authors (Renaissance period) and 17th-Century authors (Baroque period) are grouped together. Only one poet (of 52) is misclassified. It shows that topic models are able to represent distinctive characteristics of each period. Therefore, we can assume some coherence in more fine clusters.

With 20 topics but clustering authors in ten groups, we have obtained coherent groups too. All poets grouped together wrote during the same period of time. The most relevant aspects of this automatic classification are the following:

- Íñigo López de Mendoza, Marqués de Santillana, was a pre-Renaissance poet. He was the first Spanish author who wrote sonnets. It appears isolated in a specific cluster. Topic Modeling has detected clearly that this is a special poet.

- The first generation of Renaissance poets are grouped together in the same cluster: Hernando de Acuña, Juan de Timoneda, Juan Boscán, Garcilaso de la Vega, Gutierre de Cetina and Diego Hurtado de Mendoza.

- There is another cluster that groups together poets of the second Renaissance generation: authors than wrote during the second half of the 16th Century as Miguel de Cervantes, Fray Luis de León, Francisco de Figueroa, Francisco de la Torre, Diego Ramírez Pagán, Francisco de Aldana and Juan de Almeida.

- One of the poets of this generation, Fernando de Herrera, appears in isolation in a specific cluster.

- Baroque poets (who wrote during 1580 to 1650) are grouped together in varios cluster. There are two main groups: the fist one includes poets born between 1560 to 1590[10], and the second one poets born from 1600 onwards[11].

This temporal coherence in the clusters, that appears in other clusters too, shows us that, on one hand, Topic Modeling could be a reliable approach to the analysis of corpora of poetry, and on the other hand, that there is some relation between topic models and the generations of poets during these centuries. Nowadays we are analyzing the relations between the poets grouped together in the same groups in order to know the reasons of this homogeneity. We plan to run other kinds of clusters in order to analyze other possibilities.

4.1.3 Topic timeline

Taking into account an author's timeline, we are analyzing how trendy topics change during the period. We want to know about the evolution of main

[8]We have used the cluster algorithm implemented in pycluster `https://pypi.python.org/pypi/Pycluster`

[9]Only a stop-list filter has been used to pre-process the corpus.

[10]Lope de Vega (b. 1562), Juan de Arguijo (b. 1567), Francisco de Medrano (b. 1570), Tirso de Molina (b. 1579), Francisco de Quevedo (b. 1580), Francisco de Borja y Aragón (b. 1581), Juan de Jáuregui (b. 1583), Pedro Soto de Rojas (b. 1584), Luis Carrillo y Sotomayor (b. 1585), Antonio Hurtado de Mendoza (b. 1586), etc.

[11]Jerónimo de Cáncer y Velasco (c. 1599), Pantaleón de Ribera (b.1600), Enríquez Gómez (b. 1602), Bocángel y Unzueta (b. 1603), Polo de Medina (b. 1603), Agustin de Salazar y Torres (1642), Sor Juana Inés de la Cruz (b. 1651), José de Litala y Castelví (b. 1672). Only Francisco López de Zárate (b. 1580) is misclassified.

topics during the period, which authors introduce new topics, to what extent these topics are followed by other poets, etc. Nowadays we have not preliminary results to illustrate this aspect.

4.1.4 Relations between metrical patterns and semantic topics

We are analyzing possible relations between metrical patterns and topics. Our hypothesis is that for specific topics, poets use specific metrical patterns and rhythms. At this moment this is an open question.

As a preliminary analysis, we have run a cluster of sonnets based on their metrical patterns. First, we have set up the most relevant metrical patterns of each author applying LDA to the metrical patterns. Instead of using the words, each sonnet is represented only with metrical patterns. Then we have run k-means cluster algorithm with Euclidean Distance and 10 clusters.

From these clusters we have some preliminary considerations:

- Íñigo López de Mendoza, Marqués de Santillana, appears again in isolation. As we said before, hos sonnets were written in a pre-Renaissance period: their meters and rhythm are very different from the others. The cluster is correctly detecting this special case.
- Other cluster is conformed mainly by Renaissance poets: from Garcilaso de la Vega to Fray Luis de León. Even though there are two Baroque poets in this cluster, it seems that Renaissance meters are quite stable and uniform.
- The other two clusters assemble Baroque poets together. At this moment we have not detected if there are any literary criteria that justify these clusters. It is noteworthy that one cluster includes Miguel de Cervantes and Lope de Vega, who tend to use more classical rhythms, and the other Góngora and Quevedo, that tend to use more Baroque rhythms.

These clusters based on metrical patterns are similar to the previous clusters based on distribution of words. Many poets appear together in both experiments: it seems that they are sharing the same distributional topics and metrical patterns. This suggest, albeit in a very speculative way, that there must be some kind of regularity between topics and meters.

In a nutshell, as we have shown in this section, applying LDA Topics Modeling and, in general, distributional model to our corpus of sonnets it is possible to extract not evident (latent) but reliable relations between words (specially figurative language), sonnets and poets. In any case, a final close reading is necessary in order to validate or reject the relations extracted automatically and justify them according to previous studies. These computational methods attract attention to possible latent relations, but it must always be manually validated.

4.2 Compositional-distributional semantic models

Recently a new model of computational semantics has been proposed: the compositional-distributional model (Baroni, 2013). The main idea of this model is to introduce the principle of compositionality in a distributional framework.

Distributional models are based on single words. Standard Vector Space Models of semantics are based in a term-document or word-context matrix (Turney and Pantel, 2010). Therefore, as we have shown in the previous section, they are useful models to calculate similarity between single words, but they cannot represent the meaning of complex expressions as phrases or sentences.

Following Frege's principle of compositionality (Montague, 1974), the meaning of these complex expressions is formed by the meaning of their single units and the relations between them. To represent compositional meaning in a distributional framework, it is necessary to combine word vectors. How semantic vectors must be combined to represent the compositional meaning is an open question in Computational Linguistics. Some proposals are vector addiction, tensor product, convolution, etc. (Mitchell and Lapata, 2010; Clarke, 2011; Blacoe and Lapata, 2012; Socher et al., 2012; Baroni, 2013; Baroni et al., 2014; Hermann and Blunsom, 2014).

From our point of view, compositional-distributional models are useful to detect semantic relations between sonnets based on stylistic features. These models are able to detect semantic similarity according to, not only the words used in a poem, but how the author combines these words.

The combination of words in a poem is the base of its literary style.

We plan to calculate semantic similarity according to specific phrases. For example, it is very specific of an author how they use the adjectives. Compositional-distributional models allow us to extract adjective-noun patterns from sonnets and to calculate the similarities between these patterns. If two poets tend to use similar adjective-noun patterns, then it is possible to establish an influential chain between them. We are working with standard tools as DISSECT (Dinu et al., 2013). Unfortunately, at this moment we have not results to show.

5 Conclusions

In this paper we have presented the computational linguistics techniques applied to the study of a large corpus of Spanish sonnets. Our objective is to establish chains of relations between sonnets and authors and, then, analyze each author in a global literary context. Once a representative corpus has been compiled and annotated, we have focused on two aspects: metrical patterns and semantic patterns.

Metrical patterns are extracted with a scansion system developed in the project. It follows a hybrid approach than combines hand-mande and statistical rules. With all these metrical patterns we plan, on one hand, to analyze the most relevant metrical patterns of the period, as well as the most relevant patterns of each author. On the other hand, we plan to cluster sonnets and authors according to the relevant metrical pattern they use, and establish metrical relational chains.

Semantic patters are extracted following a distributional semantic framework. First, we are using LDA Topic Modeling to detect the most relevant topics of the period and the most relevant topics of each author. Then we plan to group together authors and sonnets according to the topics they share. Finally we will establish the influential chains based on these topics.

We plan to combine both approaches in order to analyze the hypothesis that poets tend to use similar metrical patterns with similar topics. At this moment it is only a hypothesis that will be evaluated during the development of the project.

Finally, we want to go one step beyond Topic Modeling and try to relate authors not by what words they use, but by how they combine the words in sonnets. We plan to apply compositional-distributional models to cluster sonnets and authors with similar stylistic features.

As a position paper, we have presented only partial results of our project. Our idea is to establish a global computational linguistic approach to literary analysis based on the combination of metrical and semantic aspects; a global approach that could be applied to other corpora of poetry.

References

Manex Agirrezabal, Bertol Arrieta, Aitzol Astigarraga, and Mans Hulden. 2013. ZeuScansion : a tool for scansion of English poetry. In *Proceedings of the 11th International Conference on Finite State Methods and Natural Language Processing*, pages 18–24, St Andrews Sctotland. ACL.

Marco Baroni, Raffaela Bernardi, and Roberto Zamparelli. 2014. Frege in Space: A Program for Compositional Distributional Semantics. *Linguistics Issues in Language Technology*, 9(6):5–110.

Marco Baroni. 2013. Composition in Distributional Semantics. *Language and Linguistics Compass*, 7(10):511–522.

William Blacoe and Mirella Lapata. 2012. A Comparison of Vector-based Representations for Semantic Composition. In *Empirical Methods in Natural Language Processing and Computational Natural Language Learning*, number July, pages 546–556.

David M Blei, Andrew Y Ng, and Michael I Jordan. 2003. Latent Dirichlet Allocation. *Journal of Machine Learning Research*, 3:993–1022.

Daoud Clarke. 2011. A context-theoretic framework for compositionality in distributional semantics. *Computational Linguistics*, 38(1):41–71.

G. Dinu, N. Pham, and M. Baroni. 2013. DISSECT: DIStributional SEmantics Composition Toolkit. In *Proceedings of the 51st Annual Meeting of the Association for Computational Linguistics. System Demonstrations.*

Antonio García Berrio. 1978. Lingüística del texto y tipología lírica (La tradición textual como contexto). *Revista española de lingüística*, 8(1).

Antonio García Berrio. 2000. Retórica figural. Esquemas argumentativos en los sonetos de Garcilaso. *Edad de Oro*, (19).

Pablo Gervas. 2000. A Logic Programming Application for the Analysis of Spanish Verse. In *Computational Logic*, Berlin Heidelberg. Springer Berlin Heidelberg.

Erica Greene, Lancaster Ave, Kevin Knight, and Marina Rey. 2010. Automatic Analysis of Rhythmic Poetry with Applications to Generation and Translation. In *Empirical Methods in Natural Language Processing*, pages 524–533, Massachusetts. ACL.

Adam Hammond, Julian Brooke, and Graeme Hirst. 2013. A Tale of Two Cultures : Bringing Literary Analysis and Computational Linguistics Together. In *Workshop on Computational Linguistics for Literature*, Atlanta, Georgia.

Michael Hammond. 2014. Calculating syllable count automatically from fixed-meter poetry in English and Welsh. *Literary and Linguistic Computing*, 29(2).

Zellig Harris. 1951. *Structural Linguistics*. University of Chicago Press, Chicago.

Karl Moritz Hermann and Phil Blunsom. 2014. Multilingual Models for Compositional Distributed Semantics. In *Proceedings of the 52nd Annual Meeting of the Association for Computational Linguistics*, pages 58–68.

Matthew L Jockers and David Mimno. 2013. Significant Themes in 19th-Century Literature. *Poetics*, 41.

Matthew L. Jockers. 2013. *Macroanalysis. Digital Media and Literary History.* University of Illinois Press, Illinois.

Dimitrios Kokkinakis and Mats Malm. 2013. A Macroanalytic View of Swedish Literature using Topic Modeling. In *Corpus Linguistics Conference*, Lancaster.

José Carlos Mainer. 2010. *Historia de la literatura española*. Crítica, Barcelona.

Andrew Kachites McCallum. 2002. Mallet: A machine learning for language toolkit.

Jeff Mitchell and Mirella Lapata. 2010. Composition in Distributional Models of Semantics. *Cognitive Science*, 34:1388–1429.

R. Montague. 1974. English as a formal language. In R. Montague, editor, *Formal philosophy*, pages 188–221. Yale University Press.

Franco Moretti. 2007. *Graphs, Maps, Trees: Abstract Models for a Literary History*. Verso.

Franco Moretti. 2013. *Distant reading*. Verso.

Lluís Padró and Evgeny Stanilovsky. 2012. FreeLing 3.0: Towards Wider Multilinguality. In *Language Resources and Evaluation Conference (LREC 2012)*, Istanbul.

Antonio Quilis. 1984. *Métrica española*. Ariel, Barcelona.

Lisa M. Rhody. 2012. Topic Modeling and Figurative Language. *Journal of Digital Humanities*, 2(1).

Francisco Rico, editor. 1980-2000. *Historia y crítica de la literatura española*. Crítica, Barcelona.

Elias L. Rivers. 1993. *El soneto español en el siglo de oro*. Akal, Madrid.

Richard Socher, Brody Huval, Christopher D Manning, and Andrew Y Ng. 2012. Semantic Compositionality through Recursive Matrix-Vector Spaces. In *Empirical Methods in Natural Language Processing and Computational Natural Language Learning*, pages 1201–1211.

Timothy R. Tangherlini and Peter Leonard. 2013. Trawling in the Sea of the Great Unread: Sub-corpus topic modeling and Humanities research. *Poetics*, 41:725–749.

Arthur Terry. 1993. *Seventeenth-Century Spanish Poetry*. Cambridge University Press.

PD Turney and Patrick Pantel. 2010. From frequency to meaning: Vector space models of semantics. *Journal of Artificial Intelligence Research*, 37:141–188.

Elena Varelo-Merino, Pablo Moíno-Sánchez, and Pablo Jauralde-Pou. 2005. *Manual de métrica española*. Castalia, Madrid.

Automated translation of a literary work: a pilot study

Laurent Besacier
LIG, Univ. Grenoble - Alpes
UJF - BP 53
38041 Grenoble Cedex 9, France
laurent.besacier@imag.fr

Lane Schwartz
Department of Linguistics
University of Illinois
Urbana, IL 61801, USA
lanes@illinois.edu

Abstract

Current machine translation (MT) techniques are continuously improving. In specific areas, post-editing (PE) can enable the production of high-quality translations relatively quickly. But is it feasible to translate a literary work (fiction, short story, etc) using such an MT+PE pipeline? This paper offers an initial response to this question. An essay by the American writer Richard Powers, currently not available in French, is automatically translated and post-edited and then revised by non-professional translators. In addition to presenting experimental evaluation results of the MT+PE pipeline (MT system used, automatic evaluation), we also discuss the quality of the translation output from the perspective of a panel of readers (who read the translated short story in French, and answered a survey afterwards). Finally, some remarks of the official French translator of R. Powers, requested on this occasion, are given at the end of this article.

1 Introduction

The task of post-editing consists of editing some text (generally produced by a machine, such as a machine translation, optical character recognition, or automatic transcription system) in order to improve it. When using machine translation in the field of document translation, the following process is generally used: the MT system produces raw translations, which are manually post-edited by trained professional translators (post-editors) who correct translation errors. Several studies have shown the benefits of the combined use of machine translation and manual post-editing (MT+PE) for a document translation task. For example, Garcia (2011) showed that even though post-editing raw translations does not always lead to significant increases in productivity, this process can result in higher quality translations (when compared to translating from scratch).[1] Autodesk also carried out an experiment to test whether the use of MT would improve the productivity of translators. Results from that experiment (Zhechev, 2012) show that post-editing machine translation output significantly increases productivity when compared to translating a document from scratch. This result held regardless of the language pair, the experience level of the translator, and the translator's stated preference for post-editing or translating from scratch.

These results from academia (Garcia, 2011) and industry (Zhechev, 2012) regarding translation in specialized areas lead us to ask the following questions:

- What would be the value of such a process (MT + PE) applied to the translation of a literary work?
- How long does it take to translate a literary document of ten thousand words?
- Is the resulting translation acceptable to readers?
- What would the official translator (of the considered author) think of it?
- Is "low cost" translation produced by communities of fans (as is the case for TV series) feasible for novels or short stories?

This work attempts to provide preliminary answers to these questions. In addition to our experimental results, we also present a new transla-

[1]The work of Garcia (2011) is somewhat controversial, because the manual translation without post-editing appears to have been done without allowing the translator to use any form of digital assistance, such as an electronic dicitonary.

Proceedings of NAACL-HLT Fourth Workshop on Computational Linguistics for Literature, pages 114–122,

tion (into French) of an English-language essay (*The Book of Me* by Richard Powers).

This paper is organized as follows. We begin in §2 by surveying related work in machine translation in the literary domain. In §3, we present our experimental methodology, including the choice of literary work to be translated and the machine translation, domain adaptation, and post-editing frameworks used. In §4, we present our experimental results,[2] including an assessment of translation quality using automated machine translation metrics. In §5, we attempt to assess machine translation quality beyond automated metrics, through a human assessment of the final translation; this assessment was performed by a panel of readers and by the official French translator of Richard Powers.

2 Related Work

While the idea of post-editing machine translations of scientific and technical works is nearly as old as machine translation (see, for example (Oettinger, 1954)), very little scholarship to date has examined the use of machine translation or post-editing for literary documents. The most closely related work (Voigt and Jurafsky, 2012) that we were able to identify was presented at the *ACL workshop on Computational Linguistics for Literature*[3] ; since 2012, that workshop has examined the use of NLP in the literary field. Voigt and Jurafsky (2012) examine how referential cohesion is expressed in literary and non-literary texts and how this cohesion affects translation (experiments on Chinese literature and news). The present paper, however, tries to investigate if computer-assisted translation of a complete (and initially un-translated) short story, is feasible or not.

For the purposes of this paper, we now define what constitutes a literary text. We include in this category (our definition is undoubtedly too restrictive) all fiction or autobiographical writing in the form of novels, short stories or essays. In such texts, the author expresses his vision of the world of his time and life in general while using literary devices and a writing technique (form) that allows him to create effects using the language and to express meanings (explicit or implied).

3 Methodology

For this study, we follow a variant of the post-editing methodology established by Potet et al. (2012). In that work, 12,000 post-edited segments (equivalent to a book of about 500 pages) in the news domain were collected through crowdsourcing, resulting in one of the largest freely available corpora of post-edited machine translations.[4] It is, for example, three times larger than that collected by Specia et al. (2010), a well known benchmark in the field.

Following Potet et al. (2012), we divide the document to be translated into three equal parts. A translation/post-edition/adaptation loop was applied to the three blocks of text according to the following process:

- The first third of the document was translated from English to French using Moses (Hoang et al., 2007), a state-of-the-art phrase-based machine translation system. This machine translation output was then post-edited.

- The post-edited data from the third of the document was used to train an updated domain-adapted English-French MT system. Given the small amount of post-edited data, adaptation at this point consisted only in adapting the weights of the log-linear SMT model (by using the corrected first third as a development corpus). A similar method is suggested by Pecina et al. (2012) for domain adaptation with a limited quantity of data (we are aware that other more advanced domain adaptation techniques could have been used but this was not the central theme of our contribution).

- Then, the second third of the text was translated with the adapted MT system, then the results were post-edited and a second adapted MT system was obtained starting from the new data. This second system was used to translate the third and last part of the text.

[2]Our translations and collected data are available at `https://github.com/powersmachinetranslation/DATA`

[3]`https://sites.google.com/site/clfl2014a`

[4]`http://www-clips.imag.fr/geod/User/marion.potet/index.php?page=download`

Our methodology differs in two important ways from Potet et al. (2012). First, our study makes use of only one post-editor, and does not use crowdsourcing to collect data. Second, once the post-editing was completed, the final text was revised: first by the post-editor and then by another reviewer. The reviewer was a native French speaker with a good knowledge of the English language. The times taken to post-edit and revise were recorded.

3.1 Choice of literary document

To test the feasibility of using machine translation and post-editing to translate a literary work, we began by selecting an essay written in English which had not yet been translated into French. The choice of text was guided by the following factors:

(a) we had a contact with the French translator of the American author Richard Powers[5] (author of the novel *The Echo Maker* which won the National Book Award and was a finalist for the Pulitzer Prize)

(b) In his writing, Powers often explores the effects of modern science and technology, and in some ways his writings contain commonalities with scientific and technical texts. We hypothesized that this characteristic may somewhat reduce the gap between translation of scientific and literary texts.

Via his French translator (Jean-Yves Pellegrin), Powers was informed by e-mail of our approach, and he gave his consent as well as his feeling on this project (Richard Powers: *"..../... this automated translation project sounds fascinating. I know that the field has taken a big jump in recent years, but each jump just furthers the sense of how overwhelming the basic task is. I would be delighted to let him do a text of mine. Such figurative writing would be a good test, to be sure. .../... "The Book of Me" would be fine, too."*).

We selected an essay by Powers, entitled *The Book of Me*, originally published in GQ magazine.[6] The essay is a first-person narrative set in 2008, in which Powers describes the process by which he became the ninth person in the world to see his genome fully sequenced. Although the topic is genetics and in spite of the simple, clinical style used by the author, *The Book of Me* is truly a work of literature in which the author, who teaches narrative technique at the university level, never puts aside his poetic ambition, his humour and his fascination for the impact of science and technology on the society.

3.2 MT system used

Our machine translation system is a phrase-based system using the Moses toolkit (Hoang et al., 2007). Our system is trained using the data provided in the IWSLT machine translation evaluation campaign (Federico et al., 2012), representing a cumulative total of about 25M sentences:

- *news-c*: version 7 of the News-Commentary corpus,
- *europarl*: version 7 of the Europarl corpus[7] (Koehn, 2005),
- *un*: the United-nations corpus,[8]
- *eu-const*: corpus which is freely available (Tiedemann, 2009),
- *dgt-tm*: DGT Multilingual Translation Memory of the Acquis Communautaire (Steinberger et al., 2012),
- *pct*: corpus of Parallel Patent Applications[9],
- *gigaword*: 5M sentences extracted from the Gigaword corpus; after cleaning, the whole Gigaword corpus was sorted at sentence level according to the sum of perplexities of the source (English) and the target (French) based on two French and English pretrained language models. Finally, the 5M subset was obtained after filtering out the whole Gigaword corpus with a cut-off limit of 300 (ppl). This leads to a subset of 5M aligned sentences.

Prior to training the translation and language models, various pre-processing steps are performed on the training data. We begin by filtering out

[5] http://en.wikipedia.org/wiki/Richard_Powers

[6] http://www.gq.com/news-politics/big-issues/200810/richard-powers-genome-sequence

[7] http://www.statmt.org/europarl/

[8] http://www.euromatrixplus.net/multi-un/

[9] http://www.wipo.int/patentscope/en/data/pdf/wipo-coppatechnicalDocumentation.pdf

badly aligned sentences (using several heuristics), filtering out empty sentences, and sentences having more than 50 words. Punctuation is normalized, and we tokenize the training data, applying specific grammar-based rules for the French tokenization. Spelling correction is applied to both source and target side, and certain words (such as *coeur*) are normalized. Abbreviations and clitics are disambiguated. Various additional cleaning steps (as described in the list above) were applied to the Gigaword corpus. Many heuristics (rules) were used in order to keep only good quality bi-texts.

From this data, we train three distinct translation models on various subsets of the parallel data (*ted; news-c+europarl+un+eu-const+dgt-tm+pct; gigaword5M*). The French part of the same corpus is used for language model training, with the addition of the *news-shuffle* corpus provided as part of the WMT 2012 campaign (Callison-Burch et al., 2012). A 5-gram language model with modified Kneser-Ney smoothing is learned separately for each corpus using the SRILM toolkit (Stolcke, 2002); these models are then interpolated by optimizing perplexity on the IWSLT dev2010 corpus. The weights for the final machine translation system are optimized using the data from the English-French MT task of IWSLT 2012. The system obtains BLEU (Papineni et al., 2002) scores of 36.88 and 37.58 on the IWSLT tst2011 and test2012 corpora, respectively (BLEU evaluated with case and punctuation).

The training data used is out-of-domain for the task of literary translation, and as such is clearly not ideal for translating literary texts. In future work, it would be desirable to at least collect literary texts in French to adapt the target language model, and if possible gain access to other works and translations of the same author. Additionally, in future work we may examine the use of real-time translation model adaptation, such as Denkowski et al. (2014).

3.3 Post-editing

We use the SECTra_w.1 post-editing interface of Huynh et al. (2008). This tool also forms the foundation that gave rise to the interactive Multilingual Access Gateway (iMAG) framework for enabling multilingual website access, with incremental improvement and quality control of the translations. It has been used for many projects (Wang and Boitet, 2013), including translation of the EOLLS encyclopedia, as well as multilingual access to dozens of websites (80 demonstrations, 4 industrial contracts, 10 target languages, 820k post-edited segments).

Figure 1 shows the post-editing interface in advanced mode. In advanced mode, multiple automatic translations of each source segment (for example, from Google, Moses, etc.) can be displayed and corrected. For this experiment, the output of our Moses system was prioritized when displaying segment translations.

Post-editing was done by a (non-English native) student in translation studies at Université Grenoble Alpes.

4 Experimental results

4.1 Corpus and post-editing statistics

The test data, *The Book of Me* (see §3.1), is made up of 545 segments comprising 10,731 words. This data was divided into three equal blocks. We apply machine translation and post-editing to the data, as described in §3.2 and §3.3.

Table 1 summarizes the number of source and target (MT or PE) words in the data. Not surprisingly, a ratio greater than 1.2 is observed between French target (MT) and English source words. However, this ratio tends to decrease after post-editing of the French output. The post-editing results reported in Table 1 are obtained after each iteration of the process; the last stage of revision is thus not taken into account at this stage.

4.2 Performance of the MT system

Table 2 summarizes machine translation performance, as measured by BLEU (Papineni et al., 2002), calculated on the full corpus with the systems resulting from each iteration. Post-editing time required for each block is also shown. The BLEU scores, which are directly comparable (because evaluated on the full corpus), show no real improvement of the system. It therefore appears that adaptation of weights alone (which resulted in improvements in (Pecina et al., 2012)) is ineffective in our case. However, post-editing time decreases slightly with each iteration (but again, the differences are small and it is unclear whether the decrease in post-editing time is due to the adaptation of the MT system or to in-

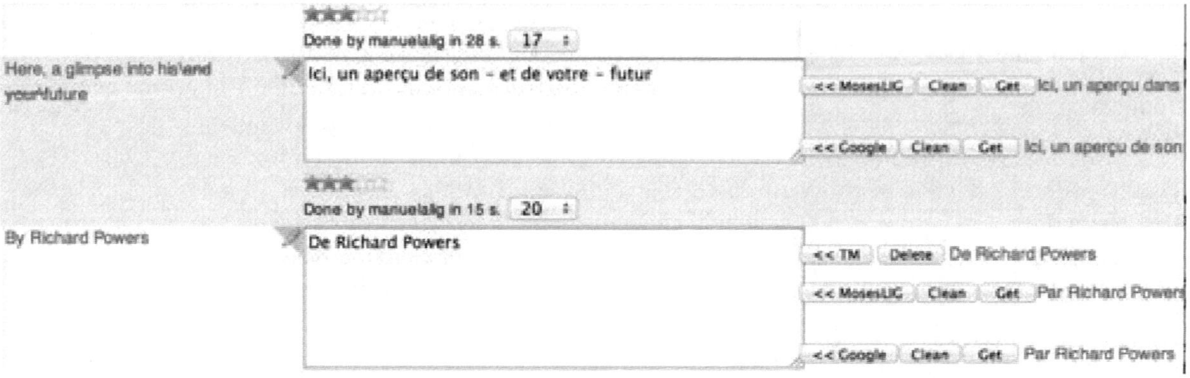

Figure 1: Post-editing interface in advanced mode

Iteration (no. seg)	English (no. words)	French MT (no. words)	French PE (no. words)
Iteration 1 (184)	3593	4295	4013
Iteration 2 (185)	3729	4593	4202
Iteration 3 (176)	3409	4429	3912
Total (545)	**10731**	**13317**	**12127**

Table 1: Number of words in each block of the English source corpus, French machine translation (MT), and French post-edited machine translation (PE).

creasing productivity as the post-editor adapts to the task). In the end, the total PE time is estimated at about 15 hours.

4.3 Analyzing the revised text

Reading the translated work at this stage (after PE) is unsatisfactory. Indeed, the post-editing is done "segment by segment" without the context of the full corpus. This results in a very embarrassing lack of homogeneity for a literary text. For this reason, two revisions of the translated text are also conducted: one by the original post-editor (4 hours) and one by a second French-English bilingual serving as a reviewer (6 hours). The final version of the translated work (which has been obtained after 15+4+6=25 hours of work) provides the basis for more qualitative assessments which are presented in the next section. The difference between the rough post-edited version (PE - 15 hours of work) and the revised version (REV - 25 hours of work) is analyzed in Table 3. It is interesting to see that while the revision takes 40% of the total time, the revised text remains very similar to the post-edited text. This can be observed by computing BLEU between the post-edited text before and after revising; the result is a BLEU score of 79.92, indicating very high similarity between the two versions. So, post-editing and revising are very different tasks. This is illustrated by the numbers of Table 3: MT and PE are highly dissimilar (post-editor corrects a lot of MT errors) while PE and REV are similar (revision probably focuses more on important details for readability and style). More qualitative analysis of the revised text and its comparison with post-edited text is part of future work (and any reader interested in doing so can download our data — see footnote 2 on page 2).

5 Human evaluation of post-edited MT

5.1 The views of readers on the post-edited translation

Nine French readers agreed to read the final translated work and answer an online questionnaire. The full survey is available on *fluidsurveys.com*.[10]. A pdf version of the test results and a spreadsheet file containing the results of the survey are also made avail-

[10] https://fluidsurveys.com/surveys/manuela-cristina/un-livre-sur-moi-qualite-de-la-traduction/?TEST_DATA=

MT system used	BLEU score (full corpus)	PE (block it.) time
Iteration 1 (not adapted)	34.79	5h 37mn
Iteration 2 (tuning on Block 1)	33.13	4h 45mn
Iteration 3 (tuning on Blocks 1+2)	34.01	4h 35mn

Table 2: BLEU after tokenization and case removal on full corpus, and time measurements for each iteration

Comparison	BLEU score
MT vs PE	34.01
MT vs REV	30.37
PE vs REV	79.92

Table 3: Automatic Evaluation (BLEU) on full corpus between unedited machine translation (MT), post-edited machine translation (PE), and revised post-edited machine translation (REV).

able on *github* (see footnote 2 on page 2).

After three questions to better understand the profile of the participant (*How old are you? Do you frequently read? If yes, what is your favorite genre?*), the first portion asks readers five questions about readability and quality of the translated literary text:

- *What do you think about text readability?*
- *Is the text easy to understand?*
- *Does the language sound natural?*
- *Do you think sentences are correct (syntactically)?*
- *Did you notice obvious errors in the text?*

The second portion (7 questions) verifies that certain subtleties of the text were understood

- *What is the text about?*
- *Who is the main character of the story?*
- *Who is funding the genome sequencing?*
- *Chronologically sort the sequence of steps involved in genome sequencing.*
- *How many base pairs are in the genome?*
- *When the novel was written, how many people had already fully sequenced their genome?*
- *Which genetic variant is associated with a high risk for Alzheimer's disease?*

The text is considered to be overall readable (5 Very Good and 3 Good), comprehensible (8 yes, 1 not) and containing few errors (8 seldom, 1 often). The easiest comprehension questions were well handled by the readers, who all responded correctly (4 questions). However, three questions led to different answers from the readers:

- 2 readers responded incorrectly to a seemingly simple question (*Who funded the genome sequencing of Powers?*)
- The question *At the time the story was written, how many people's genomes had been sequenced?* was ambiguous since the answer could be 8 or 9 (depending on whether Powers is counted), giving rise to different responses from readers
- Only 4 of 9 readers were able to give the correct sequence of steps in the process of genome sequencing; the translated text is not unclear on this point (the errors are on the part of the readers); this mixed result may indicate a lack of interest by some readers in the most technical aspects of the text.

In short, we can say that this survey, while very limited, nevertheless demonstrates that the text (produced according to our methodology) was considered to be acceptable and rather readable by our readers (of whom 3 indicated that they read very often, 4 rather often, and 2 seldom). We also include some remarks made in the free comments:

- *"I have noticed some mistakes, some neologisms (I considered them to be neologisms and not mistranslations because they made sense)"*

- *"Very fluid text and very easy reading despite precise scientific terms"*

- *"I found the text a little difficult because it contains complex words and it deals with an area I do not know at all."*

5.2 The views of R. Powers's French translator

To conclude this pilot study, the views of a tenth reader were solicited: the author's French translator, Jean-Yves Pellegrin, research professor at Paris-Sorbonne University. His comments are summarized here in the form of questions and answers.

Readability? *"The text you have successfully reproduces faithfully the content of the article by Powers. The readability bet is won and certain parts (in particular those which relate to the scientific aspects of the described experiment) are very convincing."*

So the MT+PE pipeline seems also efficient for obtaining quickly readable literary texts, as it is the case for other domain specific data types.

Imperfections? *"There are, of course, imperfections, clumsy expressions, and specific errors which require correction"*

Top mistakes?

- *"The most frequent defect, which affects the work of any novice translator, is the syntactic calque, where French structures the phrase differently .../... One understands, but it does not sound very French"*

- *"Another fairly common error is the loss of idiomatic French in favor of Anglicisms."* Sometimes these Anglicisms can be more disturbing when flirting with Franglais,[11] such as translating 'actionable knowledge' as 'connaissances actionnables' (p. 18) instead of 'connaissances pratiques / utilisables'."

- *"A third defect is due to not taking into account certain cultural references .../... For example, Powers made several references to the topography of Boston that give rise to inaccuracies in the translation: 'Charles River' for example (p. 12) is not 'une riviere' but 'un fleuve'; that is why we translate by 'la Charles River' or simply 'la Charles'"*

The errors mentioned above are considered as not acceptable by a professional translator of literary text. These are hard problems for computer assisted translation (move away from the syntactic calque, better handle idioms and multi-word expressions, take into account cultural references).

Could this text serve as a starting point for a professional literary translator? *"Instinctively, I am tempted to say no for now, because from his first cast the translator has reflexes that allow him to produce a cleaner text than the one you produced .../.... however, this translator would spend more than 25 hours to produce the 42 pages of 1500 characters that comprise Power's text. At a rate of 7 pages per day on average, it would take 6 eight-hour days. If, however, I could work only from your text (while completely forgetting Powers's) and I could be guaranteed that your translation contains no errors or omissions from the original, but just that it needs to be improved, made more fluid, more authentically French, things would be different and the time saved would be probably huge."*

As expected, the professional translator of literature wants to control the whole translation process. But the last part of his comment is interesting: if the meaning were guaranteed, he could concentrate on the form and limit going back and forth between source and target text. Thus, working more on quality assesment of MT and confidence estimation seems to be a promising way for future work on literary text translation. Based on the translation speed rates provided by Pellegrin, we can estimate the time savings of our technique. Our computer-assisted methodology can be said to have accelerated the translation factor by a factor of 2 — our process took roughly 25 hours, compared to the 50 hours estimated for a professional literary translation.

[11]Frenglish

6 Conclusion

6.1 Collected Data Available Online

The data in this article are available at https://github.com/powersmachinetranslation/DATA. There one can find:

- The 545 English source and French target (MT, PE) segments mentioned in Table 1
- The translated and revised work (REV in Table 3), in French, that was read by a panel of 9 readers
- The results of the survey (9 readers) compiled in a spreadsheet (in French)

6.2 Comments and open questions

We presented an initial experiment of machine translation of a literary work (an English text of about twenty pages). The results of an MT+PE pipeline were presented and, going beyond that, the opinions of a panel of readers and a translator were solicited. The translated text, obtained after 25 hours of human labor (a professional translator told us that he would have needed at least twice that much time) is acceptable to readers but the opinion of a professional translator is mixed. This approach suggests a methodology for rapid "low cost" translation , similar to the translation of TV series subtitles found on the web. For the author of the literary text, this presents the possibility of having his work translated into more languages (several dozen instead of a handful, this short story by Richard Powers has also been translated into Romanian using this same methodology).

But would the author be willing to sacrifice the quality of translation (and control over it) to enable wider dissemination of his works? For a reader who cannot read an author in the source language, this provides the ability to have faster access to an (admittedly imperfect) translation of their favorite author. For a non-native reader of the source language this provides a mechanism for assistance on the parts he or she has trouble understanding. One last thing: the title of the work *The Book of Me* has remained unchanged in the French version because no satisfactory translation was found to illustrate that the author refers both to a book but also to his DNA; this paradox is a good illustration of the difficulty translating a literary work!

Thanks

Thanks to Manuela Barcan who handled the first phase of post-editing machine translations in French and Romanian during the summer of 2013. Thanks to Jean-Yves Pellegrin, French translator of Richard Powers, for his help and open-mindedness. Thanks to Richard Powers who allowed us to conduct this experiment using one of his works.

References

Chris Callison-Burch, Philipp Koehn, Christof Monz, Matt Post, Radu Soricut, and Lucia Specia. 2012. Findings of the 2012 Workshop on Statistical Machine Translation. In *Proceedings of the Seventh Workshop on Statistical Machine Translation*, pages 10–51, Montréal, Canada, June. Association for Computational Linguistics.

Michael Denkowski, Alon Lavie, Isabel Lacruz, and Chris Dyer. 2014. Real time adaptive machine translation for post-editing with cdec and TransCenter. In *Proceedings of the EACL 2014 Workshop on Humans and Computer-assisted Translation*, pages 72–77, Gothenburg, Sweden, April. Association for Computational Linguistics.

Marcello Federico, Mauro Cettolo, Luisa Bentivogli, Michael Paul, and Sebastian Stüker. 2012. Overview of the IWSLT 2012 evaluation campaign. In *In proceedings of the 9th International Workshop on Spoken Language Translation (IWSLT)*, December.

Ignacio Garcia. 2011. Translating by post-editing: is it the way forward? *Journal of Machine Translation*, 25(3):217–237.

Hieu Hoang, Alexandra Birch, Chris Callison-burch, Richard Zens, Rwth Aachen, Alexandra Constantin, Marcello Federico, Nicola Bertoldi, Chris Dyer, Brooke Cowan, Wade Shen, Christine Moran, and Ondřej Bojar. 2007. Moses: Open source toolkit for statistical machine translation. In *ACL'07, Annual Meeting of the Association for Computational Linguistics*, pages 177–180, Prague, Czech Republic.

Cong-Phap Huynh, Christian Boitet, and Hervé Blanchon. 2008. SECTra_w.1: an online collaborative system for evaluating, post-editing and presenting MT translation corpora. In *LREC'08, Sixth International Conference on Language Resources and Evaluation*, pages 28–30, Marrakech, Morocco.

Philipp Koehn. 2005. Europarl: A parallel corpus for statistical machine translation. In *Proceedings of the Tenth Machine Translation Summit*, Phuket, Thailand, September.

Anthony Oettinger. 1954. *A Study for the Design of an Automatic Dictionary*. Ph.D. thesis, Harvard University.

Kishore Papineni, Salim Roukos, Todd Ward, and Zhu Wei-Jing. 2002. BLEU: A method for automatic evaluation of machine translation. In *ACL'02, 40th Annual Meeting of the Association for Computational Linguistics*, pages 311–318, Philadelphia, PA, USA.

Pavel Pecina, Antonio Toral, and Josef van Genabith. 2012. Simple and effective parameter tuning for domain adaptation of statistical machine translation. In *Proceedings of the 24th International Conference on Computational Linguistics*, pages 2209–2224, Mumbai, India.

Marion Potet, Emmanuelle Esperança-Rodier, Laurent Besacier, and Hervé Blanchon. 2012. Collection of a large database of French-English SMT output corrections. In *Proceedings of the Eighth International Conference on Language Resources and Evaluation (LREC)*, Istanbul, Turkey, May.

Lucia Specia, Nicola Cancedda, and Marc Dymetman. 2010. A dataset for assessing machine translation evaluation metrics. In *7th Conference on International Language Resources and Evaluation (LREC-2010)*, pages 3375–3378, Valetta, Malta.

Ralf Steinberger, Andreas Eisele, Szymon Klocek, Spyridon Pilos, and Patrick Schlüter. 2012. DGT-TM: A freely available translation memory in 22 languages. In *LREC 2012*, Istambul, Turkey.

Andreas Stolcke. 2002. SRILM: An extensible language modeling toolkit. In *ICSLP'02, 7th International Conference on Spoken Language Processing*, pages 901–904, Denver, USA.

Jörg Tiedemann. 2009. News from OPUS - a collection of multilingual parallel corpora with tools and interfaces. In *Proceedings of Recent Advances in Natural Language Processing*.

Rob Voigt and Dan Jurafsky. 2012. Towards a literary machine translation, the role of referential cohesion. In *Computational Linguistics for Literature, Workshop at NAACL-HLT 2012*, Montreal, Canada.

Lingxiao Wang and Christian Boitet. 2013. Online production of HQ parallel corpora and permanent task-based evaluation of multiple MT systems. In *Proceedings of the MT Summit XIV Workshop on Post-editing Technology and Practice*.

Ventsislav Zhechev. 2012. Machine translation infrastructure and post-editing performance at Autodesk. In *AMTA'12, Conference of the Association for Machine Translation in the Americas*, San Diego, USA.

Translating Literary Text between Related Languages using SMT

Antonio Toral
ADAPT Centre
School of Computing
Dublin City University
Dublin, Ireland
atoral@computing.dcu.ie

Andy Way
ADAPT Centre
School of Computing
Dublin City University
Dublin, Ireland
away@computing.dcu.ie

Abstract

We explore the feasibility of applying machine translation (MT) to the translation of literary texts. To that end, we measure the translatability of literary texts by analysing parallel corpora and measuring the degree of freedom of the translations and the narrowness of the domain. We then explore the use of domain adaptation to translate a novel between two related languages, Spanish and Catalan. This is the first time that specific MT systems are built to translate novels. Our best system outperforms a strong baseline by 4.61 absolute points (9.38% relative) in terms of BLEU and is corroborated by other automatic evaluation metrics. We provide evidence that MT can be useful to assist with the translation of novels between closely-related languages, namely (i) the translations produced by our best system are equal to the ones produced by a professional human translator in almost 20% of cases with an additional 10% requiring at most 5 character edits, and (ii) a complementary human evaluation shows that over 60% of the translations are perceived to be of the same (or even higher) quality by native speakers.

1 Introduction

The field of Machine Translation (MT) has evolved very rapidly since the emergence of statistical approaches almost three decades ago (Brown et al., 1988; Brown et al., 1990). MT is nowadays a growing reality throughout the industry, which continues to adopt this technology as it results in demonstrable improvements in translation productivity, at least for technical domains (Zhechev, 2012). Meanwhile, the performance of MT systems in research continues to improve. In this regard, a recent study looked at the best-performing systems of the WMT shared task for seven language pairs during the period between 2007 and 2012, and estimated the improvement in translation quality during this period to be around 10% absolute, in terms of both adequacy and fluency (Graham et al., 2014).

Having reached this level of research maturity and industrial adoption, in this paper we explore the feasibility of applying the current state-of-the-art MT technology to literary texts, what might be considered to be the last bastion of human translation. The perceived wisdom is that MT is of no use for the translation of literature. We challenge that view, despite the fact that – to the best of our knowledge – the applicability of MT to literature has to date been only partially studied from an empirical point of view.

In this paper we aim to measure the translatability of literary text. Our empirical methodology relies on the fact that the applicability of MT to a given type of text can be assessed by analysing parallel corpora of that particular type and measuring (i) the degree of freedom of the translations (how literal the translations are), and (ii) the narrowness of the domain (how specific or general that text is). Hence, we tackle the problem of measuring the translatability of literary text by comparing the degree of freedom of translation and domain narrowness for such texts to documents in two other domains which have been widely studied in the area of MT: technical documentation and news.

Proceedings of NAACL-HLT Fourth Workshop on Computational Linguistics for Literature, pages 123–132,
Denver, Colorado, June 4, 2015.

Furthermore, we assess the usefulness of MT in translating a novel between two closely-related languages. We build an MT system using state-of-the-art domain-adaptation techniques and evaluate its performance against the professional human translation, using both automatic metrics and manual evaluation. To the best of our knowledge, this is the first time that a specific MT system is built to translate novels.

The rest of the paper is organised as follows. Section 2 gives an overview of the current state-of-the-art in applying MT to literary texts. In Section 3 we measure the translatability of literary texts. In Section 4 we explore the use of MT to translate a novel between two related languages. Finally, in Section 5 we present our conclusions and outline avenues of future work.

2 Background

To date, there have been only a few works on applying MT to literature, for which we provide an overview here.

Genzel et al. (2010) explored constraining statistical MT (SMT) systems for poetry to produce translations that obey particular length, meter and rhyming rules. Form is preserved at the price of producing a worse translation, in terms of the BLEU automatic metric, which decreases from 0.3533 to 0.1728, a drop of around 50% in real terms. Their system was trained and evaluated with WMT-09 data[1] for French–English.

Greene et al. (2010) also translated poetry, choosing target realisations that conform to the desired rhythmic patterns. Specifically, they translated Dante's *Divine Comedy* from Italian sonnets into English iambic pentameter. Instead of constraining the SMT system, they passed its output lattice through a FST that maps words to sequences of stressed and unstressed syllables. These sequences are finally filtered with a iambic pentameter acceptor. Their output translations are evaluated qualitatively only.

Voigt and Jurafsky (2012) examined how referential cohesion is expressed in literary and non-literary texts, and how this cohesion affects translation. They found that literary texts have more dense reference chains and conclude that incorporating discourse features beyond the level of the sentence is an important direction for applying MT to literary texts.

Jones and Irvine (2013) used existing MT systems to translate samples of French literature (prose and poetry) into English. They then used qualitative analysis grounded in translation theory on the MT output to assess the potential of MT in literary translation and to address what makes literary translation particularly difficult, e.g. one objective in literary translation, in contrast to other domains, is to preserve the *experience* of reading a text when moving to the target language.

Very recently, Besacier (2014) presented a pilot study where MT followed by post-editing is applied to translate a short story from English into French. In Besacier's work, post-editing is performed by non-professional translators, and the author concludes that such a workflow can be a useful low-cost alternative for translating literary works, albeit at the expense of sacrificing translation quality. According to the opinion of a professional translator, the main errors had to do with using English syntactic structures and expressions instead of their French equivalents and not taking into account certain cultural references.

Finally, there are some works that use MT techniques in literary text, but for generation rather than for translation. He et al. (2012) used SMT to generate poems in Chinese given a set of keywords. Jiang and Zhou (2008) used SMT to generate the second line of Chinese couplets given the first line. In a similar fashion, Wu et al. (2013) used transduction grammars to generate rhyming responses in hip-hop given the original challenges.

This paper contributes to the current state-of-the-art in two dimensions. On the one hand, we conduct a comparative analysis on the translatability of literary text according to narrowness of the domain and freedom of translation. This can be seen as a more general and complementary analysis to the one conducted by Voigt and Jurafsky (2012). On the other hand, and related to Besacier (2014), we evaluate MT output for literary text. There are two differences though; first, they translated a short story, while we do so for a longer type of literary

[1] `http://www.statmt.org/wmt09/translation-task.html`

text, namely a novel; second, their MT systems were evaluated against a post-edited reference produced by non-professional translators, while we evaluate our systems against the translation produced by a professional translator.

3 Translatability

The applicability of SMT to translate a certain text type for a given pair of languages can be studied by analysing two properties of the relevant parallel data.

- Degree of freedom of the translation. While literal translations can be learnt reasonably well by the word alignment component of SMT, free translations may result in problematic alignments.
- Narrowness of the domain. Constrained domains lead to good SMT results. This is due to the fact that in narrow domains lexical selection is much less of an issue and relevant terms occur frequently, which allows the SMT model to learn their translations with good accuracy.

We could say then, that the narrower the domain and the smaller the degree of freedom of the translation, the more applicable SMT is. This is, we assert, why SMT performs well on technical documentation while results are substantially worse for more open and unpredictable domains such as news (cf. WMT translation task series).[2]

We propose to study the applicability of SMT to literary text by comparing the degree of freedom and narrowness of parallel corpora for literature to other domains widely studied in the area of MT (technical documentation and news). Such a corpus study can be carried out by using a set of automatic measures. The perplexity of the word alignment can be used as a proxy to measure the degree of freedom of the translation. The narrowness of the domain can be assessed by measuring perplexity with respect to a language model (LM) (Ruiz and Federico, 2014).

Therefore, in order to assess the translatability of literary text with MT, we contextualise the problem by comparing it to the translatability of other widely studied types of text. Instead of considering the translatability of literature as a whole, we root the study along two axes:

- Relatedness of the language pair: from pairs of languages that belong to the same family (e.g. Romance languages), through languages that belong to the same group (e.g. Romance and Germanic languages of the Indo-European group) to unrelated languages (e.g. Romance and Finno-Ugric languages).
- Literary genre: novels, poetry, etc.

We hypothesise that the degree of applicability of SMT to literature depends on these two axes. Between related languages, translations should be more literal and complex phenomena (e.g. metaphors) might simply transfer to the target language, while they are more likely to require complex translations between unrelated languages. Regarding literary genres, in poetry the preservation of form might be considered relevant while in novels it may be a lesser constraint.

The following sections detail the experimental datasets and the experiments conducted regarding narrowness of the domain and degree of translation freedom.

3.1 Experimental Setup

In order to carry out our experiment on the translatability of literary texts, we use monolingual datasets for Spanish and parallel datasets for two language pairs with varying levels of relatedness: Spanish–Catalan and Spanish–English.

Regarding the different types of corpora, we consider datasets that fall in the following four groups: novels, news, technical documentation and Europarl (EP).

We use two sources for novels: two novels from Carlos Ruiz Zafón, *The Shadow of the Wind* (published originally in Spanish in 2001) and *The Angel's Game* (2008), for Spanish–Catalan and Spanish–English, referred to as novel1; and two novels from Gabriel García Márquez, *Hundred Years of Solitude* (1967) and *Love in the Time of Cholera* (1985), for Spanish–English, referred to as novel2.

We use two sources of news data: a corpus made of articles from the newspaper *El Periódico*[3] (re-

[2] `http://www.statmt.org/wmt14/translation-task.html`

[3] `http://www.elperiodico.com/`

ferred to as news1) for Spanish–Catalan, and news-commentary v8[4] (referred to as news2) for Spanish–English.

For technical documentation we use four datasets: DOGC,[5] a corpus from the official journal of the Catalan Goverment, for Spanish–Catalan; EMEA,[6] a corpus from the European Medicines Agency, for Spanish–English; JRC-Acquis (henceforth referred as JRC) (Steinberger et al., 2006), made of legislative text of the European Union, for Spanish–English; and KDE4,[7] a corpus of localisation files of the KDE desktop environment, for the two language pairs.

Finally, we consider the Europarl corpus v7 (Koehn, 2005), given it is widely used in the MT community, for Spanish–English.

All the datasets are pre-processed as follows. First they are tokenised and truecased with Moses' (Koehn et al., 2007) scripts. Truecasing is carried out with a model trained on the caWaC corpus for Catalan (Ljubešić and Toral, 2014) and News Crawl 2012[8] both for English and Spanish.

Parallel datasets not available in a sentence-split format (novel1 and novel2) are sentence-split using Freeling (Padró and Stanilovsky, 2012). All parallel datasets are then sentence aligned. We use Hunalign (Varga et al., 2005) and keep only one-to-one alignments. The dictionaries used for Spanish–Catalan and Spanish–English are extracted from Apertium bilingual dictionaries for those language pairs.[9,10] Only sentence pairs for which the confidence score of the alignment is $>= 0.4$ are kept.[11] Although most of the parallel datasets are provided in sentence-aligned form, we realign them to ensure that the data used to calculate word alignment perplexity are properly aligned at sentence level. This is to avoid having high word alignment perplexities due, not to high degrees of translation freedom, but to the presence of misaligned parallel data.

3.2 Narrowness of the Domain

As previously mentioned, we use LM perplexity as a proxy to measure the narrowness of the domain.

We take two random samples without replacement for the Spanish side of each dataset, to be used for training (200,000 tokens) and testing (20,000 tokens). We train an LM of order 3 and improved Kneser-Ney smoothing (Chen and Goodman, 1996) with IRSTLM (Federico et al., 2008).

For each LM we report the perplexity on the testset built from the same dataset in Figure 1. The two novels considered (perplexities in the range $[230.61, 254.49]$) fall somewhere between news ($[359.73, 560.62]$) and technical domain ($[127.30, 228.38]$). Our intuition is that novels cover a narrow domain, like technical texts, but the vocabulary and language used in novels is richer, thus leading to higher perplexity than technical texts. News, on the contrary, covers a large variety of topics. Hence, despite novels possibly using more complex linguistic constructions, news articles are less predictable.

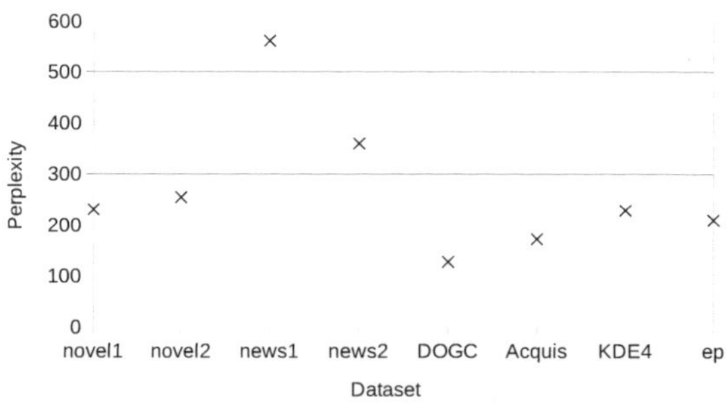

Figure 1: LM perplexity results

3.3 Degree of Translation Freedom

We use word alignment perplexity, as in Equation 1, as a proxy to measure the degree of translation freedom. Word alignment perplexity gives an indication of how well the model fits the data.

$$\log_2 PP = - \sum_s \log_2 p(e_s|f_s) \quad (1)$$

The assumption is that the freer the translations are for a given parallel corpus, the higher the per-

[4]http://www.statmt.org/wmt13/training-parallel-nc-v8.tgz

[5]http://opus.lingfil.uu.se/DOGC.php

[6]http://opus.lingfil.uu.se/EMEA.php

[7]http://opus.lingfil.uu.se/KDE4.php

[8]http://www.statmt.org/wmt13/translation-task.html

[9]http://sourceforge.net/projects/apertium/files/apertium-es-ca/1.2.1/

[10]http://sourceforge.net/projects/apertium/files/apertium-en-es/0.8.0/

[11]Manual evaluation for English, French and Greek concluded that 0.4 was an adequate threshold for Hunalign's confidence score (Pecina et al., 2012).

plexity of the word alignment model learnt from such dataset, as the word alignment algorithms would have more difficulty to find suitable alignments.

For each parallel dataset, we randomly select a set of sentence pairs whose overall size accounts for 500,000 tokens. We then run word alignment with GIZA++ (Och and Ney, 2003) in both directions, with the default parameters used in Moses.

For each dataset and language pair, we report in Figure 2 the perplexity of the word alignment after the last iteration for each direction. The most important discriminating variable appears to be the level of relatedness of the languages involved, i.e. all the perplexities for Spanish–Catalan are below 10 while all the perplexities for Spanish–English are well above this number.

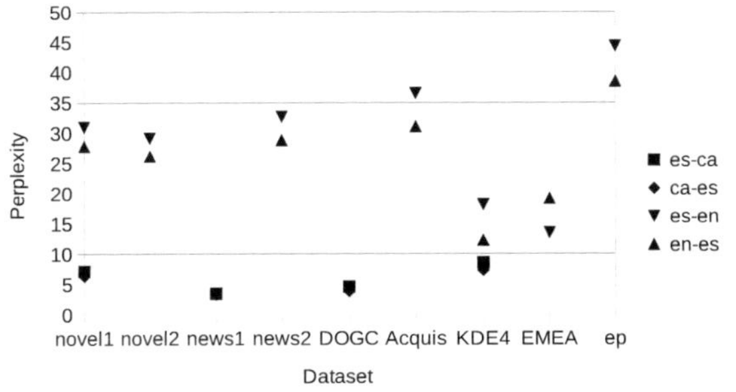

Figure 2: Word alignment perplexity results

4 MT for Literature between Related Languages

Encouraged by the results obtained for the translatability of novels (cf. Figures 1 and 2), we decided to carry out an experiment to assess the feasibility of using MT to assist with the translation of novels between closely-related languages. In this experiment we translate a novel, *The Prisoner of Heaven* (2011) by Carlos Ruiz Zafón, from Spanish into Catalan. This language pair is chosen because of the maturity of applied MT technology, e.g. MT is used alongside post-editing to translate the newspaper *La Vanguardia* (around 70,000 tokens) from Spanish into Catalan on a daily basis (Martín and Serra, 2014). We expect the results to be similar for other languages with similar degrees of similarity to Spanish, e.g. Portuguese and Italian.

Type	Dataset	# sentences	Avg length
TM	News	629,375	22.45
			21.49
	Novel	21,626	16.95
			15.11
LM	News1	631,257	22.66
	caWaC	16,516,799	29.48
	Novel	22,170	17.14
Dev	News	1,000	22.31
			21.36
	Novel	1,000	16.92
			15.35
Test	Novel	1,000	17.91
			15.93

Table 1: Datasets used for MT

The translation model (TM) of our baseline system is trained with the news1 dataset while the LM is trained with the concatenation of news1 and caWaC. The baseline system is tuned on news. On top of this baseline we then build our domain-adapted systems. The domain adaptation is carried out by using two previous novels from the same author that were translated by the same translator (cf. the dataset novel1 in Section 3.1). We explore their use for tuning (+inDev), LM (concatenated +inLM and interpolated +IinLM) and TM (concatenated +inTM and interpolated +IinTM). The testset is made of a set of randomly selected sentence pairs from *The Prisoner of Heaven*. Table 1 provides an overview of the datasets used for MT.

We train phrase-based SMT systems with Moses v2.1 using default parameters. Tuning is carried out with MERT (Och, 2003). LMs are linearly interpolated with SRILM (Stolcke et al., 2011) by means of perplexity minimisation on the development set from the novel1 dataset. Similarly, TMs are linearly interpolated, also by means of perplexity minimisation (Sennrich, 2012).

4.1 Automatic Evaluation

Our systems are evaluated with a set of state-of-the-art automatic metrics: BLEU (Papineni et al., 2002), TER (Snover et al., 2006) and METEOR 1.5 (Denkowski and Lavie, 2014).

Table 2 shows the results obtained by each of the systems built. For each domain-adapted system

System	BLEU	diff	TER	diff	METEOR	diff
baseline	0.4915		0.3658		0.3612	
+inDev	0.4939	0.49%	0.3641	-0.47%	0.3628	0.46%
+inDev+inLM	0.4948	0.67%	0.3643	-0.41%	0.3633	0.59%
+inDev+IinLM	0.5045	2.64%	0.3615	-1.18%	0.3669	1.59%
+inDev+inTM	0.5238	6.57%	0.3481	-4.85%	0.3779	4.61%
+inDev+IinTM	0.5258	6.98%	0.3510	-4.04%	0.3795	5.06%
+inDev+inLM+inTM	0.5297	7.77%	0.3433	-6.17%	0.3811	5.51%
+inDev+IinLM+IinTM	0.5376	9.38%	0.3405	-6.92%	0.3847	6.50%
inDev+inTM+inLM	0.4823	-1.87%	0.3777	3.24%	0.3594	-0.49%

Table 2: Automatic evaluation scores for the MT systems built

System	BLEU	diff	TER	diff	METEOR	diff
Google	0.4652	15.56%	0.4021	-15.31%	0.3498	9.98%
Apertium	0.4543	18.34%	0.3925	-13.25%	0.3447	11.60%
Lucy	0.4821	11.51%	0.3758	-9.40%	0.3550	8.35%

Table 3: Automatic evaluation scores for third-party MT systems

we show its relative improvement over the baseline (columns diff). The use of in-domain data to adapt each of the components of the pipeline, tuning (+inDev), LM (+inLM and +IinLM) and TM (+inTM and +IinTM), results in gains across all the metrics. Additional gains are achieved when combining the different in-domain components. Interpolation, both for LM and TM, results in gains when compared to the systems that use the same data in a concatenated manner (e.g. +IinLM vs +inLM) except for the TM in terms of TER. The best system, with in-domain data used for all the components and interpolated TM and LM (+inDev+IinLM+IinTM), yields a relative improvement over the baseline of 9.38% for BLEU, 6.92% for TER and 6.5% for METEOR. Finally we show the scores obtained by a system that uses solely in-domain data (inTM+inLM+inDev). While its results are slightly below those of the baseline, it should be noted that both the TM and TL of this system are trained with very limited amounts of data: 21,626 sentence pairs and 22,170 sentences, respectively (cf. Table 1).

We decided to compare our system also to widely-used on-line third-party systems, as these are the ones that a translator could easily have access to. We consider the following three systems: Google Translate,[12] Apertium (Forcada et al., 2011)[13] and Lucy.[14] These three systems follow different approaches; while the first is statistical, the second and the third are rule-based, classified respectively as shallow and deep formalisms.

Table 3 shows the results of the third-party system and compares their scores with our best domain-adapted system in terms of relative improvement (columns diff). The results of the third-party systems are similar, albeit slighly lower, compared to our baseline (cf. Table 2).

We conducted statistical significance tests for BLEU between our best domain-adapted system, the baseline and the three third-party systems using paired bootstrap resampling (Koehn, 2004) with 1,000 iterations and $p = 0.01$. In all cases the improvement brought by our best system is found out to be significant.

Finally we report on the percentage of translations that are equal in the MT output and in the reference. These account for 15.3% of the sentences for the baseline and 19.7% for the best domain-adapted system. It should be noted though that these tend to be short sentences, so if we consider their percentage in terms of words, they account for 4.97% and 7.15% of the data, respectively. If we consider also the translations that can reach the reference in at most five character editing steps (Volk, 2009), then the percentage of equal and near-equal translations pro-

[12]https://translate.google.com

[13]http://apertium.org/

[14]http://www.lucysoftware.com/english/machine-translation/

duced by our best domain-adapted system reaches 29.5% of the sentences.

4.2 Manual Evaluation

To gain further insight on the results, we conducted a manual evaluation. A common procedure (e.g. conducted in the MT shared task at WMT) consists of ranking MT translations. Given the source and target sides of the reference (human) translations, and two or more outputs from MT systems, these outputs are ranked according to their quality, i.e. how close they are to the reference, e.g. in terms of adequacy and/or fluency.

In our experiment, we are of course not interested in comparing two MT systems, but rather one MT system (the best one according to the automatic metrics) and the human translation. Hence, we conduct the rank-based manual evaluation in a slightly modified setting; we do not provide the target of the reference translation as reference but as one of the MT systems to be ranked. The evaluator thus is given the source-side of the reference and two translations, one being the human translation and the other the translation produced by an MT system. The evaluator of course does not know which is which. Moreover, in order to avoid any bias with respect to MT, they do not know that one of them has been produced by a human.

Two bilingual speakers in Spanish and Catalan, with a background in linguistics but without in-depth knowledge of MT (again, to avoid any bias with respect to MT) ranked a set of 101 translations. We carried out this rank-based evaluation with the Appraise tool (Federmann, 2012), using its 3-way ranking task type, whereby given two translations A and B, the evaluator can rank them as A>B (if A is better than B), A<B (if A is worse than B) and A=B (if both are of the same quality). Here we reproduce verbatim the evaluation instructions given to the evaluators:

"Given the translations by two machine translation systems A and B, the task is to rank them:
- Rank A higher than B (A>B) if the output of system A is better than the output of system B
- Rank A lower than B (A<B) if the output of system A is worse than the output of system B
- Rank both systems equally (A=B) if the outputs of both systems are of an equivalent level of quality"

The inter-annotator agreement, in terms of Fleiss' Kappa (Fleiss, 1971), is 0.49, which falls in the band of moderate agreement $[0.41, 0.60]$ (Landis and Koch, 1977).

Considering the aggregated 202 judgements, we have the breakdown shown in Table 4. In most cases (41.58% of the judgements), both the human translation (HT) and the MT are considered to be of equal quality. The HT is considered better than MT in 39.11% of the cases. Perhaps surprisingly, the evaluators ranked MT higher than HT in almost 20% of their judgements.

Judgement	Times	Percentage
HT=MT	84	41.58%
HT<MT	39	19.31%
HT>MT	79	39.11%

Table 4: Manual Evaluation. Breakdown of ranks (overall)

We now delve deeper into the results and show in Table 5 the breakdown of judgements by evaluator. For around two thirds of the sentences, both evaluators agreed in their judgement: in 28.71% of the sentences both for HT=MT and for HT>MT, and in 9.9% of the sentences for HT<MT. They disagreed in the remaining one third of the data, the two main disagreements being between HT=MT and HT>MT (13.86%) and between HT=MT and HT<MT (11.88%). The remaining case of disagreement (between HT>MT and HT<MT) is encountered less frequently (6.93%).

Judgement	Times	Percentage
HT=MT, HT=MT	29	28.71%
HT<MT, HT<MT	10	9.9%
HT>MT, HT>MT	29	28.71%
Total	68	67.33%
HT>MT, HT<MT	7	6.93%
HT=MT, HT>MT	14	13.86%
HT=MT, HT<MT	12	11.88%
Total	33	32.67%

Table 5: Manual Evaluation. Breakdown of ranks (per evaluator)

We analyse the sets of sentences where both evaluators agree, for HT=MT, HT<MT and HT>MT. First, we report on their average sentence length in tokens, as shown in Table 6. We can conclude that

Source	La habitación tenía un pequeño balcón que daba a la plaza.
Gloss	*The room had a small balcony facing the square.*
HT	La cofurna tenia un balconet que donava a la plaça.
MT	L'habitació tenia un petit balcó que donava a la plaça.
Discussion	Habitació (room) is the translation of habitación. Cofurna (hovel) has slightly different meaning.
Source	— ¿Adónde vas?
Gloss	— *Where are you going?*
HT	— ¿On vas? — hi vaig afegir.
MT	— ¿On vas?
Discussion	The snippet "hi vaig afegir" (I added) is not in the original.

Table 7: Manual Evaluation. Examples of translations ranked as HT<MT

Mode	Sentences	Tokens	Tokens/sent.
HT<MT	10	127	12.7
HT=MT	29	278	9.59
HT>MT	29	657	22.66
whole	101	1,671	16.71

Table 6: Manual Evaluation. Avg sentence length per rank

MT results in translations of good quality for shorter sentences than the average, while HT remains the best translation for longer sentences.

We now look at each of these sets of sentences and carry out a qualitative analysis, aiming at finding out what types of sentences and translation errors are predominant.

For most of the HT=MT cases (22), both translations are exactly the same. In the remaining 7 cases, up to a few words are different, with both translations being accurate.

In most of the 10 sentences ranked as HT<MT, the translator has either added some content that is not in the original or has used words that have a slightly different meaning than the corresponding words in the original, while the MT translation is accurate. Table 7 provides examples of both cases.

Finally, regarding the translations ranked as HT>MT, the translation as produced by the MT systems has some errors, in most cases affecting just one or a few words. The most common errors are related to:

- OOVs, mainly for verbs that contain a pronoun as a suffix in Spanish. E.g. "escrutándola" (*scrutinising her*).
- Pronouns translated wrongly. E.g. "lo" (him) wrongly translated as "ho" (*that*) instead of "el".
- Word choice. Either the translation looks unnatural or its meaning is closely related to the original but it is not exactly the same.

5 Conclusions and Future Work

This paper has explored the feasibility of applying MT to the translation of literary texts. To that end, we measured the translatability of literary texts and compared it to that of other datasets commonly used in MT by measuring the degree of freedom of the translations (using word alignment perplexity) and the narrowness of the domain (via LM perplexity). Our results show that novels are less predictable than texts in the technical domain but more predictable than news articles. Regarding translation freedom, the main variable is not related to the type of data but to the level of relatedness of the pair of languages involved.

Furthermore, we explored the use of state-of-the-art domain adaptation techniques in MT to translate a novel between two closely-related languages, Spanish and Catalan. This is the first time that specific MT systems are built to translate novels. Our best domain-adapted system outperforms a strong baseline by 4.61 absolute points (9.38% relative) in terms of BLEU. We provided evidence that MT can be useful to assist with the translation of novels between closely-related languages, namely (i) the translations produced by our best system are equal to the ones produced by a professional human translator in almost 20% of cases, with an additional 10% requiring at most 5 character edits, and (ii) over 60%

of the translations are perceived to be of the same (or even higher) quality by native speakers.

As this is the first work where a specific MT system has been built to translate novels, a plethora of research lines remain to be explored. In this work we have adapted an MT system by learning from previous novels from the same author. A further step would be to learn from translators while they are translating the current novel using incremental retraining techniques. We would like to experiment with less related language pairs (e.g. Spanish–English) to assess whether the current setup remains useful. As pointed out by Voigt and Jurafsky (2012), and corroborated by our manual evaluation (some of the MT errors are due to mistranslation of pronouns), we would like to explore using discourse features. Finally, as the ultimate goal of this work is to integrate MT in the translation workflow to assist with the translation of literature, we would like to study which is the best way of doing so, e.g. by means of post-editing, interactive MT, etc, with real customers.

Acknowledgments

This research is supported by the European Union Seventh Framework Programme FP7/2007-2013 under grant agreement PIAP-GA-2012-324414 (Abu-MaTran) and by Science Foundation Ireland through the CNGL Programme (Grant 12/CE/I2267) in the ADAPT Centre (www.adaptcentre.ie) at Dublin City University.

References

Laurent Besacier. 2014. Traduction automatisée d'une oeuvre littéraire: une étude pilote. In *Traitement Automatique du Langage Naturel (TALN)*, Marseille, France.

P. Brown, J. Cocke, S. Della Pietra, V. Della Pietra, F. Jelinek, R. Mercer, and P. Roossin. 1988. A statistical approach to language translation. In *Proceedings of the 12th Conference on Computational Linguistics - Volume 1*, COLING '88, pages 71–76, Stroudsburg, PA, USA. Association for Computational Linguistics.

Peter F. Brown, John Cocke, Stephen A. Della Pietra, Vincent J. Della Pietra, Fredrick Jelinek, John D. Lafferty, Robert L. Mercer, and Paul S. Roossin. 1990. A statistical approach to machine translation. *Comput. Linguist.*, 16(2):79–85, June.

Stanley F. Chen and Joshua Goodman. 1996. An empirical study of smoothing techniques for language modeling. In *Proceedings of the 34th Annual Meeting on Association for Computational Linguistics*, ACL '96, pages 310–318, Stroudsburg, PA, USA. Association for Computational Linguistics.

Michael Denkowski and Alon Lavie. 2014. Meteor universal: Language specific translation evaluation for any target language. In *Proceedings of the EACL 2014 Workshop on Statistical Machine Translation*.

Marcello Federico, Nicola Bertoldi, and Mauro Cettolo. 2008. Irstlm: an open source toolkit for handling large scale language models. In *INTERSPEECH*, pages 1618–1621.

Christian Federmann. 2012. Appraise: An open-source toolkit for manual evaluation of machine translation output. *The Prague Bulletin of Mathematical Linguistics*, 98:25–35, September.

Joseph L. Fleiss. 1971. Measuring nominal scale agreement among many raters. *Psychological Bulletin*, 76(5):378–382.

Mikel L. Forcada, Mireia Ginestí-Rosell, Jacob Nordfalk, Jim O'Regan, Sergio Ortiz-Rojas, Juan Antonio Pérez-Ortiz, Felipe Sánchez-Martínez, Gema Ramírez-Sánchez, and Francis M. Tyers. 2011. Apertium: A free/open-source platform for rule-based machine translation. *Machine Translation*, 25(2):127–144, June.

Dmitriy Genzel, Jakob Uszkoreit, and Franz Och. 2010. "Poetic" Statistical Machine Translation: Rhyme and Meter. In *Proceedings of the 2010 Conference on Empirical Methods in Natural Language Processing*, EMNLP '10, pages 158–166.

Yvette Graham, Timothy Baldwin, Alistair Moffat, and Justin Zobel. 2014. Is machine translation getting better over time? In *Proceedings of the 14th Conference of the European Chapter of the Association for Computational Linguistics*, pages 443–451, Gothenburg, Sweden.

Erica Greene, Tugba Bodrumlu, and Kevin Knight. 2010. Automatic analysis of rhythmic poetry with applications to generation and translation. In *Proceedings of the 2010 Conference on Empirical Methods in Natural Language Processing*, EMNLP '10, pages 524–533, Stroudsburg, PA, USA. Association for Computational Linguistics.

Jing He, Ming Zhou, and Long Jiang. 2012. Generating chinese classical poems with statistical machine translation models.

Long Jiang and Ming Zhou. 2008. Generating Chinese Couplets Using a Statistical MT Approach. In *Proceedings of the 22nd International Conference on Computational Linguistics - Volume 1*, pages 377–384.

Ruth Jones and Ann Irvine, 2013. *Proceedings of the 7th Workshop on Language Technology for Cultural Heritage, Social Sciences, and Humanities*, chapter The (Un)faithful Machine Translator, pages 96–101. Association for Computational Linguistics.

Philipp Koehn, Hieu Hoang, Alexandra Birch, Chris Callison-Burch, Marcello Federico, Nicola Bertoldi, Brooke Cowan, Wade Shen, Christine Moran, Richard Zens, Chris Dyer, Ondřej Bojar, Alexandra Constantin, and Evan Herbst. 2007. Moses: open source toolkit for statistical machine translation. In *Proceedings of the 45th Annual Meeting of the ACL on Interactive Poster and Demonstration Sessions*, pages 177–180.

Philipp Koehn. 2004. Statistical significance tests for machine translation evaluation. In *Proceedings of the 2004 Conference on Empirical Methods in Natural Language Processing , EMNLP 2004, A meeting of SIGDAT, a Special Interest Group of the ACL, held in conjunction with ACL 2004, 25-26 July 2004, Barcelona, Spain*, pages 388–395. ACL.

Philipp Koehn. 2005. Europarl: A Parallel Corpus for Statistical Machine Translation. In *Conference Proceedings: the tenth Machine Translation Summit*, pages 79–86, Phuket, Thailand. AAMT, AAMT.

R. J. Landis and G. G. Koch. 1977. The measurement of observer agreement for categorical data. *Biometrics*, 33(1):159 - 174.

Nikola Ljubešić and Antonio Toral. 2014. caWaC - a Web Corpus of Catalan and its Application to Language Modeling and Machine Translation. In *Proceedings of the Ninth International Conference on Language Resources and Evaluation (LREC'14)*, Reykjavik, Iceland.

Juan Alberto Alonso Martín and Anna Civil Serra. 2014. Integration of a machine translation system into the editorial process flow of a daily newspaper. *Procesamiento del Lenguaje Natural*, 53(0):193–196.

Franz Josef Och and Hermann Ney. 2003. A Systematic Comparison of Various Statistical Alignment Models. *Computational Linguistics*, 29(1):19–51.

Franz Josef Och. 2003. Minimum Error Rate Training in Statistical Machine Translation. In *Proceedings of the 41st Annual Meeting on Association for Computational Linguistics*, pages 160–167.

Lluís Padró and Evgeny Stanilovsky. 2012. Freeling 3.0: Towards wider multilinguality. In *Proceedings of the Language Resources and Evaluation Conference (LREC 2012)*, Istanbul, Turkey, May. ELRA.

Kishore Papineni, Salim Roukos, Todd Ward, and Wei-Jing Zhu. 2002. BLEU: A Method for Automatic Evaluation of Machine Translation. In *Proceedings of the 40th Annual Meeting on Association for Computational Linguistics*, pages 311–318.

Pavel Pecina, Antonio Toral, Vassilis Papavassiliou, Prokopis Prokopidis, and Josef van Genabith. 2012. Domain adaptation of statistical machine translation using web-crawled resources: a case study. In *Proceedings of the 16th Annual Conference of the European Association for Machine Translation*, pages 145–152.

Nicholas Ruiz and Marcello Federico. 2014. Complexity of spoken versus written language for machine translation. In *17th Annual Conference of the European Association for Machine Translation*, EAMT, pages 173–180, Dubrovnik, Croatia.

Rico Sennrich. 2012. Perplexity minimization for translation model domain adaptation in statistical machine translation. In *Proceedings of the 13th Conference of the European Chapter of the Association for Computational Linguistics*, pages 539–549.

Matthew Snover, Bonnie Dorr, Richard Schwartz, Linnea Micciulla, and Ralph Weischedel. 2006. A Study of Translation Error Rate with Targeted Human Annotation. In *Proceedings of the Association for Machine Translation in the Americas*.

Ralf Steinberger, Bruno Pouliquen, Anna Widiger, Camelia Ignat, Tomaz Erjavec, Dan Tufis, and Dániel Varga. 2006. The jrc-acquis: A multilingual aligned parallel corpus with 20+ languages. *CoRR*, abs/cs/0609058.

Andreas Stolcke, Jing Zheng, Wen Wang, and Victor Abrash. 2011. SRILM at Sixteen: Update and Outlook. In *Proceedings of ASRU*.

Dániel Varga, László Németh, Péter Halácsy, András Kornai, Viktor Trón, and Viktor Nagy. 2005. Parallel corpora for medium density languages. In *Recent Advances in Natural Language Processing*, pages 590–596, Borovets, Bulgaria.

Rob Voigt and Dan Jurafsky, 2012. *Proceedings of the NAACL-HLT 2012 Workshop on Computational Linguistics for Literature*, chapter Towards a Literary Machine Translation: The Role of Referential Cohesion, pages 18–25.

Martin Volk. 2009. The automatic translation of film subtitles. A machine translation success story? *JLCL*, 24(3):115–128.

Dekai Wu, Karteek Addanki, and Markus Saers. 2013. Modelling hip hop challenge-response lyrics as machine translation. In *Machine Translation Summit XIV*, pages 109–116, Nice, France.

Ventsislav Zhechev. 2012. Machine Translation Infrastructure and Post-editing Performance at Autodesk. In *AMTA 2012 Workshop on Post-Editing Technology and Practice (WPTP 2012)*, pages 87–96, San Diego, USA.

Author Index